THE MASTER

AP*
ENGLISH LITERATURE
& COMPOSITION

TEST

TEACHER-TESTED STRATEGIES AND

TECHNIQUES FOR SCORING HIGH

2002

ARCO

THOMSON LEARNING™

Australia • Canada • Mexico • Singapore • Spain • United Kingdom • United States

ARCO
THOMSON LEARNING

An ARCO Book

ARCO is a registered trademark of Thomson Learning, Inc., and is used herein under license by Peterson's.

About Peterson's

Founded in 1966, Peterson's, a division of Thomson Learning, is the nation's largest and most respected provider of lifelong learning resources, both in print and online. The Education Supersite^{SM} at www.petersons.com—the Internet's most heavily traveled education resource—has searchable databases and interactive tools for contacting U.S.-accredited institutions and programs. In addition, Peterson's delivers unmatched financial aid resources and test-preparation tools. Peterson's serves more than 100 million education consumers annually.

Peterson's is a division of Thomson Learning, one of the world's largest providers of lifelong learning. Thomson Learning serves the needs of individuals, learning institutions, and corporations with products and services for both traditional and distributed learning. Headquartered in Stamford, Connecticut, with offices worldwide, Thomson Learning is a division of The Thomson Corporation (www.thomson.com), one of the world's leading e-information and solutions companies in the business, professional, and education marketplaces. For more information, visit www.thomsonlearning.com.

For more information, contact Peterson's, 2000 Lenox Drive, Lawrenceville, NJ 08648; 800-338-3282; or find us on the World Wide Web at: www.petersons.com/about

Fifth Edition

ISBN 0-7689-0740-3

Printed in the United States of America

10 9 8 7 6 5 4 3 2 1   04 03 02

CONTENTS

PART 1: OVERVIEW OF THE AP TEST IN ENGLISH LITERATURE AND COMPOSITION   **1**

What is the Advanced Placement Program? 1

Why Take an AP Course? 1

The Advanced Placement Courses in English 2

The Format of the AP Literature and Composition Exam 2

   The Multiple-Choice Section 2

   The Essay Section 3

Overview of the Scoring System 4

How Essays are Scored 4

   General Essay Grading Rubric 5

   Specific Essay Grading Rubric 6

The Multiple-Choice Questions: Should You Guess? 7

Preparing to Take the Examination 7

FAQs: Sure-Fire Test-Taking Strategies for Success on the AP English Literature and Composition Exam 8

For Additional Information 10

PART 2: DIAGNOSTIC TEST AND ANSWER KEY   **11**

PART 3: STRATEGIES FOR SUCCESS ON THE MULTIPLE-CHOICE QUESTIONS   **41**

FAQs: The Multiple-Choice Section of the AP Literature and Composition Exam 42

Overall Guidelines for Answering Multiple-Choice Questions 43

   Top Ten Hints for Scoring High on Multiple-Choice Questions 43

   Answering Multiple-Choice Vocabulary Questions 45

   Answering Multiple-Choice AP Questions on Poetry 45

   Questions about Theme 46

   Questions about Speaker 48

   Questions about Poetic Language 48

      Similes, Metaphors, and Personification 49

      Symbols and Symbolism 51

      Conceits and Allusions 53

      Imagery 57

      Tone 61

Answering Multiple-Choice AP Questions on Prose Passages 63

   Questions about Genre 63

   Questions about Structure 63

   Questions about Rhetoric 64

Practice Multiple-Choice Questions on Prose 65

   Sample Passage 1 65

   Sample Passage 2 69

PART 4: STRATEGIES FOR SUCCESS ON THE ESSAY QUESTIONS   73
Overall Essay Guidelines 73
Writing an Essay on Poetry 75
The Basic Poetry Analysis Question 75
Five-Step Method to a High Score 77
Sample Poetry Questions and Model Responses 77
  Sample 1 77
  Sample 2 79
  Sample 3 82
Practice Poetry Analysis Questions 84
Writing an Essay on a Prose Passage 86
The Basic Prose Analysis Question 86
Five-Step Method to a High Score 89
Sample Prose Passage Essay Questions and Model Responses 89
  Sample 1 89
  Sample 2 92
  Sample 3 96
Practice Prose Analysis Questions 98
Writing an Open-Ended Literary Response 101
The Basic Open-Ended Question 101
Five-Step Method to a High Score 103
Recommended Books 103
Sample Open-Ended Questions and Model Responses 105
  Sample 1 105
  Sample 2 108
  Sample 3 110
Practice Open-Ended Literary Response Questions 112

PART 5: ADDITIONAL PRACTICE TESTS   113
Test 1 and Answer Key 114
Test 2 and Answer Key 143
Test 3 and Answer Key 172
Test 4 and Answer Key 201

PART 6: GLOSSARY OF LITERARY TERMS   231

PART 7: GUIDE TO GRAMMAR AND USAGE   251

ACKNOWLEDGMENTS

My deepest thanks to all the people who helped me with this book.

To F.L. for her unflagging support of this project and great help in seeing it to completion. Her professionalism and consideration combined to make this mammoth undertaking so much easier.

My thanks to Stephanie Hammett, who spoke to me first about revising my original AP book. Thank you, Stephanie. I hope we get a chance to work together.

Several gifted and unselfish teachers tested questions for me and guided their students to write and contribute papers. In addition, several curriculum supervisors and administrators provided support for this project. These generous and accomplished people include the following:

- Dr. Sue Kelly, English Chairperson, New Hyde Park Memorial High School
- Richard Rozakis, Assistant Principal, New Hyde Park Memorial School
- Dennis Biagi, English teacher, New Hyde Park Memorial School
- Kathleen Devine, English teacher, New Hyde Park Memorial School
- Mike Lomonico, English teacher, Farmingdale High School

And to all the generous, talented, and hard-working AP students who contributed their papers. These wonderful young scholars include the following:

Alexis Acevedo	Alyson Bernstein
Merry Benner	Oleg Bitman
Christina Caruso	Claire Casaccio
Sibi Chacko	Rita Chang
Susan Choinski	Stephen Cipot
Kevin Cordova	Melissa Costa
Ashley Dunne	Brian Eilbott
Will Fellini	Megan Fortunato
William Frischeisen	Nicole Fulgieri
Meredith Gran	Jessica Hacker
Kimberley Harris	Jack Hall
Jennifer Heller	Daisy Ho
Christia Ignatiadis	Jonathan Kadishon
Kenneth Ko	Ray Kuhn
Karen Kwok	Gina Lewis
Adam Lowenstein	Scott Lustig
Ashley Klein	Ryan Mannix
Lindsay Martin	Christine Maulion
Alex Morales	Michael Nathan
Laura Orgill	Heather Ozgerian
Sevan Ozcentenkaya	Kristine Peterson
Michelle Piwowarski	Karina Petoe
Paul Rachita	Jason Rostoker
Charles Rozakis	Sammi Rozakis
Katie Rhindress	Vanessa Rudeman
Lauren Sakowich	Lindsay Sarne
Staci Scianablo	Heather Schultz
Lindsay Stern	Michelle Stern
Laura Suarez	Matt Smith
Princy Thottathil	Robert Trasolini
Helen Yeung	Jane Youn
Danielle Young	Lisa Weickert
Rashmi Varma	

WORKS CITED

Overview of the AP Test in English Literature and Composition

WHAT IS THE ADVANCED PLACEMENT PROGRAM?

Advanced Placement (AP) is a program of college-level courses and examinations that allows high school students to earn advanced placement and/or college credit. The Advanced Placement program is administered by the College Entrance Examination Board, a division of the Educational Testing Service (ETS).

In May 1998, AP reached a milestone; for the first time in the history of the program, more than one million students took an AP exam. These students represent more than 3,500 secondary schools; credit is accepted by more than 2,000 colleges and universities. More than 100,000 examinations a year are taken in English alone.

Currently, AP courses and exams are given in thirty-three different subjects, including art, biology, calculus, chemistry, Chinese, computer science, economics, English literature, English language, environmental science, French, German, history (European, United States, and World), Latin, music theory, physics, psychology, Spanish, statistics, and U.S. government and politics.

WHY TAKE AN AP COURSE?

Aside from the obvious pleasure inherent in studying more challenging material, earning advanced placement in college lets you skip work you've already done in high school and, perhaps, even participate in an internship or study abroad. You may be able to graduate from college earlier, enter graduate school sooner, or begin a career more quickly. Because of AP credit, you may also be able to take additional courses and explore areas of interest that would not otherwise fit into a busy school program.

Advanced Placement courses also represent a very significant savings in college tuition. Tuition for a full year's course can be as much as $2,500. If you save a semester's work in a private college, you can save as much as $18,000 (including tuition, fees, and room and board) at current prices. However, no college is obligated to accept your AP credit — no matter what score you earn.

ROAD MAP

- *What is the Advanced Placement Program?*
- *Why Take an AP Course?*
- *The Advanced Placement Courses in English*
- *The Format of the AP English Literature and Composition Exam*
- *Overview of the Scoring System*
- *How Essays are Scored*
- *The Multiple-Choice Questions: Should You Guess?*
- *Preparing to Take the Examination*
- *FAQs*
- *For Additional Information*

THE ADVANCED PLACEMENT COURSES IN ENGLISH

The Advanced Placement program now offers two courses and examinations in English:

- English Literature and Composition

- English Language and Composition

- The two different Advanced Placement courses are designed to represent the two types of freshman English generally offered in colleges and universities. Each examination represents a full-year college introductory English course. Either course can substitute for a year's worth of English credit, always depending on the specific policy of the college or university. *Consequently, students may take either examination—but not both.*

- The English Literature and Composition course is for students trained in literary analysis.

- The English Language and Composition course is designed for students who have attained the reading and writing skills generally expected at the end of the freshman year of college but who may not have studied literary analysis.

- Each examination is 3 hours long. One hour is devoted to multiple-choice questions; 2 hours to essays. The multiple-choice questions count as 45 percent of the grade; the essays count as 55 percent of the grade.

THE FORMAT OF THE AP ENGLISH LITERATURE AND COMPOSITION EXAM

The English Literature and Composition exam tests both your writing ability and knowledge of literature. This is done through the two parts of the test: multiple-choice questions and essays.

THE MULTIPLE-CHOICE SECTION

The multiple-choice section consists of approximately 50–60 questions. The exact number varies from year to year. The questions consist of four passages from literature, including both poetry and prose. (Very rarely, the test will contain five passages instead of four.)

- If the test pattern continues as it has in the past, there will be two prose passages and two poems.

- The works will be drawn from different literary periods. For example, the test might contain literature that spans the sixteenth century to the present.

The questions are the sort that a teacher might ask in class to elicit a close analytical reading of a prose passage or a poem. You will be expected to be familiar with such literary terms as connotation, denotations, metaphor, simile, irony, syntax, and tone. Of course, you will be expected to understand the theme or main idea of the work of literature you are analyzing.

As mentioned earlier, you will have 1 hour to complete this section.

THE ESSAY SECTION

The essay section consists of 3 questions:

- a poem or pair of poems to analyze

- a close reading of a prose passage. This might be part of a novel, an essay, or a short story, for example. In rare cases, an entire short story will be included for analysis.

- an open-ended literary response question. A list of suggested literary texts is provided, but you are free to choose any well-respected work of literature that applies to the specific question. Students usually choose novels, plays, a biographies, or autobiographies.

You will have 2 hours to complete all 3 essays. This gives you about 40 minutes per essay. However, you won't be told how much time to allocate to each essay; how you allocate your time will be left to you. Nonetheless, savvy test takers spread their time equally to give adequate time to each essay. Clearly, one of the skills necessary to do well on this part of the exam is the ability to balance your time wisely.

Examinations can be divided in a number of ways. Some typical examinations may look like the following:

NOTE
You are required to write all 3 essays.

Sample AP English Literature and Composition Format

Section I	multiple-choice questions	53 questions	1 hour
	passage from a sixteenth-century play	14 questions	
	excerpt from a modern novel	15 questions	
	passage from a Victorian essay	15 questions	
	contemporary American poem	9 questions	

Section II	essay questions	3 questions	2 hours
	analysis of a nineteenth-century poem		40 minutes
	analysis of a contemporary essay		40 minutes
	open-ended essay response on a character, setting, or theme		40 minutes

Sample AP Literature and Composition Format

Section I	multiple-choice questions	55 questions	1 hour
	passage from a modern novel	15 questions	
	excerpt from a eighteenth-century essay	15 questions	
	passage from a Victorian poem	15 questions	
	contemporary British poem	10 questions	

Section II	essay questions	3 questions	2 hours
	analysis of a twentieth-century poem		40 minutes
	analysis of a eighteenth-century essay		40 minutes
	open-ended essay response contrasting two novels or plays		40 minutes

Sample AP Literature and Composition Format

Section I	multiple-choice questions	54 questions	1 hour
	passage from a nineteenth-century play	14 questions	
	excerpt from an eighteenth-century poem	15 questions	
	passage from a seventeenth-century speech	15 questions	
	contemporary American poem	10 questions	

Section II	essay questions	3 questions	2 hours
	analysis of a seventeenth-century poem		40 minutes
	analysis of a modern essay		40 minutes
	open-ended essay response on a nineteenth-century short story		40 minutes

OVERVIEW OF THE SCORING SYSTEM

The AP English Literature and Composition exam is graded according the following scale:

5   extremely well qualified

4   well qualified

3   qualified

2   possibly qualified

1   no recommendation

How do you get an overall grade on the AP English Literature and Composition exam? The process has four steps:

1. The multiple-choice section is scored.

2. The free-response section is scored.

3. The composite score is calculated.

4. The composite score is converted to an AP grade: a 5, 4, 3, 2, or 1. This is the grade that you receive.

HOW ESSAYS ARE SCORED

The essays are scored by English teachers from around the country who gather in a central location. They spent about a week reading the essays. "Table leaders," scorers with extensive experience grading AP English Literature essays, are appointed to direct the scoring.

For three days before the essay exams arrive at the scoring site, Educational Testing Service graders and "table leaders" create a grading scale. This is called a *rubric*. While each rubric is tailored to an individual question, there are general qualities that define a paper and determine its score. When the rest of the grading staff arrives on the first formal day of scoring, the first morning is spent grading sample papers so that the grades can be as accurate as possible. At this time, the rubric may be adjusted to match expectations. Every few hours during the scoring, readers pause to check their accuracy by grading sample papers and comparing their scores.

Notice that the rubric is calibrated from 9–0, even though the final score you receive is calibrated from 5–1.

General Essay Grading Rubric

"9–8" papers demonstrate originality and imagination. They are clearly focused discussions made up of coherent arguments of exceptional clarity. These papers leave the reader convinced of the soundness of the discussion, impressed with the quality of the writing style, and stimulated by the intelligence and insight of the writer.

"7–6" papers demonstrate solid, logical, and persuasive discussion, but they lack the originality or insight of the "5" papers. Further, the development lacks the grace and style of the "5" papers and may seem a bit predictable and plodding.

"5" papers demonstrate a thorough but not totally convincing discussion of the topic, marked by the sense that the writer has not completely thought out the issue. In addition, there are some writing errors that may distract the reader from the argument and the writer's point.

"4–3" papers demonstrate an attempt made to organize the essay, but the structure is flawed and the supporting detail is weak. There may be serious problems with the mechanics of correct written English.

"2–1" papers demonstrate a lack of understanding; either they do not address the topic directly or fail to answer the question. They draw obscure, irrelevant, or bizarre conclusions and are seriously deficient in the conventions of standard written English.

"0" papers demonstrate papers that barely touch on the topic or write on a topic that has nothing to do with the essay question at all.

Below is a simulated free-response question.

Most villains in literature are characters who harm others in order to satisfy their own needs and self-interest. Select a novel or play that includes such a character and, in a focused essay, explain what the villain wants, how it will serve the villain's interest, and whom the villain hurts to get what he or she wants. You may choose a work from the list below or another novel or play of recognized literary merit.

Mrs. Dalloway	*Invisible Man*
David Copperfield	*Cry, the Beloved Country*
Hamlet	*The Dead*
Macbeth	*The Glass Menagerie*
Othello	*The Color Purple*
The Great Gatsby	*Jane Eyre*
Our Town	*Pride and Prejudice*
The Sound and the Fury	*Moby-Dick*
The Scarlet Letter	*1984*
Gulliver's Travels	*The Adventures of Huckleberry Finn*
McTeague	*A Clockwork Orange*

Specific Essay Grading Rubric

"9–8" papers demonstrate how a villain harms others and why. The essays focus on the villain's motivations and how they shape his or her actions. The writers of these essays understand how a villain functions as an antagonist in a literary work. The writers may summarize specific scenes but are careful to link all summaries to a greater understanding of the entire literary work. These essays may contain a few minor errors, but they amply demonstrate the writer's ability to discuss a literary work with insight and to convey ideas with clarity, sophistication, and coherence.

"7–6" papers demonstrate a villain's reasons for acting as he or she does and the results of those actions. In addition to some minor flaws in interpretation, the analysis here is not as well supported with details and examples. As a result, the analysis is less incisive and convincing. While these essays demonstrate the writer's ability to articulate ideas clearly, they lack the mastery and control of rhetoric shown by writers in the 9–8 range. In addition, there may be minor errors in grammar, usage, and mechanics, but these do not seriously affect the argument.

"5" papers demonstrate superficial analysis. Instead of focusing on the specific actions of a villainous character, these essays may discuss the character's general harmful qualities. The writer may also choose a character whose actions are harmful but caused by accident or unavoidable circumstances rather than being motivated by self-interest. These essays reveal shallow thinking, focus on trivial incidents, and do not contribute significantly to a greater meaning of the work or character. These essays are not well planned, well organized, or coherent. However, the writing style is sufficient to convey the writer's ideas.

"4–3" papers demonstrate a general discussion rather than the focus on a specific character. In addition, these papers may incorrectly identify a character as a villain or seriously misinterpret the character's actions and motivation and the outcome of the machinations. These essays may contain inadequate supporting evidence, and/or plot summary rather than analysis. Any analysis may be unconvincing, irrelevant, or misguided. While the writing may convey the student's ideas, there are serious omissions or stylistic issues. The style is flat and dull with little sentence variation, few figures of speech, and repetitious punctuation.

"2–1" papers demonstrate little clarity or coherence. Even though the writers may have attempted to answer the question, they choose an inappropriate character, make only obvious points about the character, or seriously misread the literary work. In addition, these essays may be too brief to convey a point in any detail. They contain distracting errors in grammar, usage, and mechanics. Overall, the essay is empty of both content and style.

"0" papers demonstrate no more than a passing reference to the question and any discernible character or work of literature.

As you can see, the essay section stresses your skill in organizing your thoughts coherently, developing ideas fully, responding to general questions with specific evidence, and writing clearly and vividly. The Advanced Placement Grading Committee will look especially for your ability to mold language, to utilize and recognize imagery and symbolism, point of view, audience, mood, and tone. But a knowledge of literary convention alone by no means guarantees success on the exam.

THE MULTIPLE-CHOICE QUESTIONS: SHOULD YOU GUESS?

Should you guess wildly? No.

Your score on the multiple-choice questions is based on the number of questions you answer correctly minus a percentage for incorrect answers. Here's the math:

What You Do...	What You Get...
a correct answer:	1 point
a blank:	0 points
an incorrect answer:	minus .25

Therefore, just running down the page and filing in answers will not help you earn a better grade. But, *do make educated guesses*—eliminate one or more choices and then guess from the remaining choices.

PREPARING TO TAKE THE EXAMINATION

January:	Talk about taking the examination with your English teacher, guidance counselor, and the AP Coordinator at your school. Make sure that these people understand that you wish to take the examination. If you need special accommodations, such as a Braille exam, speak with your school's AP Coordinator or write to the College Board.
Fees:	The exam carries a fee. The College Board will reduce fees by $12–15 for qualified students who can demonstrate financial need. Do not send money to the College Board. Your school's AP Coordinator will have this information.
May:	Examinations are given.
June:	If you do not want all your AP grades reported to your colleges, you must notify the College Board by June 15.
July:	The scores are sent to you and your designated colleges and universities. In cases of a scoring conflict, the College Board allows up to one year for the multiple-choice section to be rescored and retotaled by hand. The essay sections cannot be reread.

In 1992, the AP program introduced three awards to honor those students who have earned outstanding AP achievement.

- The Scholar Award honors students who earn grades of 3 or higher on three or more AP examinations.

- The Scholar with Honor and Scholar with Distinction awards are available for those students who go beyond these criteria.

FAQS: SURE-FIRE TEST-TAKING STRATEGIES FOR SUCCESS ON THE AP ENGLISH LITERATURE AND COMPOSITION EXAM

Q: *When should I use this book?*
A: If possible, look at the book early in the year to familiarize yourself with the test's content and format. Then as you learn specifics about literature, literary analysis, and writing throughout the year, you can apply that knowledge to the test. If you have just purchased the book and the test is around the corner, you can still see marked benefits from reviewing the instruction and taking the practice tests.

Q: *How should I use this book?*
A: Work from beginning to end, concentrating on the parts of the test that present the greatest challenge. For example, if you're having trouble writing essays, spend most of your time reviewing the essay section.

Q: *What about reading novel and play study guides?*
A: Save your money. There's no substitute for reading the literature itself. Discuss the literature in class and with your friends to be sure that your interpretation is valid, but don't waste your time on quick fixes.

Q: *What should I do a week before the test?*
A: Select four books of recognized literary merit that you enjoyed the most and review them in detail. Try to get an array of genres, including at least one novel and one full-length play. If possible, know one Shakespearean tragedy in depth, since they can be used to answer nearly all free-response questions. It's not enough to memorize the characters, plot, setting, and theme: be sure you *understand* the work.

Q: *What should I do the night before the test?*
A: Stay home and relax. Lay out your clothes for the next day, gather any identification you may need to get into the test site, and get your writing implements. Get plenty of sleep.

Q: *Should I cram?*
A: If by cramming you mean staying up all night before the test frantically reading novels of recognized literary value, skimming old AP tests, and biting your nails, the answer is a clear "No!" If by cramming you mean reviewing literary terms a week before the test, I'd say "Sure." The AP English Literature and Composition exam measures years of study in English, so cramming the night before will get you nothing more than a headache.

Q: *Should I eat breakfast?*
A: Chow down, even if you normally skip the morning meal. Studies have repeatedly shown that test takers who eat breakfast do appreciably better than those who do not. And while we're on the subject of food, no coffee or cola. The last thing you want during an exam is a caffeine jolt. Even if you think you need caffeine to wake up, it will make you edgy and fidgety. Ditto on sugar: donuts, toaster pastries, etc. Stick with the basics: juice, cereal, toast, and eggs. Eating a nourishing breakfast is a simple and successful way to give yourself an edge.

Q: *What should I wear during the test?*
A: Shakespeare realized that clothes make the man and woman, so dress for test success. Wear comfortable clothes so you can concentrate on the test.

Q: *When should I get to the school on test day?*

A: Get to the test site with ample time to spare. Allow yourself enough time to settle in the seat, lay out your pens and pencils, and relax. This is not the day to be rushing out the door in a frenzy.

Q: *Does my seat at the test matter?*

A: Yes! Choose your seat carefully because sitting near friends during a test can be disrupting. If you see your friends handing in their papers early, you may feel pressured to do the same, even if you're not finished with the test. Therefore, try not to sit near your friends.

Q: *Does listening to the proctor matter, or can I zone out for a minute?*

A: Pay close attention to <u>all</u> directions. Even though you'll be completely familiar with the test format, the proctor may say something very important, such as safety procedures in the event of a fire drill or an actual fire.

Q: *How should I budget my time?*

A: If you don't complete a question in the time you have allotted, leave it and move on. You can return to the question if you have extra time at the end of the test.

Q: *What should I do if I have time left over?*

A: Stay focused and use your time to advantage.

- Return to questions you couldn't answer the first time and work on them now.

- Double-checking your answers.

- Make sure you have marked all test bubbles correctly. You surely don't want to lose credit because you mismarked answers!

- Proofread your essay for errors in grammar, usage, and punctuation.

- Recopy messy parts of your essays.

Q: *What can I do about panic?*

A: Few test situations are as high-pressured as an AP exam, especially the AP Exam in English Literature and Composition, because there's no "right" answer on the essay questions. If you still have some last-minutes jitters, take a few deep breaths and focus on a pleasant scene. Try not to think about anything but the test in front of you.

Q: *What should I do if some questions seem harder than others?*

A: Don't panic if some questions seem much harder than others. They probably are. That's the way the test was designed.

Q: *What should I do if other students are writing and I'm not?*

A: Relax. They may be working on another part of the test or not have thought enough. By thinking a bit longer before you answer, you might do better than someone who plunges right in.

Q: *What if other students finish before I do?*

A: Finishing early doesn't guarantee the best grade. Usually the better papers are handed in by students who have spent more time thinking about their answers and checking their papers over.

Q: *And if I can't get an answer?*

A: Just skip the question and move on. If you have enough time, you can return to the question later. If you run out of time before you can return to it, you were still better off answering more questions correctly than wasting time on a question you didn't know.

Q: *If I freeze and just can't go on?*

A: If this happens, there are many different things that you can do. First, remind yourself that you have studied and so you are well prepared. Then remember that every question you have answered is worth points. Third, stop working and close your eyes. Take two or three deep breaths. Breath in and out to the count of five. Then go on with the test.

FOR ADDITIONAL INFORMATION

For additional information about the AP Program and its policies, you can contact the College Board and/or ETS.

General e-mail inquiries: www. collegeboard.org
AP questions: apexams@info.collegeboard.org

The College Board
45 Columbus Avenue
New York, NY 10023-6992
Telephone: 212-713-8000

Educational Testing Service
Rosedale Road
Princeton, NJ 08541
Telephone: 888-CALL-4-AP (toll-free)
                              609-771-7300
                              609-921-9000
E-mail: etsinfo@ets.org
Fax: 609-734-5410
                              609-530-0482

Diagnostic Test and Answer Key

GENERAL DIRECTIONS FOR THE DIAGNOSTIC TEST

This test was constructed to be representative of what you will encounter on the AP exam. Take the test in a quiet room without distractions, following all directions carefully and observing all time limits. Try to get as close as possible to actual test conditions, and take the test in one sitting. The more carefully you match test conditions, the more accurate your results will be and the better able you will be to evaluate your strengths and weaknesses.

ROAD MAP

- *General Directions for the Diagnostic Test*
- *Section I: Multiple-Choice Questions*
- *Section II: Essay Questions*
- *Answers and Explanations*

ENGLISH LITERATURE AND COMPOSITION

SECTION I: MULTIPLE-CHOICE QUESTIONS

Time—1 hour

Directions: This section contains selections from two passages of prose and two poems with questions on their content, style, form, and purpose. Read each selection closely and carefully. Then choose the best answer from the five choices.

Questions 1–14. Read the following selection carefully before you mark your answers.

Mrs. Knowles affected to complain that men had much more liberty allowed them than women.

JOHNSON. "Why, Madam, women have all the liberty they wish to have. We have all the labor and danger, and women all the advantage. We go to sea, we build houses, we do everything, in short, to pay our court to women."

MRS. KNOWLES. "The Doctor reasons very wittily, but not convincingly. Now, take the instance of building; the mason's wife, if she is ever seen in liquor, is ruined; the mason may get himself drunk as often as he pleases, with little loss of character; nay, may let his wife and children starve."

JOHNSON. "Madam, you must consider, if the mason does get himself drunk, and let his wife and children starve, the parish will oblige him to find security for their maintenance. We have different modes of restraining evil. Stocks for men, a dunking-stool for women, and a pound for beasts. If we require more perfection from women than from ourselves, it is doing them honor. And women have not the same temptations that we have: they may always live in virtuous company; men must mix in the world indiscriminately. If a woman has no inclination to do what is wrong, being secured from it is no restraint to her. I am at liberty to walk into the Thames, but if I were to try it, my friends would restrain me to Bedlam, and I should be obliged to them."

MRS. KNOWLES. "Still, Doctor, I cannot help thinking it is a hardship that more indulgence is allowed to men than to women. It gives a superiority to men, to which I do not see how they are entitled."

JOHNSON. "It is plain, Madam, one or another must have the superiority. As Shakespeare says, 'If two men ride on a horse, one must ride behind.'"

DILLY. "I suppose, Sir, Mrs. Knowles would have them to ride in panniers, one on each side."[1]

JOHNSON. "The, Sir, the horse would throw them both."

MRS. KNOWLES. "Well, I hope that in another world the sexes will be equal."

BOSWELL. "That is being too ambitious, Madam. *We* might as well desire to be equal with the angels. We shall all, I hope, be happy in a future state, but we must not

---

[1]*panniers:* a pair of baskets hung across the back of a horse for carrying produce.

expect to be all happy in the same degree. It is enough to be happy according to our several capacities. A worthy carman[2] will get to heaven as well as Sir Isaac Newton. Yet, though equally good, they will not have the same degree of happiness."

JOHNSON. "Probably not."

1. This essay is framed as a(n)
   (A) autobiography.
   (B) short story.
   (C) dialogue.
   (D) parable.
   (E) conceit.

2. As used in the second paragraph, the phrase "to pay court" means
   (A) to pay for justice.
   (B) to carry out our responsibilities.
   (C) to attend formal royal functions with women.
   (D) to deal with inequality.
   (E) to show admiration and deference.

3. The third paragraph (Mrs. Knowles' first argument) is marked by
   (A) metaphors.
   (B) symbols.
   (C) parallelism.
   (D) understatement.
   (E) hyperbole.

4. The stylistic element in the third paragraph serves to
   (A) convey the speaker's intelligence and conviction.
   (B) undercut the speaker's argument with gratuitous embellishment.
   (C) suggest the seriousness of the problem she is discussing.
   (D) undermine her point through misplaced comparisons.
   (E) reinforce her point by showing the true scope of the situation.

5. Johnson addresses Mrs. Knowles as "Madam" to show
   (A) contempt.
   (B) respect.
   (C) humor.
   (D) irony.
   (E) loathing.

6. You can infer from this passage that
   (A) Mrs. Knowles and Dr. Johnson are working for full equality for both men and women.
   (B) Johnson brushes asides Mrs. Knowles' arguments because she is a woman.
   (C) Johnson very much enjoys the privileges he has as a male in his society.
   (D) Johnson feels helpless to change the social order.
   (E) Johnson justifies a double standard whereby men do not have to be perfect but women must be.

---

[2]*carman:* a carriage driver.

7. Johnson justifies his conclusions by arguing that
   (A) men and women are both mistreated by society.
   (B) it is far more difficult to be a man than to be a woman.
   (C) men are out in the world and subject to temptation, but women are sheltered and thus can choose to be virtuous.
   (D) society justly punishes those who violate the social order.
   (E) men are often tempted to drown themselves to escape their unfair burdens.

8. When he quotes Shakespeare ("If two men ride on a horse, one must ride behind,") Johnson is using
   (A) an allusion.
   (B) a simile.
   (C) personification.
   (D) irony.
   (E) ambiguity.

9. When he says, "Sir, the horse would throw them both," Johnson is
   (A) using sarcasm to underscore the natural order of the universe.
   (B) being bitter at Mrs. Knowles' expense.
   (C) twisting his earlier metaphor at Boswell's expense.
   (D) using wit and humor to suggest that men and women can never be equal.
   (E) suggesting that men are as badly treated as women.

10. You can infer from his comments that Boswell
    (A) realizes that Johnson needs his help to win the argument.
    (B) secretly sides with Mrs. Knowles against Johnson.
    (C) concludes that women are like angels.
    (D) believes that women are inferior to men.
    (E) thinks that Johnson has fallen in love with Mrs. Knowles.

11. Boswell likely believes that upper-class people will find more joy in heaven than lower-class people because
    (A) Boswell came from humble beginnings.
    (B) Boswell is a snob who does not have much respect for the lower classes.
    (C) Johnson has convinced him of this side of the argument.
    (D) lower-class people are smarter and more intuitive than their "betters."
    (E) Boswell is close to death himself.

12. From the diction and syntax used in this passage, you can conclude that
    (A) the writer was poorly educated.
    (B) the writer was restraining his anger over inequality between the sexes.
    (C) the writer is trying to impress his readers by parading his learning.
    (D) the passage was written in the late eighteenth century.
    (E) the passage is contemporary.

13. Which of the following words best describes the writer's attitude toward Dr. Johnson?
    (A) Contemptuous
    (B) Amazement
    (C) Neutral
    (D) Scornful
    (E) Admiring

14. The best title for this selection would be
    (A) Women are Better than Men.
    (B) Men are Superior to Women.
    (C) On Equality of the Sexes.
    (D) Heaven Can Wait.
    (E) Argue at Your Own Peril.

Questions 15–30. Read the following selection carefully before you mark your answers.

   Thou sorrow, venom elf.
   Is this thy play,
   To spin a web out of thyself
   To catch a fly?
5 For why?

   I saw a pettish wasp
   Fall foul therein:
   Whom yet thy whorl pins did not
      clasp
   Lest he should fling
10 His sting.

   But as afraid, remote
   Didst stand hereat,
   And with thy little fingers stroke
   And gently tap
15 His back.

   Thus gently him didst treat
   Lest he should pet,
   And in a froppish, waspish heat
   Should greatly fret
20 Thy net.

   Whereas the silly fly,
   Caught by its leg,
   Thou by the throat took'st hastily,
   And 'hind the head
25 Bite dead.

   This goes to pot, that not
   Nature doth call.
   Strive not above what strength hath
      got,
   Lest in the brawl
30 Thou fall.

   This fray seems thus to us:
   Hell's Spider sets
   His entrails spun to whip cords thus,
   And wove to nets,
35 And sets.

   To tangle Adam's race
   In's stratagems
   To their destructions, spoil'd, made
      base
   By venom things,
40 Damn'd sins.

   But mighty, Gracious Lord,
   Communicate
   Thy Grace to break the cord; afford
   Us glory's gate
45 And state.

   We'll nightingale sing like,
   When perched, on high
   In glory's cage, Thy glory, bright:
   Yea, thankfully,
50 For joy.

15. The rhyme scheme in this poem is best described as
    (A) abbaa.
    (B) ababb.
    (C) aabaa.
    (D) aabca.
    (E) ababa.

16. Who is "Hell's Spider" in line 32?
    (A) Satan
    (B) Man
    (C) The black widow spider
    (D) The venom elf
    (E) A representative of Adam's race

17. What is the analogy in the sixth stanza?

    (A) The spider bit the fly's head off. In a similar manner, "Hell's Spider" (line 32) is poised to bite off the venom elf's head.
    (B) The venom elf (line 1) calls man to brawl, but "Hell's Spider" comes between them.
    (C) People will go to ruin if they do not follow natural reason. The spider "bags" his victim, just as Satan catches his victim, humanity.
    (D) People must allow themselves to be called by Nature. If they fail to respond to this natural summons, Satan will "bag" them.
    (E) People "fly" as the insect does; nonetheless, Satan is ready to "bag" people.

18. What are the "venom things" in line 39?

    (A) Base metals that poison people
    (B) "Damn'd sins" that sting people to death and destruction
    (C) Strands of the web that entangle people
    (D) The entrails of "Hell's Spider"
    (E) The spider's poison

19. What is the "cord" in line 43?

    (A) The cord that guards Heaven's gate. The poet wants to break it and be allowed to enter Heaven.
    (B) The cord that connects a child to his or her mother
    (C) The whip cord that the spider uses to trap the fly
    (D) The cord that the devil uses to trap humanity
    (E) The cord that the venom elf uses to trap humanity

20. The figure of speech in the seventh stanza is a(n)

    (A) metaphor.
    (B) simile.
    (C) analogy.
    (D) example of personification.
    (E) example of hyperbole.

21. What does that figure of speech in the seventh stanza mean?

    (A) The activity of the spider is similar to humanity's fall from grace.
    (B) The activity of the fly is similar to humanity's fall from grace.
    (C) The activity of the nightingale is similar to humanity's fall from grace.
    (D) Entrails are compared to the venom elf and the spider's whip cords.
    (E) God's grace is personified in the spider.

22. What is the figure of speech in the last stanza?

    (A) Metonymy
    (B) Synecdoche
    (C) Metaphor
    (D) Simile
    (E) Mixed metaphor

23. In the final stanza, the nightingale symbolizes

    (A) the spider.
    (B) the fly.
    (C) humanity.
    (D) God.
    (E) the sweet bird of youth.

24. How is the entire poem an analogy?

    (A) Fly : spider :: humanity: devil
    (B) Spider : fly :: humanity : devil
    (C) Venom elf : spider :: devil : humanity
    (D) Venom elf : nightingale :: spider : fly
    (E) God : humanity :: spider : venom elf

25. The poet switches topics to make his comparison in line

    (A) 31.
    (B) 15.
    (C) 36.
    (D) 20.
    (E) 46.

26. This poem is best described as

    (A) pedestrian and trite.
    (B) characterized by many elaborate and surprising figures of speech.
    (C) comparing two very similar things.
    (D) narrative.
    (E) didactic and preachy.

27. The author is most likely

    (A) an atheist.
    (B) an agnostic.
    (C) religious.
    (D) irreligious.
    (E) a biologist.

28. The tone of this poem is

    (A) intense and agitated.
    (B) thoughtful and morose.
    (C) witty and light.
    (D) resigned and pessimistic.
    (E) irreligious.

29. Which of the following statements is NOT true about the poem?

    (A) The poem compares two very dissimilar things.
    (B) The poet is a very learned man.
    (C) The poet believes Satan is ready to catch his victims at any moment.
    (D) Humanity is silly, vulnerable, and easily destroyed by Satan's traps.
    (E) The poet is little concerned with religion; he is actually dealing with the material world of insects.

30. Which title best fits this poem?

(A) Humanity's Sorrow
(B) The Glory of Goodness
(C) Upon a Spider Catching a Fly
(D) Upon a Fly Catching a Spider
(E) Upon What Base?

Questions 31–38. Read the following selection carefully before you mark your answers.

These are the times that try men's souls: The summer soldier and the sunshine patriot will, in this crisis, shrink from the service of his country; but he that stands it NOW deserves the love and thanks of man and woman. Tyranny, like hell, is not easily conquered; yet we have this consolation with us, that the harder the conflict, the more glorious the triumph. What we obtain too cheap, we esteem too lightly:—'Tis dearness only that gives everything its value. Heaven knows how to put a proper price upon its goods; and it would be strange indeed, if so celestial an article as FREEDOM should not be highly rated. Britain, with an army to enforce her tyranny, has declared that she has a right (not only to) TAX but "to BIND us in ALL CASES WHATSOEVER," and if being bound in that manner is not slavery, then is there not such a thing as slavery upon earth. Even the expression is impious, for so unlimited a power can belong only to GOD.

I have as little superstition in me as any man living, but my secret opinion has ever been, and still is, that God Almighty will not give up a people to military destruction, or leave them unsupportedly to perish, who have so earnestly and so repeatedly sought to avoid the calamities of war, by every decent method which wisdom could invent. Neither have I so much of the infidel in me, as to suppose that he has relinquished the government of the world, and given us up to the care of devils; and as I do not, I cannot see on what grounds the king of Britain can look up to Heaven for help against us: a common murderer, a highwayman, or a housebreaker, has as good a pretense as he.

I once felt all that kind of anger, which a man ought to feel against the mean principles that are held by the Tories: A noted one, who kept a tavern at Amboy, was standing at his door, with as pretty a child in his hand, about eight or nine years old, as I ever saw, and after speaking his mind as freely as he thought was prudent, finished with this unfatherly expression, "Well! give me peace in my day." Not a man lives on the continent but fully believes that a separation must some time or other finally take place, and a generous parent should have said, "If there must be trouble, let it be in my day, that my child may have peace," and this single reflection, well applied, is sufficient to awaken every man to duty. Not a place upon earth might be so happy as America. Her situation is remote from all the wrangling world, and she has nothing to do but to trade with them. A man can distinguish himself between temper and principle, and I am as confident as I am that GOD governs the world, that America will never be happy till she gets clear of foreign dominion. Wars, without ceasing, will break out till that period arrives, and the continent must in the end be conqueror; for though the flame of liberty may sometimes cease to shine, the coal can never expire.

The heart that feels not now is dead; the blood of his children will curse his cowardice, who shrinks back at a time when a little might have saved the whole and made them happy. I love the man that can smile in trouble, that can gather strength from distress, and grow brave by reflection. 'Tis the business of little minds to shrink; but he whose heart is firm, and whose conscience approves his conduct, will pursue his principles unto death. My own line of reasoning is to myself as straight and clear as a ray of light. Not all the treasures of the world, so far as I believe, could have induced me to support an offensive war, for I think it murder; but if a thief breaks into my house, burns and destroys my property, and kills or threatens to kill me, or those that are in it, and to "bind me in all cases whatsoever" to his absolute will, am I to suffer it? What signifies it to me, whether he who does it is a king or a common man; my countryman or not my countryman; whether it be done by an individual villain, or an army of them? If we reason to the root of things we shall find no difference; neither can any just cause be assigned why we should punish in the one case and pardon in the other.

31. The phrase "summer soldier and the sunshine patriot" is an example of

   (A) personification and irony.
   (B) alliteration and apostrophe.
   (C) alliteration and metaphor.
   (D) apostrophe and ambiguity.
   (E) imagery and assonance.

32. The tone of this passage is best described as

   (A) calm.
   (B) annoyed.
   (C) upset.
   (D) angry.
   (E) fiery.

33. The phrase "the harder the conflict, the more glorious the triumph" is an example of

   (A) romanticism.
   (B) a figure of speech.
   (C) an aphorism.
   (D) the superiority of people who share his opinion.
   (E) bias.

34. The writer uses the phrase cited in item 33 and others like it to

   (A) create the impression that the specific argument being presented has a more general application.
   (B) display his learning.
   (C) attack the opposition.
   (D) suggest that it is easier to fight in the summer than in the winter.
   (E) applaud the people who have supported him for the duration of the struggle.

35. The writer draws his imagery from all the following EXCEPT

   (A) nature.
   (B) the Bible.
   (C) crime and lawbreakers.
   (D) water, especially the ocean.
   (E) fire.

36. The metaphor in the second paragraph compares the king's actions to those of

   (A) a conqueror.
   (B) an angel.
   (C) a loyal tavernkeeper.
   (D) a thief and murderer.
   (E) an eternal flame.

37. What point does the author make with his anecdote about the tavernkeeper at Amboy?

    (A) Americans must stamp out the scourge of alcoholism or the country will be destroyed.
    (B) Children should not be allowed to become embroiled in the conflict.
    (C) The colonists must remain loyal to England.
    (D) We can never have peace in our day because people refuse to listen to reason.
    (E) The tavernkeeper is more interested in keeping the status quo than securing peace for his children.

38. The writer uses the simile "My own line of reasoning is to myself as straight and clear as a ray of light" to covey the idea that

    (A) the colonists are fighting for a just cause and should not lose sight of their purpose.
    (B) people who do not think as he does are deluded.
    (C) he has special insight into the situation that others lack.
    (D) ironically, the situation is far more complex than people believe.
    (E) it is important to use reason, not emotion, in complex situations such as this one.

Questions 39–51. Read the following selection carefully before you mark your answers.

    1   As a fond mother, when the day is o'er,
        Leads by the hand her little child to bed,
        Half willing, half reluctant to be led,
        And leave his broken playthings on the floor,
    5   Still gazing at them through the open door,
        Nor wholly reassured and comforted
        By promises of others in their stead,
        Which, though more splendid, may not please him more;
        So Nature deals with us, and takes away
    10 Our playthings one by one, and by the hand
        Leads us to rest so gently, that we go
        Scarce knowing if we wish to go or stay,
        Being too full of sleep to understand
        How far the unknown transcends the what we know.

39. What two situations are being compared in this poem?

    (A) A mother reassuring her child that his broken toys will be replaced compared to Nature's destruction of the world's "toys"
    (B) Life to sleep
    (C) Death to sleep
    (D) Parenthood to childhood
    (E) A "fond mother" and her sleepy child to "Mother Nature" and natural disasters

40. What is such a comparison called?

    (A) Simile
    (B) Hyperbole
    (C) Pun
    (D) Oxymoron
    (E) Synesthesia

41. What is the author's attitude toward his subject matter?

(A) We have much to fear from death's embrace, he says.
(B) Death ought to hold little fear.
(C) To avoid being surprised by the suddenness of death, we should consider suicide.
(D) Life usually terminates abruptly, but this is good, for it relieves us of the trials of parenthood.
(E) Life is a boring affair at best, and death is preferable because it is exciting.

42. How does the author's use of comparison illuminate his theme?

(A) It shows that the mother-child relationship is central to Nature.
(B) It really doesn't illuminate the theme to any great extent; rather, he uses poetic devices to illuminate the theme.
(C) It portrays life's dilemma accurately, as our "toys" often break, and we may not always be solaced by others.
(D) It pictures the approach of death and casts it in a light of calm reassurance.
(E) It describes the enormous difficulty of raising children and reassures us that all parents share these emotions.

43. What are the "playthings" in line 10?

(A) All the people and things with which we fill our lives
(B) All the minor annoyances of daily life
(C) High status items
(D) Leisure activities
(E) Wicked and evil habits

44. What does the use of the word "playthings" tell you about the speaker's view of life?

(A) Life is best appreciated by the young.
(B) Life is an extended childhood.
(C) People are immature and subject to folly all their lives.
(D) People are unaware of the true value of life until it is terminated.
(E) Life is a bitter affair at best.

45. What is the form of this poem?

(A) An ode
(B) Free verse
(C) A sonnet
(D) A ballad
(E) Light verse

46. What is the rhyme scheme of this poem?

(A) abbaabba cdecde
(B) ababcdcdefefgg
(C) aaaa bbbb cccc dd
(D) aaba aaba cde cde
(E) It is unrhymed.

47. What is the tone of this poem?

    (A) Hostile
    (B) Baroque
    (C) Gentle and contemplative
    (D) Bewildered
    (E) Straightforward

48. The speaker shifts point of view in which of the following lines?

    (A) Line 9
    (B) Line 4
    (C) Line 5
    (D) Line 3
    (E) Line 2

49. Which line best states the poem's meaning?

    (A) Line 14
    (B) Line 9
    (C) Line 4
    (D) Line 11
    (E) Line 12

50. The author states that

    (A) life far exceeds death.
    (B) we have an enormous amount to fear from death.
    (C) we shall never know what awaits us after death.
    (D) we have little to fear from death because the afterlife exceeds all our expectations.
    (E) there is nothing after life.

51. The poet's attitude toward life and death shows that he was most likely influenced by

    (A) the death of a loved one.
    (B) the Transcendentalists of the 1830–1860s.
    (C) the rhythm of nineteenth-century slave verse.
    (D) the Puritan attitudes of the seventeenth century.
    (E) the Revolutionary War.

SECTION II: ESSAY QUESTIONS

Time—2 hours

Question 1
Suggested Time: 40 minutes

Directions: Read the following excerpt from Mark Twain's essay "Fenimore Cooper's Literary Offenses." Then write a careful analysis to show how Twain does or does not follow his own advice as he criticizes Cooper's writing style.

There are nineteen rules governing literary art in the domain of romantic fiction—some say twenty-two. In *Deerslayer,* Cooper violated eighteen of them. These eighteen require:

1. That a tale shall accomplish something and arrive somewhere. But the *Deerslayer* tale accomplishes nothing and arrives in the air.

2. They require that the episodes of a tale shall be necessary parts of the tale, and shall help to develop it. But as the *Deerslayer* tale is not a tale, and accomplishes nothing and arrives nowhere, the episodes have no rightful place in the work, since there was nothing for them to develop.

3. They require that the personages in a tale shall be alive, except in the case of corpses, and that always the reader shall be able to tell the corpses from the others. But this detail has often been overlooked in the *Deerslayer* tale....

In addition to these large rules, there are some little ones. These require that the author shall

1. Say what he is proposing to say, not merely come near it.

2. Use the right word, not its second cousin.

3. Eschew surplus.

4. Not omit necessary details.

5. Avoid slovenliness of form.

6. Use good grammar.

7. Employ a simple and straightforward style.

Even these seven are coldly and persistently violated in the *Deerslayer* tale.

Question 2
Suggested Time: 40 minutes

Directions: Carefully read the following poem by Henry Wadsworth Longfellow. Then write a well-organized essay in which you discuss the poem's use of literary devices to express his view of life. You may wish to consider some or all of the following literary devices: allusions, tone, metaphors, diction, parallelism, similes, and imagery.

A Psalm of Life

Tell me not, in mournful numbers,
    Life is but an empty dream!—
For the soul is dead that slumbers,
    And things are not what they seem.

Life is real! Life is earnest!
    And the grave is not its goal;
Dust thou art, to dust returnest,
    Was not spoken of the soul.

Not enjoyment, and not sorrow,
    Is our destined end or way;
But to act, that each tomorrow
    Find us farther than today.

Art is long, and Time is fleeting,
    And our hearts, thought stout and brave,
Still, like muffled drums, are beating
    Funeral marches to the grave.

In the world's broad field of battle,
    In the bivouac of Life,
Be not like dumb, driven cattle!
    Be a hero in the strife!

Trust no future, howe'er pleasant!
    Let the dead Past bury its dead!
Act—act in the living Present!
    Heart within, and God o'erhead!

Lives of great men all remind us
    We can make our lives sublime,
And, departing, leave behind us
    Footprints in the sands of time.

Question 3
Suggested Time: 40 minutes

Directions: The balance between the extremes of good and bad make us "human," and this is true in literature as well as life. Select a major character from any work of recognized literary merit and show how that character is human in that he or she possesses both good and bad traits. Be sure to include specific examples from the work under discussion to make your point. If you wish, you may select from the following list:

Madame Bovary	Ethan Frome
Vanity Fair	Moby Dick
Lord Jim	Catch-22
The Turn of the Screw	To the Lighthouse
Native Son	Invisible Man
Like Water for Chocolate	The Great Gatsby
The Sun Also Rises	Nicholas Nickleby
Cry, the Beloved Country	Julius Caesar
Othello	Romeo and Juliet
Jane Eyre	Our Town
Pride and Prejudice	The Sound and the Fury

QUICK-SCORE ANSWERS

1.	C	18.	B	35.	D
2.	E	19.	D	36.	D
3.	C	20.	C	37.	E
4.	A	21.	A	38.	A
5.	B	22.	D	39.	C
6.	E	23.	C	40.	A
7.	C	24.	A	41.	B
8.	A	25.	A	42.	D
9.	D	26.	B	43.	A
10.	D	27.	C	44.	B
11.	B	28.	C	45.	C
12.	D	29.	E	46.	A
13.	E	30.	C	47.	C
14.	C	31.	C	48.	A
15.	B	32.	E	49.	B
16.	A	33.	C	50.	D
17.	C	34.	A	51.	B

COMPUTING YOUR SCORE

You can use the following worksheet to compute an approximate score on the practice test. Since it is difficult to be objective about your own writing and since you are not a trained ETS scorer or English teacher, you may wish to ask a friend who has already taken the test (and earned a high score of 4 or 5) to score your three essays.

Recognize that your score can only be an approximation (at best), as you are scoring yourself against yourself. In the actual AP English Literature and Composition Exam, you will be scored against every other student who takes the test as well.

Section I: Multiple-Choice Questions

	_____	number of correct answers
−	_____	.25 × number of wrong answers
=	_____	raw score
	_____	raw score
×	_____	1.25
=	_____	scaled score (out of a possible 67.5)

Section II: Essays

_____	essay 1 (0–9)
_____	essay 2 (0–9)
_____	essay 3 (0–9)
× _____	3.055
= _____	scaled score (out of a possible 82.5)

Scaled Score

_____	multiple-choice scaled score
+ _____	essay scaled score
= _____	final scaled score (out of a possible 150)

AP Score Conversion Chart

Scaled Score	Likely AP Score
150–100	5
99–86	4
85–67	3
66–0	1 or 2

ANSWERS AND EXPLANATIONS

SECTION I: MULTIPLE-CHOICE QUESTIONS

1. **The correct answer is (C).** This essay is framed as a dialogue, as the speakers alternate sides. This is shown by each speaker's name in capital letters, as readers would find in a play script. The dialogue cannot be an *autobiography,* choice (A), because it is not written in the first person. It can't be a *short story,* choice (B), because it is fact, not fiction; it is not a *parable,* choice (D), because it argues a point rather than teaches a lesson. Finally, it cannot be a *conceit,* choice (E), because it is not an ornate extended metaphor.

2. **The correct answer is (E).** As used in the second paragraph, the phrase "to pay court" means to show admiration and deference. This can be inferred from context, as the men "go to sea, build houses, and do everything" to further their chances for marriage. Choice (A) is another use of the word "court" but not the meaning used in this context. Choice (B) is only part of the answer; men are carrying out these "responsibilities" to further their aim of winning a woman. Don't confuse the verb "court" with the noun "court," as is the case in choice (C). Choice (D) has nothing to do with the word or its context.

3. **The correct answer is (C).** The third paragraph (Mrs. Knowles' first argument) is marked by *parallelism.* The speaker matches parts of speech, phrases, and clauses, such as "reasons *very wittily,* but not *very convincingly.*" There are no comparisons, choice (A); symbols, choice (B); understatement, choice (D); or exaggeration, choice (E).

4. **The correct answer is (A).** The stylistic element in the third paragraph serves to convey the speaker's intelligence and conviction. *Parallelism* (also called "parallel structure") gives writing style and vigor, serving to convince readers of the writer's command of examples. Parallelism may suggest the seriousness of the problem the writer is discussing, but it may also convey many other moods, so choice (C) is wrong. Since there is no gratuitous embellishment, choice (B) cannot be correct. Choice (D) is far from the mark since there are no comparisons, misplaced or otherwise. Choice (E) is half true: the parallelism does reinforce her point, but it does not show the true scope of the situation. Rather, it does so by strength of language and syntax.

5. **The correct answer is (B).** Johnson addresses Mrs. Knowles as "Madam" to show respect. Beware of "overreading" by forcing relationships that do not exist: he is not showing *contempt,* choice (A); *humor,* choice (C); *irony,* choice (D); or *loathing,* choice (E). Sometimes, a word is just what it appears to be.

6. **The correct answer is (E).** You can infer from this passage that Johnson justifies a double standard whereby men do not have to be perfect but women must be. You can infer this from these lines: "And women have not the same temptations that we have: they may always live in virtuous company; men must mix in the world indiscriminately. If a woman has no inclination to do what is wrong, being secured from it is no restraint to her." Johnson's belief in a double standard for men and women is also shown in this line: "It is plain, Madam, one or another must have the superiority. As Shakespeare says, 'If two men ride on a horse, one must ride behind.'" This directly contradicts choice (A). Since Johnson counters Mrs. Knowles' arguments with arguments of his own, it is plain that he is taking her point seriously, so you can discount choice (B). While choice (C) may be true, you cannot infer that from the information provided in this passage. Finally, Johnson does not want to change the social order, so choice (D) cannot be correct.

7. **The correct answer is (C).** Johnson justifies his conclusions by arguing that men are out in the world and subject to temptation, but women are sheltered and thus can choose to be virtuous. This is shown directly in the following line: "And women have not the same temptations that we have: they may always live in virtuous company; men must mix in the world indiscriminately. If a woman has no inclination to do what is wrong, being secured from it is no restraint to her." This directly contradicts choice (B). There is no proof that Johnson believes that anyone is being mistreated, so you can eliminate choice (A). Since punishment is meted out equally to men and women (and animals) that violate the social order, you can eliminate choice (D). Choice (E) is a misreading of Johnson's metaphor about jumping into the Thames River.

8. **The correct answer is (A).** When he quotes Shakespeare ("If two men ride on a horse, one must ride behind"), Johnson is using an *allusion;* he is making a reference to Shakespeare. Recall that an *allusion* is a reference to a well-known place, event, person, work of art, or other work of literature. Allusions enrich a story or poem by suggesting powerful and exciting comparisons. It is not a *simile* (a comparison using "like" or "as"), *personification* (giving human traits to nonhuman objects), or *irony* (a reversal of expectations.) Neither is it *ambiguity*, statements that are open to interpretation on several levels.

9. **The correct answer is (D).** When he says, "Sir, the horse would throw them both," Johnson is using wit and humor to suggest that men and women can never be equal. His witty rejoinder here builds on his earlier allusion to Shakespeare. This directly contradicts choice (E). Choice (A) is too strong; he is being witty but not sarcastic. The same is true of choice (B). He is not mocking Boswell, nor even referring to him in any way, so choice (C) is off the mark.

10. **The correct answer is (D).** You can infer from his comments that Boswell believes that women are inferior to men. Since Johnson has already won the argument, choice (A) is wrong. The same can be said for choice (B) since it directly contradicts the point. There is no support for choice (C) or choice (E).

11. **The correct answer is (B).** Boswell likely believes that upper-class people will find more joy in heaven than lower-class people because Boswell is a snob who does not have much respect for the lower classes. There is no support for choice (A). Choice (C) is too vague. Choice (D) is the direct opposite of the truth: Boswell believes that *upper-class* people are smarter and more "intuitive" than their betters. Finally, there is no proof for choice (E) nor is it germane to the argument here.

12. **The correct answer is (D).** From the diction and syntax used in this passage, you can conclude that the passage was written in the late eighteenth century. This is shown in words such as "Nay" and "Madame" and the long sentences. This is the direct opposite of choice (E). Since the style is so elegant, choice (A) is not likely correct. Choice (B) directly contradicts the writer's feelings that Johnson is correct. Finally, there is no proof that the writer is trying to impress his readers by parading his learning, choice (C). Rather, he is using what appears to be his natural and usual style of writing.

13. **The correct answer is (E).** The writer's attitude toward Dr. Johnson is best described as *admiring*. Dr. Johnson gets the best in the argument; Boswell and Dilly echo his points. This directly contradicts choice (A), *contemptuous*, and choice (D), *scornful*. He cannot be *neutral,* choice (C), if he is admiring. Finally, he is admiring but not *amazed,* choice (B), which is too strong.

14. **The correct answer is (C).** The best title for this selection would be "On Equality of the Sexes." Since it is an argument, using either choice (A) or (B) would tip the writer's hand to the outcome and spoil any sense of suspense. Choice (D) is too narrow for the one reference to heaven. Since Johnson clearly wins, choice (E) does not apply.

15. **The correct answer is (B).** You can figure out a poem's rhyme scheme by assigning a letter to each word that rhymes. For example, Cat (A)/ Bat (A)/ Mat (A) would all be assigned the same letter because they all rhyme. The next word that does not rhyme, such as "like," would be assigned the letter "B." This continues for the length of the poem. Choice (B) is the correct choice, as the following example shows:

Thou sorrow, venom elf.	A
Is this thy play,	B
To spin a web out of thyself	A
To catch a fly?	B
For why?	B

16. **The correct answer is (A).** "Hell's Spider" is Satan, the devil. We can tell this is so by the eighth stanza, specifically in the phrase "Adam's race," in line 36, referring to mankind. Only the devil would be able to entrap man. Thus, choice (B), *Man,* cannot be correct. Choice (C) is equally wrong, for nowhere in the poem is a black widow spider mentioned. Choice (D), *the venom elf* mentioned in the first line, refers to a spider spinning a net to catch a fly, not to the devil himself, and choice (E) is the one being trapped, not the one doing the trapping.

17. **The correct answer is (C).** The poem is using the analogy of a spider and a fly to show how Hell's spider—Satan—traps Adam's race—man. Choice (A) is partly correct, for the spider did indeed bite the fly's head off, as the lines "Whereas the silly fly,/Caught by its leg,/Thou by the throat took'st hastily,/And 'hind the head/Bite dead" (stanza 5) tell us. The rest of the statement is not correct, however, because the "venom elf" mentioned in the first line does not refer to the fly, as the answer choice implies, but rather to the spider. Choice (B) is not correct, for again, the "venom elf" refers to the spider, not the fly. Choice (D) is not correct, as the poem does not say that humanity must allow itself to be called by Nature. Rather, the sixth stanza explains that humans must listen to their inborn ability to tell right from wrong. This choice is far too general and thus fails to answer the question. Choice (E) is wrong, because the poem does not say that man flies. An ability to fly would have nothing to do with Satan's power to ensnare humanity.

18. **The correct answer is (B).** In keeping with the analogy between the spider (Satan) and the fly (man) set up above, it follows that the "venom things" that trap man would be his sins. Choice (A) cannot be correct, for base metals have nothing to do with spiders and flies and the battle between Satan and man. Choice (C) is partly correct, for man is indeed tangled in a web, but the comparison is more fully expressed in choice (B). Choice (D) and choice (E) may appear to be correct, but a closer examination reveals that nowhere is poison considered.

19. **The correct answer is (D).** The cord is the devil's way to trap man. Choice (A) makes no sense, for the poet would not beg God's grace to break the cord. God's grace is awarded to man to ease sins. Since there is no mother-child discussion here, choice (B) is incorrect. Choice (C) looks like a correct answer at first glance, but by this point in the poem, we are beyond the spider-fly analogy, and so an answer with the devil and man is more suitable. The same is true for choice (E).

20. **The correct answer is (C).** The figure of speech here is an *analogy,* as a comparison is constructed between the spider of the beginning of the poem and the devil. Each sets traps to ensnare its prey. Choice (A) is wrong, for a *metaphor* is a comparison between two objects in a brief and succinct manner. Unless it is an extended metaphor, it would rarely stretch more than a line and certainly not through a whole poem. Choice (B) is wrong because a *simile* is a type of metaphor that uses either "like" or "as" to make the comparison, as in "He eats like a horse." Choice (D) is wrong because *personification*

gives human attributes to objects, and *hyperbole,* choice (E), is exaggeration for literary effect.

21. **The correct answer is (A).** The spider traps the fly as the devil traps man; each constructs clever snares for its unsuspecting prey. Choice (B) may appear to be a correct answer, but the analogy between the fly and man is not close enough to select this as a better answer than choice (A). A fly cannot reason and escape from a trap; a fly cannot stop himself from sinning. Choice (C) is wrong, for nowhere in stanza 7 is a nightingale mentioned. Choice (D) is wrong, for entrails are not compared to the spider. Choice (E) is wrong because we cannot see God's grace in the spider, for the spider is identified with the devil.

22. **The correct answer is (D).** A *simile* is a brief comparison using "like" or "as." The line in the last stanza, "We'll nightingale sing like," as man in heaven is likened to a bird singing with joy, is the correct choice here. Choice (A) means using the name of one object for that of another of which it is a part or related, such as "scepter" for "sovereignty." Choice (B) is a figure of speech in which part is used for the whole, as when modern poet and dramatist T.S. Eliot said a "pair of ragged claws" in referring to crab in his poem "The Love Song of J. Alfred Prufrock." Choice (E) is a *metaphor* that contains parts that do not fit together, as in "sailing to the crosswalk of life," for a crosswalk would not be found on the ocean.

23. **The correct answer is (C).** Humanity, washed free of sins, will sing gloriously in heaven, says the poet. Lines 43–44, "Thy Grace to break the cord; afford/Us glory's gate," is a clue to this, especially the word "Us."

24. **The correct answer is (A).** The fly is trapped by the spider as humans are trapped by the devil. Both the spider and the devil construct clever snares for their unsuspecting prey. Choice (B) appears to be a correct answer, but the analogy between the fly and man is not close enough to select this as a better answer than choice (A). A fly cannot reason and escape from a trap; a fly cannot stop himself from sinning. Choice (C) is wrong, for nowhere in stanza 7 is a nightingale mentioned. Choice (D) is wrong, for entrails are not compared to the spider. Choice (E) is wrong because we cannot see God's grace in the spider, for the spider is identified with the devil.

25. **The correct answer is (A).** The switch is made in line 31, where the poet says "This fray seems thus to us" and ties the spider to the devil and the fly to humanity to make his point.

26. **The correct answer is (B).** This poem is best described as characterized by many elaborate and surprising figures of speech. This best shown in the surprising comparisons. Therefore, choice (A) and choice (C) cannot be true. The poem does not tell a story so much as make a comparison, so choice (D) is wrong. While the poem is religious, it is not *didactic and preachy,* so choice (E) is incorrect.

27. **The correct answer is (C).** The final two couplets tell us that the author is most likely a very religious person, as the poem concludes with the wish that God will wash away the devil's traps and afford us all His grace. In this light, choices (A), (B), and (D) would not fit. Choice (E) has little to do with the poem, as it does not focus on what we would consider "natural" or "nature" phenomena.

28. **The correct answer is (C).** *Witty and light* best expresses the tone of the poem. The *tone* of a work of literature is the particular manner or style, the mood of a piece of writing. It is determined through the author's choice of words and their placement. Here, the very comparison between Satan and the spider and a fly and man establishes the general tone, for were the author to be *intense and agitated,* choice (A), or *resigned and pessimistic,* choice (D), we would have had a different choice of analogy. The

ending, with its vision of redemption, also would not fit in with choices (A) and (D). The very subject of the work contradicts choice (E).

29. **The correct answer is (E).** As established in previous answers, the poet is very much concerned with religion. Thus, the only answer that is not true would be choice (E). The questions that have the word *not* or *only*, or any other qualifier, must be read very carefully. They are often answered incorrectly because they are read too quickly and the qualifier is overlooked.

30. **The correct answer is (C).** The spider catches a fly (Satan catches humanity sinning), so choice (C) is the best title. Choice (D) cannot be true because it reverses the relationship. Choices (A) and (E) are too vague to accurately reflect the poem's contents. Choice (B) does not reflect the poem's theme, the danger humanity faces when it strays from the path of goodness.

31. **The correct answer is (C).** The phrase "summer soldier and the sunshine patriot" is an example of *alliteration* and *metaphor*. *Alliteration* is the repetition of initial consonant sounds in several words in a sentence or line of poetry. Writers use alliteration to create musical effects, link related ideas, stress certain words, or mimic specific sounds. Here, the initial consonant "s" is repeated. A *metaphor* is a figure of speech that compares two unlike things. The more familiar thing helps describe the less familiar one. In this passage, soldiers and patriots are being compared to good weather, implying that they will fight only when it is easy and pleasant. When the weather and the battle turn foul, they will desert.

32. **The correct answer is (E).** The tone of this passage is best described as *fiery*. The author goes so far as to call the King a murderer, highwayman, or thief: "Neither have I so much of the infidel in me, as to suppose that he has relinquished the government of the world, and given us up to the care of devils; and as I do not, I cannot see on what grounds the king of Britain can look up to Heaven for help against us: a common murderer, a highwayman, or a housebreaker, has as good a pretense as he." The tone is so strong that you can eliminate choices (B), (C), and (D) because they are not strong enough. Obviously, choice (A) is far from the mark.

33. **The correct answer is (C).** The phrase "the harder the conflict, the more glorious the triumph" is an example of *an aphorism*, a brief witty statement designed to be memorable. Choice (B) is both inaccurate and too general; choice (E) is inaccurate. Choice (A) has nothing to do with the subject at hand, nor does choice (D).

34. **The correct answer is (A).** The writer uses the phrase cited in item 34 and others like it to create the impression that the specific argument being presented has a more general application. He is specifically arguing against King George and generally arguing against tyranny. He is trying to convince his audience that his point is valid, and *displaying his learning*, choice (B), would work against that. He does attack the opposition, choice (C), but neither in this instance nor through the aphorisms. Choice (D) makes no sense. The same is true of choice (E).

35. **The correct answer is (D).** The writer draws his imagery from all the following EXCEPT *water*, especially the ocean. The *nature imagery*, choice (A), is displayed by his reference to "The summer soldier and the sunshine patriot." The repeated references to heaven and hell are allusions to the Bible, choice (B). When he calls the King a murderer, highwayman, or thief, he is referring to crime and lawbreakers, choice (C). Finally, we see fire imagery in the line "though the flame of liberty," choice (E). Only water imagery is not used.

36. **The correct answer is (D).** The metaphor in the second paragraph compares the king's actions to those of a thief and murderer. This is directly shown in the following line: "Neither have I so much of the infidel in me, as to suppose that he has relinquished the

government of the world, and given us up to the care of devils; and as I do not, I cannot see on what grounds the king of Britain can look up to Heaven for help against us: a common murderer, a highwayman, or a housebreaker, has as good a pretense as he."

37. **The correct answer is (E).** The author uses the anecdote about the tavernkeeper at Amboy to make the point that the tavernkeeper is more interested in keeping the status quo than securing peace for his children. You can infer this from the following statement: "...a separation must some time or other finally take place, and a generous parent should have said, 'If there must be trouble, let it be in my day, that my child may have peace,' and this single reflection, well applied, is sufficient to awaken every man to duty."

38. **The correct answer is (A).** The writer uses the simile "My own line of reasoning is to myself as straight and clear as a ray of light " to covey the idea that the colonists are fighting for a just cause and should not lose sight of their purpose. Choice (B) is far too strong and undercuts the writer's point. The same is true of choice (C). Choice (D) is reading far more into the simile than the writer intended. The same is true for choice (E). Be careful not to "over-reason" or "over-think" the answer. The questions on the AP English Literature and Composition exam are detailed but not deceptive.

39. **The correct answer is (C).** The poet is using the Italian (also known as Petrarchan) sonnet form to compare death to sleep, a common theme in sonnets. Lines 1–8 describe a mother leading her child to bed and rest at day's end; lines 9–14 describe Nature leading a person to death.

40. **The correct answer is (A).** The poet uses a *simile* here, a direct comparison of two unlike objects, using "like" or "as." The first line, "As a fond mother . . . " tells us this. *Hyperbole,* choice (B), is overstatement or great exaggeration for effect. A *pun,* choice (C), is the humorous use of words to stress their different meanings or the use of words that are alike or almost alike in sound but different in meaning—a play on words (e.g., "tail" and "tale"). An *oxymoron,* choice (D), consists of contradictory terms brought together to express a paradox in order to establish a strong poetic effect. *Synesthesia,* choice (E), occurs when the stimulus applied to one sense triggers another; for example, when hearing a certain sound induces a person to visualize color.

41. **The correct answer is (B).** The poet uses the mother-child comparison to reassure the reader and to remove death's sting. Furthermore, words such as "gently" in line 11 suggest the calmness with which we ought to approach death. The final line clarifies his attitude: What lies after our mortal existence far exceeds what meager "playthings" we might have relinquished. The afterlife promises far more splendid treasures.

42. **The correct answer is (D).** The author pictures the approach of death and casts it in a light of calm reassurance, as explained in item 41.

43. **The correct answer is (A).** As a child has his treasures, so adults fill their lives with the people and things they value.

44. **The correct answer is (B).** The poet does not condemn humanity for their diversions, as choice (C) implies. Rather, people are unaware of what lies beyond, and so we remain in a state of childlike innocence, not realizing what is of value until we have passed through life.

45. **The correct answer is (C).** A *sonnet* is a lyric poem of fourteen lines written in iambic pentameter. Originated by the Italian poets during the thirteenth century, it reached perfection a century later in the work of Petrarch and later came to be known as the Italian or Petrarchan sonnet. When the English poets of the sixteenth century discovered Petrarch, they were challenged by his format and adopted the number of lines but changed the rhyme scheme, as will be discussed later. An *ode*, choice (A), is

an elaborate lyric verse that usually deals with an important and dignified theme. *Free verse*, choice (B), has unrhymed lines without regular rhythm. A *ballad*, choice (D), is a simple verse that tells a story to be sung or recited. *Light verse*, choice (E), falls into a general group of poems written to entertain. Epigrams and limericks show the less serious side of light verse; parody or satire illustrates its more profound aspects.

46. **The correct answer is (A).** This is the rhyme scheme of the Italian sonnet. The first group, called the *octave*, presents the poet's subject; the second group, called the *sestet*, indicates the importance of the facts set forth in the octave. The sestet may resolve the problem presented in the octave. The rhyme scheme of a poem is determined by assigning a letter to each new sound found at the end of a line of verse.

47. **The correct answer is (C).** A poem's *tone* is derived from the author's attitude toward his audience and subject matter. Here, the tone is gentle and contemplative, as the mother-child situation suggests. Choice (A), *hostile*, suggests outright anger, which is directly at odds with the poem's gentle, soothing tone. Choice (B), a *baroque* tone, would be elaborate and extravagantly ornamented. Choice (D) is wrong because far from bewildered, the speaker is certain that the unknown afterlife exceeds that which we know. The compassion and tenderness evidenced argue against a straightforward tone. Therefore, you can eliminate choice (E) as well.

48. **The correct answer is (A).** The speaker shifts point of view in line 9: "So Nature deals with us, and takes away..."

49. **The correct answer is (B).** Line 9, "So Nature deals with us," best states the poem's meaning.

50. **The correct answer is (D).** The author states that we have little to fear from death because the afterlife exceeds all our expectations, as previously discussed.

51. **The correct answer is (B).** The poet's attitude toward life and death shows that he was most likely influenced by the Transcendentalists of the 1830s–1860s. The Transcendentalists believed that there was some knowledge of reality or truth that people grasp not through logic or the laws of nature but through our intuition. There is obviously no way that the poet could have known of the afterlife. Choice (A) cannot be true because readers have no way of knowing from the poem if the poet suffered a personal loss. Eliminate choice (C) because again we cannot link this poem to slavery. Choice (D) is wrong because the Puritans preached God's wrath and the fearsomeness of the afterlife for all but a few who were "elect" or saved. There is no way of knowing prior to one's death if one was saved or not. Finally, choice (E) is too general a response to suffice as a correct answer.

SECTION II: ESSAY QUESTIONS

QUESTION 1:

This question requires you to analyze Twain's writing to analyze whether he uses stylistic devices to underscore his advice. For example, does he write clearly, as he advises Fenimore Cooper to do, or does he obscure meaning with intricate sentences? Does he omit superfluous words and phrases or load his writing with "dead wood"?

This question represents a very typical AP Literature question: discuss Writer A's evaluation of another writer and the stylistic devices that Writer A uses. To earn a high score on this question,

- be sure to answer the question you are asked. Responses often earn low scores because they do not directly focus on the question being asked.

- provide background or additional information only if it directly pertains to the issue at hand. Don't parade your learning for the sake of impressing your reader. Also be sure that you have your facts right.

- focus on stylistic devices. These include sentence structure and length, diction (word choice), punctuation, figures of speech, and imagery.

- cite specific examples from the text and your own knowledge to make your point.

- demonstrate a sophisticated use of language and an awareness of its power to communicate meaning.

- revise your essay to make sure that *you* have used all words correctly. After all, you don't want to misuse words when you're analyzing another writer's style.

- check your essay for errors in grammar, usage, punctuation, capitalization, and spelling.

The following model response would earn a top score because it fulfills the requirements of this question and the standards of good writing:

James Fenimore Cooper's *Deerslayer* series was a remarkable
1   accomplishment: America's first "native" novels, concerned with American themes and characters, set on American soil. Previously, the best-selling novels in America were all imported from England. By writing these novels, Fenimore Cooper succeeded in putting America on the literary map. Unfortunately, Fenimore Cooper's prose was bloated and his characters wooden.

1. Background establishes writer's knowledge.

2   Mark Twain, noted for his precise diction, humorous prose, and lively characters, takes Fenimore Cooper to task in his essay "Fenimore Cooper's Literary Offenses." Twain reinforces his points by following his own advice. This is shown in his clear, clean, and direct writing style.

2. Thesis stated directly.

We see this in Twain's first point: "That a tale shall accomplish something and arrive somewhere. But the *Deerslayer* tale accomplishes nothing and arrives in the air." These two simple sentences are straight and unadorned. As a result,
3   Twain directly nails Cooper's stylistic defects by contrast: his simple sentences show clear writing at its best.

3. Specific examples from the text.

Points 12–18 are all simple sentences, brief and to the point. Twain is showing readers by his example that the most effective writing style is concise and carefully crafted. Notice also that

4. Sophisticated use of language makes the writer's point.

5. Examples reinforce the writer's thesis.

6. "Bombastic" shows sophisticated use of language.

7. Conclusion reinforces the writer's point.

4   Twain uses the more familiar "reader" rather than the stiff "one" to keep his writing from becoming overly formal and off-putting.

Further, each point Twain makes does exactly what he says it should. For example, Point 12—"Say what he is proposing to say, not merely come near it."—does just that. Twain makes his point clearly, adding a touch of humor to make the advice go down more smoothly. Twain reinforces the importance of choosing the precise word in item 13: "Use the right word, not its second cousin." The phrase "not its second cousin" is a humorous

5   way of emphasizing the importance of diction in effective writing. You can't be much more simple and straightforward than point 18: "Employ a simple and straightforward style." Twain pares away the pronoun ("you"), using a command to make his writing even more immediate.

6   Twain matches form to function to reinforce his criticism of Fenimore Cooper's bombastic writing style. By writing simple, direct sentences, Twain reinforces his advice about writing crisp, precise prose. He instructs readers to choose exact words, pare down redundancies, correct errors, and follow the conventions of standard written English. His writing follows each of these rules.

7   "Do as I say *and* as I do," is Twain's advice. And as with any good teacher, he follows his own advice!

QUESTION 2

This is another archetypal AP question: analyze a specific work of literature to reveal its meaning. With these questions, you are expected to use the literary techniques as tools to uncover the writer's theme or main idea.

Try these suggestions as you answer these types of literary analysis questions:

- Start by reading the poem (essay, short story excerpt, etc.) several times through. Each time you read, look for different literary elements, such as figures of speech and diction. As you read, see how all the literary elements fit together to help the writer express his or her insight about life.

- Go with the obvious interpretation. If a poem is called "A Psalm of Life," for example, assume that the main idea concerns a hymn (psalm) to existence (life.) If a close reading proves that this is not the case, you can readjust your expectations. However, always start by assuming that the literary work is what it appears to be. In general, these questions are not designed to trip you up; rather, they are crafted to test what you have learned about literary analysis in class and on your own.

- Unless you're desperately stuck for an opening gambit, don't rephrase the question in your opening sentence. Remember that the scorers are reading hundreds of essays on the same topic, so they're not likely to be impressed if the opening to your essay is just like the opening of the previous fifty essays they have read. Instead, get right to your point by stating your thesis.

- If you *do* want to try crafting an interesting opening, try using a well-known quotation, anecdote (brief story), or fact. These techniques will be explained in detail in the essay Part IV: Strategies for Success on the Essay Questions.

- Follow with specific examples drawn from the work of literature under analysis. Relate each point to your main idea.

- Interweave all the elements together into a meaningful whole. You may treat metaphor, irony, and allusions in each paragraph, for example, examining different examples of each literary element to make your point. In general, don't separate the literary elements out, one in each paragraph, as this usually results in a choppy and redundant essay.

- Sum up by briefly reiterating your point. Don't introduce any new information, but reach for an insight or point that ties everything together in an intelligent and logical way.

- Be sure to proofread your essay for errors in grammar, usage, punctuation, capitalization, and spelling. You won't get clobbered for a few minor errors, but why not improve your chances of earning a top score by being letter perfect?

The following model response would earn a top score because it fulfills the requirements of this question and the standards of good writing:

1   "A Psalm of Life" expresses Longfellow's view that life is brief and real. As a result, he exhorts us to make the most of the time we have been allotted by trying to make our lives a template for those who follow. He suggests that individuality and self-reliance are very important to a meaningful life.

1. Get right to the point without restating the question.

2   Longfellow opens with the metaphor "Tell me not, in mournful numbers, Life is but an empty dream!" (lines 1–2) to convey the point that life is real, not a fantasy. Whether or not there is an

2. Uses a specific literary element and example to make the point.

3. Stylistic devices woven in to make the point.

4. Examples directly relate to the point.

5. Allusion and simile make the point.

6. Point treated in the order presented in the topic paragraph.

7. Topic summed up with a direct reference to the poem.

3   afterlife, he suggests, we must be concerned with the here and now. "Life is real! Life is earnest!" he admonishes us in line 5. He drives his point home by using parallel sentences that end in exclamation points. The positive tone of these two sentences reinforces Longfellow's optimistic view of life's possibilities.

4   Longfellow applies the Biblical allusion in line 7—" Dust thou art, to dust returnest /Was not spoken of the soul"—to reinforce his point that we must make the most of the time we have on this earth. While our bodies will die, our legacy lives on. Therefore, we must "... act, that each tomorrow/Find us farther than today" (lines 11–12).

5   In the fourth stanza, Longfellow makes an allusion to the Latin saying *Ars longa, vita brevis est* when he says that "Art is long, and Time is fleeting." This allusion, with its echoes of the long record of human achievement, reminds us to make the most of the time we have to make our own positive impact on history. The simile in line 15 hastens us on our way to achievement: "And our hearts, thought stout and brave,/Still, like muffled drums, are beating/Funeral marches to the grave."

6   How can we make a difference for those to follow? We can start with the simile in lines 20–21: "Be not like dumb, driven cattle!/Be a hero in the strife!" Then we can obey the command in line 20: "Be a hero in the strife!" The memorable image in lines 27–28—"And, departing, leave behind us/Footprints in the sands of time"—reminds us that we *can* make a mark on the world by being active and optimistic.

An assured and optimistic view of life's possibilities, "A Psalm of Life" advises readers to live meaningful lives filled with positive actions. Longfellow encourages his audience to live in such a way that future generations can take courage from our acts. His hymn to a meaningful existence provides a blueprint for

7   action: "Act—act in the living Present!"

QUESTION 3

This is the third type of essay question that you will encounter on the AP test: the free-choice opened-ended response. With these questions, be especially sure to choose a literary work that contains the information you need to answer the question. Don't be trapped into choosing a book just because you know it well or think that the scorer will applaud your choice. Instead, select a literary work that has what you need in this instance. To answer this question, for example, you need a literary work that contains

- a character who possesses good traits and bad traits

- a character who is fully rounded and thus emerges as "human"

Therefore, you can't use a character who is all bad (such as the villain Iago from Shakespeare's tragedy *Othello*) or all good (the saintly Uncle Tom from Harriet Beecher Stowe's *Uncle Tom's Cabin*). Neither can you use a flat or stock character such as Shakespeare's jolly Falstaff, the stereotypical good-time Charlie.

As you answer these questions, be sure to address each part. For instance, in this case you would

- identify the character's traits.

- use specific examples to make your point.

- demonstrate how the character springs to life.

The following model response would earn a top score because it fulfills the requirements of this question and the standards of good writing:

1   Huckleberry Finn, the protagonist in Mark Twain's *The Adventures of Huckleberry Finn*, springs from the page as a real person because he possesses both good and bad traits. By showing both sides of Huck's character, Twain succeeds in creating a fully rounded real person rather than a two-dimensional literary figure.

    We see Huck's less-than-admirable side in the tricks he plays on his friend Jim. The first trick, involving a nickel and a hat, is relatively innocuous, but as Huck continues with his childishness, the tricks become progressively more dangerous and humiliating. The second trick, involving a snake, results in Jim getting bitten. While Jim recovers without lasting damage, the trick has the potential to kill him. The final trick, however, is the worst of all. Huck and Jim get separated on their journey down the Mississippi River during a foggy night. Jim is disconsolate

2   because he assumes that Huck has died. When they are reunited in the morning, Jim says, "Goodness gracious, is dat you, Huck?

3   En you ain't dead—you ain't drowned—you's back agin?" Unable to pass up the chance to play a joke on his friend, Huck convinces Jim that they had never been separated. Rather, Jim dreamed the entire incident. Huck tricks Jim into interpreting every part of the "dream" until they see the pile of leaves, twigs, and the smashed oar on the raft. Jim looks at the trash and realizes that Huck has tricked him. He stares at the pile of trash

4   and says, "Dat truck dah is *trash*; en trash is what people is dat puts dirt on de head er dey fren's en makes 'em ashamed." But Huck learns from his folly. Although it takes him fifteen minutes to work up the courage, he apologizes to Jim for humiliating him.

1. Identifies the character's traits.

2. Specific details prove the point.

3. Consider memorizing key quotes to use as examples.

4. Quote nails the main idea.

Huck never plays any more mean tricks on Jim and realizes that he should never have played any tricks on him at all.

5. Smoothly transitions into the next part of the question.

5 As any real person, Huck also has an admirable side. In Chapter 31, Huck is faced with the key moral dilemma of his life: does he return Jim to his rightful owner, Miss Watson, or continue to harbor a fugitive? At first, Huck decides to turn Jim in, as he has been taught by a corrupt society that slavery is acceptable. Huck writes a letter to Miss Watson, revealing Jim's whereabouts. The more Huck thinks about his actions, however, the more he realizes the conflict between what he has been taught about slavery and what he knows is morally right about owning another human being. Huck decides to follow his conscience and risk eternal damnation rather than return his friend to slavery. "All

6. Novel's climax used to prove the point.

6 right, then, I'll go to hell," Huck says and tears up the letter. It's the rare person who does not face a crisis of conscience at least once in their life. Like Huck, we're torn between what we have been taught and what we know in our hearts is right. It would be gratifying if we all had Huck's courage to choose the right path.

7. Conclusion sums up the main idea.

7 By showing the two sides of Huck's character, Mark Twain succeeds in fashioning a fully rounded human being. Like all of us, Huck can be childish, thoughtless, and even cruel. However, like the heroes among us, he can also be courageous. Huck defies society and risks eternal damnation to follow his conscience. Humans make mistakes, and they act with great bravery. Huck leaps from the page because he is like us: imperfect yet filled with heart.

Strategies for Success on the Multiple-Choice Questions

You'll recall from Part I of this book and the sample AP English Literature and Composition exams you've taken that the multiple-choice portion of this exam consists of 50–60 questions. The exact number varies from year to year. This portion of the test contains four passages from literature, including both poetry and prose. (Very rarely, the test will contain five passages instead of four.)

- If the test pattern continues as it has in the past, there will be two prose passages and two poems. The poems are complete, but the prose passages are almost always excerpts from longer works.

- The passages will be drawn from different literary periods. For example, the test might contain literature that spans the sixteenth century to the present.

- The passages will represent a wide variety of authors, including minorities and women as well as the traditional white male writers.

- Even if the passages were written by famous authors, the passages will almost always be drawn from the writers' lesser-known works. Therefore, it's very unlikely that you will have studied these passages in class or read them on your own, since they rarely appear in anthologies or textbooks.

- One passage will have at least fifteen questions and is used on future exams.

The multiple-choice questions are the sort that a teacher might ask in class to elicit a close analytical reading of a prose passage or a poem. To earn a high score on the multiple-choice part of the test...

You *won't* have to know...	You *will* have to know...
biographical information about the author	how to analyze both poetry and prose
historical information that might relate to the passage	literary terms such as *connotation, denotation, metaphor, simile, irony, syntax, tone*, etc.
the author's other works	allusions to well-known people, places, things, mythology, art, and other famous literary texts
	diction and syntax used in sixteenth-, seventeeth-, eighteenth-, and nineteenth-century literature era

ROAD MAP

- *FAQs: The Multiple-Choice Section of the AP Literature and Composition Exam*

- *Overall Guidelines for Answering Multiple-Choice Questions*

- *Answering Multiple-Choice AP Questions on Poetry*

- *Answering Multiple-Choice AP Questions on Prose Passages*

- *Practice Multiple-Choice Questions on Prose*

This book contains five practice exams and many simulated multiple-choice questions that you can use to practice. However, the Advanced Placement program of the College Board owns all the rights to the actual exams they've administered in the past. Therefore, if you wish to practice on actual past AP exams, you will have to order them directly from the College Board.

FAQS: THE MULTIPLE-CHOICE SECTION OF THE AP ENGLISH LITERATURE AND COMPOSITION EXAM

Q: *Are there any trick questions on the multiple-choice part of the exam?*

A: No. Some of the questions may seem sneaky, but they're surprisingly straight-forward for a standardized test. Read carefully, stay cool and focused, and you'll find most of the answers.

Q: *What happens if I can't answer all the multiple-choice questions?*

A: You'll have plenty of company! Few students answer all the questions—and fewer still answer them all correctly. You can miss a few questions and still earn a 4 or 5 on the exam if you earn a high score on the essays.

Q: *What should I do if I skip a question?*

A: If you do skip a question and move on, be very careful to mark your answer sheet correctly.

Q: *What pattern of answers can I expect?*

A: None. Mark the answers that you think are correct, not the ones that make a pleasing pattern. Therefore, even if you have written four A's in a row and you're sure that the fifth answer is an A, write down A. (You may want to go back and check those other A's, however. You might have misread a question or mismarked an answer.)

Q: *How many multiple-choice questions do I have to answer correctly to do well on the test?*

A: Your final score depends on how well you do on the essays as well as the multiple-choice questions. Your final score also depends on how well everyone else does on the test. As a very, very rough gauge, figure that you would have to earn near-perfect scores on all three essays and answer about half the multiple-choice questions correctly to get a "3."

OVERALL GUIDELINES FOR ANSWERING MULTIPLE-CHOICE QUESTIONS

While half the passages will be prose and the other half poetry, every multiple-choice question demands the same reasoning process. The following hints can help you boost your score.

TOP TEN HINTS FOR SCORING HIGH ON MULTIPLE-CHOICE QUESTIONS

1. **Know what to expect on the multiple-choice part of the AP test.** Complete all the practice exams in this book so you know what you're facing when you take the real test. That way, you won't waste precious time reading directions (since you'll already have them memorized) and trying to figure out what comes next (since you'll be thoroughly familiar with the test format).

2. **Study.** You can't win it if you're not in it. Getting college credit for freshman English by earning a high AP score can save you some serious money—thousands and thousands of dollars in most private colleges. Therefore, it's clearly in your best interests to do your very best on the AP English Literature and Composition exam so you earn the credit. Set up a study schedule months before the exam and stick to it. Even if you're blessed with an exceptionally gifted and hard-working AP teacher, how well you do on the test has a lot to do with the amount of reading, writing, and studying *you* do on your own.

3. **Use your time wisely.** The multiple-choice questions are arranged in order of difficulty, from least difficult to most difficult. Most test takers get many of the easy questions correct, but few students get the most difficult questions right. Since every question is worth the same number of points, you're better off spending your time making sure you get the easier and middle questions right rather than rushing to finish the entire multiple-choice section.

4. **Develop a test strategy.** There are three ways you can approach any multiple-choice test:
   - Work from beginning to end, answering every question in order. Answer every single question, even if you have to guess.
   - Answer the easy questions first, and then go back and work on the harder questions.
   - Answer the hardest questions first, and then go back and answer the easy ones.

None of these test-taking methods is right or wrong. However, for most people, Method 2 works best. If you decide to use this strategy, answer the easier questions first and then go back to figure out the more difficult ones.

As you work from the beginning to the end, put a checkmark next to any question you skip. Write in pencil so you can erase the checkmarks to avoid leaving stray marks. When you get to the end of the multiple-choice questions, go back to the beginning of the section and start answering the items you skipped.

5. **Slow down!** If you work too fast, you risk making careless errors. You're better off skipping a few of the last (most difficult) questions rather than working so fast that you make costly blunders.

6. **Guess.** If you can eliminate any of the answer choices, it's always in your favor to guess. The more choices you can eliminate, the better your chances of selecting the right choice. Don't just guess willy-nilly, but if you can eliminate some choices, guessing is likely to earn you some extra points.

    NEVER just fill in blanks in an attractive, random pattern to make it appear that you've legitimately answered every question. If you do, you'll lose far more credit than you'll gain.

7. **Use process of elimination.** Multiple-choice test writers know that you're looking for the correct answer, so they include a lot of answers that *look* correct but are really wrong. Rather than looking for the right answer, start by looking for the wrong answers. Start by eliminating these ringers because each wrong answer you knock out brings you one step closer to finding the correct answer.

8. **Think before you switch answers.** Don't go back and change answers unless you're positive that your second choice is correct. Studies have shown that in nearly all cases, your first choice is more likely to be correct than subsequent choices, unless you suddenly recall some relevant information.

9. **Stay cool.** Don't get rattled. The answer to every question is somewhere in the poem or passage. All you have to do is find it or find the details that enable you to make the inference you need.

10. **Deal with panic.** Convince yourself that you can succeed by working carefully and resolutely. If you start losing control, pause for a second to calm yourself. Take a few deep breaths, imagine a pleasant scene, and then keep working.

ANSWERING MULTIPLE-CHOICE VOCABULARY QUESTIONS

A number of multiple-choice questions on both poetry and prose passages require you to define a word as it is used in the poem or passage. The questions may be on difficult words or easier words that have uncommon meanings. In either case, follow these four steps as you work through these test items:

1. Go back to the poem or passage and find the word.

2. Fill in your own word for the one you are asked to define.

3. Eliminate the answer choices that don't match your word.

4. Choose the best answer choice.

Vocabulary questions will be phrased like this:

- In line 10, "amorphous" is best interpreted as...

- "Seraphic" in line 11 most nearly means...

- From its context, you can deduce that "wan" (line 15) must mean...

- What does "vain" mean as used in this context: "Miss Nightingale pleaded in vain"?

As you're looking for the correct meaning, always use context clues.

- *Definition clues* have the definition right in the poem or passage. The definition is a *synonym* (word that means the same). It may come before or after the unfamiliar word. For example: "*Tsunamis,* or seismic sea-waves, are gravity waves set in motion by underwater disturbances associated with earthquakes." "Seismic sea-waves" is a synonym for the unfamiliar word *tsunamis.*

- *Contrast clues* tell you what something isn't rather than what it is. Often, you'll find contrast clues set off with *unlike, not,* or *instead of.* For example, "Then arrange a handful of mulch, not fresh leaves, on the top." *Mulch* must be the opposite of fresh leaves. It must mean "decayed leaves."

- *Common sense clues* encourage you to use what you already know to define the word. For example, "Airplanes make daily *ascents* to gather data." Since airplanes go into the air, *ascent* must mean "to rise."

ANSWERING MULTIPLE-CHOICE AP QUESTIONS ON POETRY

While there are different methods of approaching poetry, the following steps have proven helpful for many students taking the AP exam:

1. Read the poem through once, and see how much of the author's meaning you can immediately grasp.

2. Then go back through the poem a second time, line by line, and define all the unfamiliar words, concepts, ideas, and references. Consider all the images and symbols, too.

3. If you're having difficulty understanding the poem, try "translating" each line into prose or simply substituting simpler words for the more difficult ones. When you understand all the basic words and ideas, reread the poem a few more times and pull it all back together.

Read the following poem. Using the method outlined, see what meaning you can extract.

NOTE
Currently, tuition at an elite "Ivy League" university runs more than $35,000 per year. The average private university charges around $22,000 per year; state universities, around $10,500. Because the cost of goods and services continues to rise, college costs are projected to rise about 3–4 percent per year. Many students who count on getting financial aid often receive far less than they projected. As a result, the vast majority of college students take out loans to pay the cost of their education.

From "A Pindaric Ode"

1 It is not growing like a tree
    In bulk, doth make man better be;
    Or, standing long an oak, three hundred year,
    To fall a log at last, dry, bald, and sear:

5 A lily of a day
    Is fairer far, in May,
    Although it fall and die that night;
    It was the plant and flower of light.
    In small proportions we just beauties see,

10 And in short measures life may perfect be.

—Ben Jonson

There are three basic parts of any poem: its vision, the speaker who expresses that vision, and the language the poet uses to create the vision and voice. You will be asked multiple-choice questions on each of these literary elements as well as the poem's structure, the author's purpose, the poem's mood or tone, and the poem's unity.

QUESTIONS ABOUT THEME

The poetic "vision" is the poem's theme or main idea. The theme can be stated outright in the poem, but that's highly unlikely on poems chosen to be tested on the AP exam. Rather, you will have to infer the theme from language, figures of speech, images, details, and other poetic elements. When you *make inferences*, you combine what you already know with details from the poem. In effect, you are "reading between the lines" to find unstated information and draw conclusions.

Questions about theme are phrased in different ways on the AP test. Notice the variations on the same question:

- The subject (or topic) of the poem is ... [you must know the subject or topic before you can infer the theme]

- The theme of this poem is best stated as . . .

- The theme of this poem can most precisely be stated as follows...

- The poet's main idea is...

- What does (specific element) symbolize in line 23?

- The poem as a whole introduces contrasts between all of the following EXCEPT...

- (Specific quote from the poem) makes a suitable ending for all of the following reasons EXCEPT . . .

- The poem presents a movement from...

- The best title for this poem would be...

- What poetic techniques does the author use in this passage to convey his or her main idea? [This is a cross-over question, involving both theme and figures of speech.]

Poets create their vision in two main ways. The first way is by expressing their view so clearly that we feel that we are seeing what the poet wishes us to see with a new closeness and clarity. The second way involves using figures of speech, unexpected comparisons, or juxtapositions of words that force us to make comparisons we have never before imagined.

A look at two poems that use these different methods will show how language is used to create the poet's vision.

The Eagle

1   He clasps the crag with crooked hands;
    Close to the sun in lonely lands,
    Ring'd with the azure world, he stands.
    The wrinkled sea beneath him crawls;
5   He watches from his mountain walls,
    And like a thunderbolt he falls.
        —Alfred, Lord Tennyson

The Dalliance of the Eagles

1   Skirting the river road, (my forenoon walk, my rest,)
    Skyward in air a sudden muffled sound, the dalliance of the eagles,
    The rushing amorous contact high in space together,
    The clinching interlocking claws, a living, fierce, gyrating wheel,
5   Four beating wings, two beaks, a swirling mass tight grappling,
    In tumbling turning clustering loops, straight downward falling,
    Till o'er the river pois'd, the twain yet one, a moment's lull,
    A motionless still balance in the air, then parting, talons loosing,
    Upward again on slow-firm pinions slanting, their separate diverse flight,
10 She hers, he his, pursuing.
        —Walt Whitman

It is easy to see that these poems are very different. Tennyson's work, depicting a lone eagle who remains still throughout most of the poem, creates a feeling of space and solitude. In contrast, Whitman's poem deals with two eagles and seems to have captured a constant rush of movement. This difference in feeling is created in part by the sounds of the words the poets have selected.

Tennyson's words, lines, and sentences are all short, and they stop abruptly at the end of each line. Whitman uses longer lines with less sharp breaks between them, and his sentences are complex and involved. This technique keeps the poem in almost constant motion—like that of the eagles' flight. Yet the basic difference in the presentation of these two poems lies not in the motion or motionlessness of the eagles, but rather in the imagery used to describe them.

Whitman uses many adjectives, especially participles (adjectives formed from verbs), such as "clinching," "interlocking," "living," "beating," and "grappling" to convey a sense of motion and action. These words contribute much of the force of the poet's description. The poet is an observer here. Taking a walk, he has been startled first by the "sudden muffled sound" and then by the sight of the eagles. He describes these two sensations as "The clinching interlocking claws, a living, fierce, gyrating wheel,/ Four beating wings, two beaks, a swirling mass tight grappling."

Tennyson's verse is also descriptive, but it varies greatly from Whitman's word choice when describing the eagle. Where Whitman uses words that could easily be applied to eagles, Tennyson uses words that are not usually associated with birds. His eagle is compared to other things: an old man, grown crooked with age; an explorer in "lonely lands"; and a thunderbolt. By calling our attention to the comparison between the eagle and other objects, he draws upon our feelings for these other objects (respect or awe, for example) and uses those emotions to influence our feelings about the eagle itself. Thus, instead of saying, as Whitman does, that the eagle has "clinching claws," Tennyson gives his eagle "crooked hands." He "stands"—a human rather than a birdlike act—and "watches," as both people and birds do. The landscape is also humanized. The lands are described as "lonely"; the sea is pictured as "wrinkled," and it "crawls." There are examples of hyperbole (exaggeration) as well. The eagle is said to have a perch "close to the sun," which of course is impossible. In the same way, the sky against which he is pictured is an entire "azure world," and the eagle falls like "a thunderbolt." High and remote, yet in these very qualities very human, Tennyson's eagle presents a stunning image of isolation.

By linking things that we would not ourselves associate, the poet creates new images and calls forth new emotions that make the reader look at things in a different light. Abstract ideas become specific through the use of precise visual images and specific words. The reader derives very different feelings from Whitman's waterfall of precisely denotative adjectives and Tennyson's careful balance of connotations of space, people, and isolation. For definitions of these terms and all other types of poetic language and figures of speech, see Part VI: Glossary of Literary Terms.

QUESTIONS ABOUT THE SPEAKER

Questions about the speaker in a poem challenge you to distinguish between the poet and the personae he or she assumes in the poem. *Never* assume that the poet and the speaker are the same. Even in autobiographical poems, distance exists between the poet and the mask he or she assumes, revealed as the speaker.

Questions about speaker will often take this form:

- Who is the speaker in the poem?

- How do the speaker and poet differ?

QUESTIONS ABOUT POETIC LANGUAGE

Many (if not most) of the multiple-choice questions on poems concern an analysis of poetic language and techniques. These questions are designed not only to determine how well you know the elements of poetry, but also to judge how well you can integrate these literary techniques with the poet's purpose and theme.

Questions on poetic language will be expressed the following ways. Note the different variations on the exact same question:

- The following line is an example of which poetic technique? (specific line quoted)

- What figure of speech is used in line xx?

- What does the (element from the poem) personify?

- (Figure of speech) (line reference) is an example of...

- In line 14, (figure of speech) is an example of a(n) . . .

- What poetic technique does the author use in the final two lines?

- Which figure of speech does the poet use to unify the poem?

- Which of the following literary devices most significantly contributes to the unity of the poem?

- The poet's style is marked by...

- Throughout the poem, the imagery suggests that...

- The metaphors in lines xx and xx are derived from . . .

- In the context of the passage, the phrase ("specific phrase") (line reference) is used as a metaphor for the . . .

- The language of the poem can best be described as . . .

- The mood of the poem is best described as...

- The tone of the poem is best characterized as...

- All of the following are true about the language of the poem EXCEPT . . .

- In lines xx–xx, the primary effect of using clauses that elaborate on one another is to . . .

The following section examines figures of speech in great detail. I've provided practice AP multiple-choice questions in each section to help you see how these literary elements are tested on this portion of the test.

Similes, Metaphors, and Personification

Similes are comparisons using the words "like," "as," or a similar word of comparison. Usually the objects under comparison resemble each other in only one or two ways, differing in all other aspects. For example, an eagle and a thunderbolt are not very similar, but the fact that they both can travel from the sky to the ground allows Tennyson to use this comparison to say that the eagle falls "like a thunderbolt." The strength of the simile lies in the difference between the eagle and the thunderbolt. The fact that the thunderbolt is much more powerful and dangerous than the eagle gives a sense of speed, power, and danger to the bird's fall.

Metaphors, like similes, are comparisons of two unlike objects. In this instance, though, the joining of the two objects is more complete, for there is no intervening word such as "like" or "as." Instead, the metaphor simply states that A is B; one element of the comparison becomes the other. Some metaphors go one step further and omit the "is." They talk about A as though it were B and in some cases may not even use the name for B at all, forcing the reader to guess what B is by the language used. In this instance, the poet creates an *implied metaphor.*

Personification is a type of implied metaphor that involves speaking about something nonliving as though it were living. Or, as in the case of Tennyson's eagle, personification is the attribution of human characteristics ("crooked hands") to something nonhuman (the bird).

As you read a poem on the AP exam, decide what the speaker's feelings are toward the subject and how many subjects of comparison are used. Ask yourself these questions:

- Is each subject compared to one thing, or is one subject compared to several?

- Is the comparison developed at length? If it is, to what purpose?

- What is the point that the poet is making through an extended metaphor?

- If the subject is compared to several things, how do the different images fit together? Are they unrelated so that the job of fixing them into a pattern is left to the reader? Or does the poet suggest some sort of relationship or contrast between/among them?

- How does the pattern of comparison form your sense of the poet's vision, meaning, and progression?

Finally, read the poem through once again to see if the conclusions you have reached hold up.

In the following poem, John Keats used metaphors to convey theme. Read the poem and answer the practice AP questions that follow.

On First Looking Into Chapman's Homer

1 Much have I travelled in the realms of gold,
    And many goodly states and kingdoms seen;
    Round many western islands have I been
    Which bards in fealty to Apollo hold.
5 Oft of one wide expanse had I been told
    That deep-brow'd Homer ruled as his demesne;
    Yet did I never breathe its pure serene ·
    Till I heard Chapman speak out loud and bold:
    Then felt I like some watcher into his ken;
10 When a new planet swims of the skies
    Or like stout Cortez when with eagle eyes
    He star'd at the Pacific—and all his men
    Look'd at each other with a wild surmise—
    Silent, upon a peak in Darien.
          —John Keats

1. The vocabulary in the first eight lines of this poem is drawn mainly from

    (A) prospecting for gold.
    (B) exploring Europe.
    (C) poetic traditions.
    (D) the Middle Ages and its system of feudalism.
    (E) Greek and Roman mythology.

2. As it is used in this poem, "realms" most nearly means

    (A) bundle.
    (B) good fortune.
    (C) places.
    (D) fortunes.
    (E) kingdoms.

3. The allusion to "Apollo" is drawn from

    (A) classical mythology.
    (B) the Middle Ages.
    (C) the Renaissance.
    (D) Homer.
    (E) Chapman.

4. In lines 9–10, the poet creates a simile when he

    (A) makes a reference to a watcher.
    (B) repeats the initial "s" sound in *swims* and *skies.*
    (C) compares his feelings to those of an astronomer discovering a new planet.
    (D) rhymes "skies" and eyes."
    (E) describes how the planet "swims."

5. Throughout the poem, the similes combine to suggest

    (A) that great explorers are like readers, discovering uncharted new lands.
    (B) there are far more wonders in the world than we can comprehend.

(C)   the Middle Ages was a richer and more astonishing world than the present day.

(D)   the poet's great excitement and wonder at discovering great literature.

(E)   the poet prefers reading to exploring.

Answers

1.   **The correct answer is (D).**

2.   **The correct answer is (E).**

3.   **The correct answer is (A).**

4.   **The correct answer is (C).**

5.   **The correct answer is (D).**

The vocabulary in the first eight lines of this poem is drawn mainly from the Middle Ages and its system of feudalism. For example, the word "realms" is used for kingdoms, "bards" for poets, and "fealty" for the system under which a nobleman owed his allegiance to a king or other nobleman with more extensive power. "Demesne" is the word for the nobleman's domain, and "ken" means knowledge. In the same way, we no longer use "serene" for air or "oft" for often. "Apollo," in contrast, is drawn from classical mythology and stands for the god of poets. Homer is an ancient Greek poet, and Chapman is a sixteenth-century English poet who was noted for his translation of Homer's *Iliad* into English.

As you analyze this poem, ask yourself why the poet would use the language of the Middle Ages and the metaphor of traveling to talk about his joy in reading poetry and the delight he experienced with his discovery of Chapman's translations of Homer. Perhaps he created the Middle Ages metaphor to show the timelessness of true verse and how it transcends the boundaries of time to speak for all people at all times.

In lines 11–14, the speaker compares his feelings about Chapman's Homer to Cortez's feelings at discovering a new ocean (the Pacific). From these two similes we can sense the poet's great excitement and wonder at discovering great literature (question 5).

Symbols and Symbolism

A *symbol* is a person, place, or object that represents an abstract idea. For example, a dove may symbolize peace or a rose may symbolize love. Similes and metaphors are used to make us take a closer look at a subject or to look at a subject in a new light. In contrast, symbols force readers to look beyond the literal meaning of the poem's statement or action. The following poem provides an example:

The Tyger

1 Tyger! Tyger! burning bright
    In the forests of the night,
    What immortal hand or eye
    Could frame thy fearful symmetry?

5 In what distant deeps or skies
    Burnt the fire of thine eyes?
    On what wings dare he aspire?
    What the hand, dare seize the fire?

    And what shoulder, & what art,
10 Could twist the sinews of thy heart?
    And when thy heart began to beat,
    What dread hand? & what dread feet?

What the hammer? what the chain?
In what furnace was thy brain?
15 What the anvil? What dread grasp
Dare its deadly terrors clasp?

When the stars threw down their spears,
And water'd heaven with their tears,
Did he smile his work to see?
20 Did he who made the Lamb make thee?

Tyger! Tyger! burning bright
In the forests of the night,
What immortal hand or eye
Dare frame thy fearful symmetry?
          —William Blake

In this poem, Blake focuses readers' attention not on the topic of tigers but on the awesome qualities suggested by the tiger's beauty and the godlike powers involved in its creation. This poem may lead the reader to the question of the existence of evil as symbolized by the tiger's murderous nature. How far the symbol or allegory is carried is frequently left in the reader's hands, as shown in this poem.

The following sonnet presents a symbolic tale of a king's fall from power:

Ozymandias

1 I met a traveler from an antique land
Who said: Two vast and trunkless legs of stone
Stand in the desert—Near them, on the sand,
Half sunk, a shattered visage lies, whose frown,
5 And wrinkled lip, and sneer of cold command,
Tell that its sculptor well those passions read
Which yet survive, stamped on these lifeless things,
The hand that mocked them, and the heart that fed:
And on the pedestal these words appear:
10 "My name is Ozymandias, king of kings:
Look on my works, ye Mighty, and despair!"
Nothing beside remains. Round the decay
Of that colossal wreck, boundless and bare
The lone and level sands stretch far away.
          —Percy Bysshe Shelley

The story of the king's loss of power is symbolic. Within the story, the most striking symbol is the broken statue with its boastful inscription. The symbolism of the broken statue can be interpreted in three different ways:

1. the inescapable destruction of human lives and civilization by the unceasing motion of time

2. the fall of pride, which lends a moral interpretation to the poem

3. the fall of tyranny, which throws a political cast on the poem's theme

The tyrant with his "sneer of cold command" is unsavory enough for the reader to welcome his overthrow. But the sculptor, with "the hand that mocked," is dead too, and even the work that was to endure is half destroyed.

Conceits and Allusions

A *conceit* is a comparison between two very unlike objects. Unlike metaphors and similes, conceits are usually developed at length, comparing and contrasting many different aspects of two objects to make their meaning clear. In traditional love verse, conceits often derive from the Renaissance tradition that paints the woman as the walled village and the man as the conquering warrior; he attacks, and she defends or surrenders. Or she might be the warrior, harming him with sharp looks and sharp words. Some poets take these poetic conventions very seriously; others use them in fun, working from the surprise that comes from turning an expected comparison upside down.

The Metaphysical poets of the seventeenth century used conceits to create surprising and complex poems. Science (especially physics, astronomy, and navigation) was often used as the basis of a conceit that charted the soul's progress in relation to the physical universe. This is shown in the following poem, "Hymn to God My God, In My Sickness." Read the poem and answer the practice AP questions that follow.

Hymn to God My God, In My Sickness

1   Since I am coming to that holy room,
    Where, with thy choir of Saints for evermore,
    I shall be made thy music; as I come
    I tune the instrument here at the door,
5   And what I must do then, think now before.

    Whilst my physicians by their love are grown
    Cosmographers, and I their map, who lie
    Flat on this bed, that by them may be shown
    That this is my Southwest discovery
10 Per fretum febris, by these straights to die,

    I joy, that in these straits, I see my west;
    For, though their currents yield return to none,
    What shall my west hurt me? As west and east
    In all flat maps (and I am one) are one,
15 So death doth touch the Resurrection.

    Is the Pacific Sea my home? Or are
    The eastern riches? Is Jerusalem?
    Anyan, and Magellan, and Gibraltàr,
    All straits, and none but straits, are ways to them,
20 Whether where Japhet dwelt, or Cham, or Shem.

    We think that Paradise and Calvary,
    Christ's Cross, and Adam's tree, stood in one place;
    Look Lord, and find both Adams met in me;
    As the first Adam's sweat surrounds my face,
25 May the last Adam's blood my soul embrace.

    So, in his purple wrapped receive me, Lord,
    By these thorns give me his other crown;
    And as to others' souls I preached thy word,
    Be this my text, my sermon to mine own,
30 Therefore that he may raise, the Lord throws down.
      —John Donne

1. The first conceit concerns

   (A) church and choirs.
   (B) illness.
   (C) travel and discovery.
   (D) death.
   (E) maps and voyages.

2. The conceit in stanza 5 is created from images of

   (A) Christ as the second Adam.
   (B) the Bible.
   (C) unfamiliar and exotic locations.
   (D) blood and suffering.
   (E) escape from pain.

3. The two conceits are interwoven by the theme of

   (A) the importance of travel to a well-educated soul.
   (B) the distortions in perception caused by suffering.
   (C) the Lord's unfair treatment of His followers.
   (D) the soul's journey to salvation as an annihilation of time and space.
   (E) life's triumphs and tragedies.

Answers

1. **The correct answer is (E).**
2. **The correct answer is (A).**
3. **The correct answer is (D).**

Conceits demand that readers bring some outside knowledge to the poem under study. For example, you must be able to grasp the distortions of space involved in making a flat map represent a round world if you are to fully grasp Donne's hymn.

As you read "Sonnet 15" and answer the practice AP questions that follow, look carefully at the imagery. It will help you decode the conceit and the theme. Also note the poet's use of *apostrophe* (direct address) and the poem's tone. You may find the language in the sonnet challenging because of the unfamiliar spelling and syntax. If so, read slowly and carefully, sounding out the words as you go.

From Amoretti—Sonnet 15

1 Ye tradefull Merchants, that with weary toyle,
    Do seeke most pretious things to make your gain,
    And both the Indias of their treasure spoile,
    What needeth you to seeke so farre in vaine?
5 For loe, my love doth in her selfe containe,
    All this worlds riches that may farre be found:
    If saphyres, loe her eies be saphyres plaine;
    If rubies, loe hir lips be rubies sound;
    If pearles hir teeth be pearles both pure and round;
10 If yvorie, her forehead yvory weene;
    If gold, her locks are finest gold on ground;
    If silver, her faire hands are silver sheene:
    But that which fairest is but few behold:—
    Her mind, adornd with vertues manifold.
        —Edmund Spenser

1. Toward whom is the poet addressing his remarks?

   (A) His beloved
   (B) Himself
   (C) Treasure hunters
   (D) Native Americans
   (E) Merchants

2. What do the phrases "weary toyle" and "in vaine" suggest about this audience or their activities?

   (A) It is very difficult to make a large fortune.
   (B) Making money and gaining fame are brutally hard but ultimately well worth the effort.
   (C) All their hard work is useless, for real riches rest in love, not commodities.
   (D) Poets work far harder than even tradesmen and travelers.
   (E) To be truly happy, people need both love and wealth.

3. How are the metaphors in lines 7–12 connected to create the poem's conceit?

   (A) The poet describes the beauty of his love in terms of the most precious substances on earth: gems, gold, silver, and ivory.
   (B) The poem catalogues the precious gems he has received for his labors at his pen.
   (C) The poet argues that all the wealth in the world cannot replace true art.
   (D) The speaker claims that people value gems more than art or love.
   (E) The speaker describes his ideal woman, an imaginary creation of indescribable splendor.

4. In the conclusion, the poet suggests that

   (A) love may fade with time, but art is immortal.
   (B) poets need sufficient wealth to have the leisure they require to create great art.
   (C) few people are able to appreciate the beauty of a great work of art.
   (D) his beloved's virtues, the most valuable of her treasures, cannot be gathered like so many jewels.
   (E) poetry must come from the mind, not the heart or soul.

5. What new questions does the conclusion raise about the merchants' quest for precious things?

   (A) The merchant's quest is valuable because the world abounds with untold treasure.
   (B) The merchant's quest is absurd, for all we should seek are the virtues hidden in a fine mind, not the outward show of precious metals and stones.
   (C) The merchant's quest is imaginary; only art is real.
   (D) The merchant's quest is valiant because of the dangers it entails.
   (E) The merchant's quest is irrelevant because the beauty of art is the only real treasure.

6. The poem's theme is best expressed as

   (A) the importance of striving in a competitive world.
   (B) the difficulty of succeeding.
   (C) the inevitable battle between art and commerce.
   (D) love is brief, but art is long.
   (E) all the riches of the world are right at home, in the person of his loved one.

Answers

1. **The correct answer is (E).**
2. **The correct answer is (C).**
3. **The correct answer is (A).**
4. **The correct answer is (D).**
5. **The correct answer is (B).**
6. **The correct answer is (E).**

In the following poem, earthly riches are once again equated with the beauty of a woman and then are devalued by it, as time gives way to timelessness. As you read, compare and contrast Donne's treatment of these conceits to Spenser's. How are they the same? How are they different?

The Sun Rising

1 Busy old fool, unruly sun,
   Why dost thou thus
   Through windows and through curtains call on us?
   Must to thy motions lovers' seasons run?
5 Saucy, pedantic wretch, go chide
   Late schoolboys and sour 'prentices,
   Go tell court huntsmen that the king will ride,
   Call country ants to harvest offices.
   Love, all alike, no season knows nor clime,
10 Nor hours, days, months, which are the rags of time.
   Thy beams, so reverend and strong
   Why shouldst thou think?
   I could eclipse and cloud them with a wink,
   But that I would not lose her sight so long.
15 If her eyes have not blinded thine,
   Look, and tomorrow late tell me
   Whether both th' Indias of spice and mine
   Be where thou left'st them, or lie here with me;
   Ask for those kings whom thou saw'st yesterday,
20 And thou shalt hear: All here in one bed lay.
   She's all states, and all princess I;
   Nothing else is.
   Princes do but play us; compared to this,
   All honor's mimic, all wealth alchemy.
25 Thou, sun, art half as happy as we,
   In that the world's contracted thus;
   Thine age asks ease, and since thy duties be
   To warm the world, that's done in warming us.
   Shine here to us, and thou art everywhere;
30 This bed thy center is, these walls thy sphere.
       —John Donne

Like in Spenser's work, earthly riches are equated with the beauty of a woman and then are devalued by it, as time gives way to timelessness. However, Spenser simply praises the woman for her beauty and virtues, while Donne makes further arguments. Donne's poem is far more earthly than Spenser's, making specific reference to their love.

Imagery

An *image* is a word or a phrase that appeals to the sense—sight, smell, taste, touch, or sound—to create pictures in the reader's mind and aid in conveying the poem's theme.

Renaissance poems tended to begin with a position and then build on it, showing little movement within the verse. Metaphysical poems showed more movement, often following a speaker's mind through the ramifications of an idea or situation. Modern poets may create scenes, moods, and speakers with even greater movement and further use of sound and imagery. The nineteenth-century American poet Walt Whitman, for example, relied on a pattern of imagery to give structure to his verse rather than on the more conventional rhymes and meters. "There Was a Child Went Forth" is one example. Read it and answer the practice AP questions that follow.

There Was a Child Went Forth

1   There was a child went forth every day,
     And the first object he look'd upon, that object he became,
     And that object became part of him for the day or a certain part of the day,
     Or for many years or stretching cycles of years.

5   The early lilacs became part of this child,
     And grass and white and red morning-glories, and white and red clover, and the song
        of the phoebe-bird,
     And the Third-month lambs and the sow's pink-faint litter, and the mare's foal and the
        cow's calf,
     And the noisy brood of the barnyard or by the mire of the pond-side,
     And the fish suspending themselves so curiously below there, and the beautiful curious
        liquid,
10 And the water-plants with their graceful flat heads, all became part of him.
     The field-sprouts of Fourth-month and Fifth-month became part of him,
     Winter-grain sprouts and those of the light-yellow corn, and the esculent roots of the
        garden,
     And the apple-trees cover'd with blossoms and the fruit afterward, and woodberries,
        and the commonest weeds by the road,
     And the old drunkard staggering home from the outhouse of the tavern whence he had
        lately risen,
15 And the schoolmistress that pass'd on her way to the school,
     And the friendly boys that pass'd, and the quarrelsome boys,
     And the tidy and fresh-cheek'd girls, and the barefoot Negro boy and girl,
     And all the changes of city and country wherever he went.
     His own parents, he that had father'd him and she that had conceiv'd him in her womb
       and birth'd him,
20 They gave this child more of themselves than that,
     They gave him afterward every day, they became part of him.

     The mother at home quietly placing the dishes on the supper-table,
     The mother with mild words, clean her cap and gown, a wholesome odor falling off
       her person and clothes as she walks by,
     The father, strong, self-sufficient, manly, mean, anger'd, unjust,
25 The blow, the quick loud word, the tight bargain, the crafty lure,
     The family usages, the language, the company, the furniture, the yearning and swelling
       heart,
     Affection that will not be gainsay'd, the sense of what is real, the thought if after all it
       should prove unreal,
     The doubts of day-time and the doubts of night-time, the curious whether and how,
     Whether that which appears so is so, or is it all flashes and specks

30 Men and women crowding fast in the streets, if they are not flashes and specks what
   are they?
   The streets themselves and the facades of houses, and goods in the windows,
   Vehicles, teams, the heavy-plank'd wharves, the huge crossing at the ferries,
   The village on the highland seen from afar at sunset, the river between,
   Shadows, aureola and mist, the light falling on roofs and gables of white or brown two
   miles off,
35 The schooner near by sleepily dropping down the tide, the little boat slack-tow'd
   astern,
   The hurrying tumbling waves, quick-broken crests, slapping,
   The strata of color'd clouds, the long bar of maroon-tint away solitary by itself, the
   spread of purity it lies motionless in,
   The horizon's edge, the flying sea-crow, the fragrance of salt marsh and shore mud.
   These became part of that child who went forth every day, and who now goes, and will
   always go forth every day.
   —Walt Whitman

1. What images are found in lines 1–13?

   (A) Childhood
   (B) Animals
   (C) A winter afternoon, the sunset of the seasons
   (D) An unending cycle of love and happiness
   (E) Spring morning in the country, the beginning of both plant and animal life

2. The images in lines 14–17 are best described as

   (A) tragic in their brevity.
   (B) fall and re-entry into the town and the world of people.
   (C) the sorrowful waste of human life.
   (D) the obligations we must fulfill in life.
   (E) the importance of friendship and human connection.

3. Which images can you find in lines 19–26?

   (A) Home and the child's parents
   (B) Birth and death
   (C) Obligations we owe to our parents
   (D) The restrictions of childhood
   (E) Following traditional gender roles

4. The images in lines 30–34 mainly describe

   (A) the filth and decay of the city.
   (B) the limitations of city life.
   (C) the movement of the city.
   (D) the freedom of country life over the restrictions of city life.
   (E) the great advantage of city life.

5. The images in lines 34–38 combine to create a word picture of

   (A) sunrise at the ocean.
   (B) a storm building.

(C)   travel and frantic activity.
(D)   the shore and nightfall.
(E)   death.

6. The poem's images combine to form every pattern EXCEPT

(A)   a movement from evening to morning.
(B)   a movement from childhood to adulthood and home to shore.
(C)   a movement from country to city and self outward to others.
(D)   the progression of the seasons (spring-summer-fall).
(E)   a movement from acceptance to doubt and finally back to a reaffirmation of life and the goodness of the universe.

7. What primary image serves to unify and connect the poem?

(A)   The child
(B)   The mother
(C)   The poet
(D)   Nature
(E)   Death

8. How did the child's parents become "part of him" in lines 19–21?

(A)   The child is the result of love between his parents.
(B)   The child's development depends on the continued care of his parents.
(C)   The child has their precise self-image.
(D)   The child's parents leave him alone to decide how he wishes to live his life.
(E)   The child's parents bring him all over the country and the city.

9. What is the poet describing through the use of the images in line 37?

(A)   The Northern Lights
(B)   A fierce storm brewing
(C)   Sunrise over the city
(D)   Sunset over the water
(E)   His own death

10. How long is the time span in the poem?

(A)   One hour
(B)   One afternoon, from noon to sunset
(C)   One day, from sunrise to sunset
(D)   One week
(E)   One year

Answers

1. **The correct answer is (E).**
2. **The correct answer is (B).**
3. **The correct answer is (A).**
4. **The correct answer is (C).**
5. **The correct answer is (D).**
6. **The correct answer is (E).**

7. **The correct answer is (A).**

8. **The correct answer is (B).**

9. **The correct answer is (D).**

10. **The correct answer is (C).**

Read "To Helen" by Edgar Allan Poe and answer the practice AP questions that follow. As you read, pay close attention to the poem's imagery.

To Helen

1 Helen, thy beauty is to me
   Like those Nicean barks of yore,
   That gently, o'er a perfumed sea,
   The weary, wayworn wanderer bore
5 To his own native shore.

   On desperate seas long wont to roam,
   Thy hyacinth hair, thy classic face,
   Thy Naiad airs, have brought me home
   To the Glory that was Greece
10 And the grandeur that was Rome.

   Lo! in yon brilliant window niche
   How statuelike I see thee stand,
   The agate lamp within thy hand!
   Ah, Psyche, from the regions which
15 Are Holy Land!

1. In the first stanza, Poe creates a simile that compares Helen's beauty to a(n)

   (A) ancient boat that is unable to complete its appointed voyage.
   (B) homeland that is sorely missed.
   (C) desperate longing that can never be sated.
   (D) gentle and sweet-smelling ocean of love.
   (E) ship that can carry him to the heights of happiness experienced by a weary traveler brought home at last.

2. Helen's "hyacinth hair" creates an image of

   (A) curls.
   (B) a garden.
   (C) beauty.
   (D) nature.
   (E) glory that cannot be attained.

3. As portrayed in this poem, Helen is best described as

   (A) an idealized portrait, removed and abstract.
   (B) a real woman, familiar to us all.
   (C) mortal but always beautiful.
   (D) elegant and classical.
   (E) majestic and desirable.

Answers

1. **The correct answer is (E).**
2. **The correct answer is (C).**
3. **The correct answer is (A).**

The poem's meaning has been much discussed. It may be that the author was drawing from the people of what is now Nice, France, who were a great seapower in the later part of the Middle Ages. The phrase "perfumed sea" calls forth Nicea (now called Iznik), located just southeast of the Bosporos. This city was important because it was located on the early trade routes to the Orient, but it was not on the sea. The Phaeacians—"lovers of the sea"—are another reference to classical imagery. They were the ones to whom Odysseus recounted his adventures and who sent him home in their enchanted bark (ship).

"Naiad airs" may refer to the Ulysses story and also reinforces the impression of beauty. "Psyche" in the third stanza is also a classical reference. Psyche was separated from her lover, Cupid, when she ignored his instructions and took a lamp to look at him. She searched for Cupid for years, and finally she was reunited with him.

The theme of this poem revolves around the contemplation of Helen's beauty. By thinking of Helen, the ideally remembered figure from his childhood, the poet is able to recapture the classic beauty of the state of mind he enjoyed during his youth. He implies that this state of mind must have been common when the world itself was "young"—in the classical age.

Tone

Tone is the writer's or speaker's attitude toward the subject, audience, or self. Tone is a vital part of a poem's meaning because it brings emotional power to the language.

To figure out a poem's tone, analyze the writer's use of language, imagery, and allusions. Look especially at imagery, simile, metaphor, personification, irony, and diction (language). Now read "Crossing the Bar" and answer the practice AP questions that follow. As you read, try to restate the poem's tone in your own words.

Crossing the Bar

1 Sunset and evening star,
    And one clear call for me!
    And may there be no moaning of the bar
    When I put out to sea,

5 But such a tide as moving seems asleep,
    Too full for sound and foam,
    When that which drew from out the boundless deep
    Turns again home.

    Twilight and evening bell,
10 And after that the dark!
    And may there be no sadness of farewell
    When I embark;

    For though from out our bourne of Time and Place
    The flood may bear me far,
15 I hope to see my Pilot face to face
    When I have crossed the bar.
         —Alfred, Lord Tennyson

1. What two different symbols does the poet use to herald death?
   - (A) Moaning of the bar; the flood
   - (B) The tide; my Pilot
   - (C) The boundless deep; sadness of farewell
   - (D) Time and Place; crossing the bar
   - (E) Sunset and the evening star; twilight and the evening bell

2. What is the exact moment of death in each instance?
   - (A) Lines 1–2 and line 5
   - (B) Line 9 and line 14
   - (C) Line 12 and line 14
   - (D) Lines 7–8 and line 16
   - (E) Lines 11–12 and lines 15–16

3. In this poem, the speaker wishes for a death that is
   - (A) public and attended with much pomp and circumstance.
   - (B) neither painful nor protracted.
   - (C) filled with extended leave-takings.
   - (D) marked by people gathering around his beside.
   - (E) conducted at sea.

4. What does the "boundless deep" symbolize?
   - (A) Death itself
   - (B) A long, painful death
   - (C) That which awaits us after death
   - (D) The feelings of those we have left behind
   - (E) The ocean

5. The tone of this poem is best described as
   - (A) grudging acceptance.
   - (B) fierce resistance.
   - (C) calm resignation.
   - (D) deep sorrow.
   - (E) bitter anger.

Answers

1. **The correct answer is (E).**
2. **The correct answer is (D).**
3. **The correct answer is (B).**
4. **The correct answer is (C).**
5. **The correct answer is (C).**

ANSWERING MULTIPLE-CHOICE AP QUESTIONS ON PROSE PASSAGES

Many of the techniques you learned in this chapter for answering multiple-choice questions on poetry are equally useful for answering multiple-choice questions on prose. That's because prose writers use many of the same literary techniques as poetry writers, especially figures of speech, symbols, allusions, imagery, and tone.

In addition, both the poetry and prose passages present the questions in chronological order. For example, you can find the information you need to answer question 10 between the information for questions 9 and 11. Taken together, the questions present a story map or chronological reading of the poem or passage. Therefore, try to answer the questions in order rather than skipping around.

However, analyzing prose passages is different from analyzing poetry in several significant ways: *genre, structure,* and *rhetoric*.

QUESTIONS ABOUT GENRE

Poetry can take different forms (such as sonnets, odes, and lyrics, for instance), but regardless of form, all poems are the same genre. Prose, in contrast, can be fiction or nonfiction—two very different genres. The following examples of fiction and nonfiction can appear on the AP English Literature and Composition exam:

- *Fiction*: short stories, excerpts from novels

- *Nonfiction*: essays, autobiographies, biographies, articles

Fiction and nonfiction are analyzed differently. As you read, you focus on very different elements:

- Analyze fiction for *plot, setting, characters, narrator, point of view*.

- Analyze nonfiction for *topic, speaker, purpose, structure*.

Questions about genre will often take this form:

- This essay is framed as a(n)...

- This passage takes the form of a(n)...

- This excerpt is likely part of a(n)...

QUESTIONS ABOUT STRUCTURE

Structure is the arrangement of details in a work of literature. Most fiction is arranged in *chronological order*, the order of time. The events unfold in the order in which they occurred. Clue words include *first, second, then, next, finally*, and so on. Nonfiction can also be arranged in chronological order, but it can have many other methods of organization as well. Identifying the structure of a prose passage is a key AP skill because it helps you determine the author's purpose (to entertain, to explain, to persuade, to describe).

The most common methods of organization for nonfiction include

- cause and effect (what happened and why).

- comparison and contrast (how two people, places, things, or ideas are the same or different).

- problem and solution.

- most- to least-important details.

NOTE

In this section, I have isolated the various figures of speech to discuss each one individually, but as you answer the multiple-choice poetry questions on the AP exam, always consider the various poetic devices together, as they interact with each other to create meaning. When you first begin to read a poem, you may focus on one striking aspect, but when you reread the poem, the entire pattern should come together as the various figures of speech will enter into your understanding of the poem's meaning.

- process analysis (how-to essays), which are usually in chronological order.

- spatial order (up and down, down and up, side to side, etc.).

Questions about structure will often take this form:

- This essay is constructed primarily on...

- The author's thesis in the third paragraph is developed through...

- The passage suggests contrasts between...

QUESTIONS ABOUT RHETORIC

Rhetoric is the strategic use of language to accomplish the author's purpose. On the poetry passages, most multiple-choice questions concern figurative language; on prose passages, most multiple-choice questions concern rhetoric.

Questions about rhetoric will often take this form:

- The language of this essay is best described as...

- In the first paragraph, what rhetorical strategy does the writer use with the word ("insert word")?

- The third paragraph is marked by...

- When she quotes Shakespeare ("quote,") the author is using a(n)...

- The phrase ("specific phrase") is an example of...

- The writer uses the simile ("simile") to covey the idea that...

- The writer draws his imagery from all the following EXCEPT...

- The writer uses the word ("word") in relation to (part of the poem) to suggest...

- The phrase ("phrase") functions here as a(n)
   I. simile.
   II. example.
   III. personification.

- The writer concludes the third paragraph with a series of metaphors to suggest...

- The long sentences in paragraph 2 serve to...

- The phrase "I must acknowledge" in the second paragraph does which of the following?

- The phrase ("phrase") in the second paragraph does which of the following things?

- The tone of this passage is best described as...

- The writer uses the phrase cited in item (item number) and others like it to... [rhetoric combined with main idea]

- From the diction and syntax used in this passage, you can conclude that... [rhetoric combined with main idea]

- The stylistic element in the third paragraph serves to... [rhetoric combined with main idea]

Practice Multiple-Choice Questions on Prose

Read the following passages and answer the practice AP questions that follow.

SAMPLE PASSAGE 1

About forty years ago I was an instructor in the military academy at Woolwich. I was present at one of the sections when young Scoresby underwent his preliminary examinations. I was touched to the quick with pity; for the rest of the class answered up brightly and handsomely, while he—why, dear me, he didn't know *anything*, so to speak. He was evidently good, and sweet, and lovable, and guileless; and so it was exceedingly painful to see him stand there, as serene as a graven image, and deliver himself of answers which were veritably miraculous for stupidity and ignorance. All the compassion in me was aroused in his behalf. I said to myself, when he comes to be examined, he will be flung over, of course, so it would be simply a harmless act of charity to ease his fall as much as I can. I took him aside, and found that he knew a little of Caesar's history, as he didn't know anything else; I went to work and drilled him like a galley slave on a certain line of stock questions concerning Caesar which I knew would be used. If you'll believe me, he went through with flying colors on examination day! He went through on that purely superficial "cram," and got compliments too, while others, who knew a thousand times more than he, got plucked. By some strangely lucky accident—an accident not likely to happen twice in a century—he was asked no questions outside of the narrow limits of his drill.

It was stupefying. Well, all through his course I stood by him, with something of the sentiment which a mother feels for a crippled child; and he always saved himself—just by a miracle, apparently.

Now of course the thing that would expose him and kill him at last was mathematics. I resolved to make his death as easy as I could; so I drilled him and crammed him and crammed him and drilled him, just on the line of questions which the examiners would be most likely to use, and then launched him on his fate. Well, sir, try to conceive of the result: to my consternation he took the first prize! And with it he got a perfect ovation in the way of compliments.

Sleep? There was no more sleep for me for a week. My conscience tortured me day and night. What I had done I had done purely through charity, and only to ease the poor youth's fall—I had never dreamed of any such preposterous result as the thing that had happened. I felt as guilty and miserable as the creator of Frankenstein. Here was a woodenhead whom I had put in the way of glittering promotions and prodigious responsibilities, but one thing could happen: he and his responsibilities would all go to ruin together at the first opportunity.

The Crimean War had just broken out. Of course there had to be a war, I said to myself: we couldn't have peace and give this donkey a chance to die before he is found out. I waited for the earthquake. It came. And it made me reel when it did come. He was actually gazetted to a captaincy in a marching regiment! Better men grow old and gray in the service before they climb to a sublimity like that. And who would ever have foreseen that they would go and put such a load of responsibility on such green and inadequate shoulders? I could just barely have stood it if they had made him a coronet; but a captain—think of it! I thought my hair would turn white.

1. In the context of the passage, the simile "as serene as a graven image" (paragraph 1) is used

    (A) to suggest the importance of belief in shaping a person's character.
    (B) to contrast Scoresby's promise to his lack of achievement.
    (C) as a metaphor for Scoresby's total lack of intelligence and potential.
    (D) to convey Scoresby's dignity and self-possession.
    (E) to hint that Scoresby will soon be worshipped for his academic accomplishments.

2. What tone does the author create by describing Scoresby giving answers "veritably miraculous for stupidity and ignorance"?

    (A) Irony
    (B) Humor
    (C) Sarcasm
    (D) Sorrow
    (E) Pity

3. Why does Scoresby's behavior arouse compassion in the narrator?

    (A) The narrator feels that Scoresby cannot possibly succeed without help.
    (B) The narrator is Scoresby's father as well as his teacher.
    (C) Since he isn't much more intelligent than Scoresby, the narrator understands how the young man suffers.
    (D) Only the narrator realizes that Scoresby is putting on a brilliant act.
    (E) The narrator pities all the other people in the class who will be eclipsed by Scoresby's achievements.

4. The simile "drilled him like a galley slave" in the first paragraph implies that

    (A) Scoresby is not getting paid for his efforts.
    (B) Scoresby is being held against his will.
    (C) Scoresby will be a sailor.
    (D) the narrator makes Scoresby exercise his body as well as his mind.
    (E) the narrator worked Scoresby brutally hard.

5. In the context of the passage, the phrases "flung over" and "plucked" (paragraph 1) are used to mean that

    (A) Scoresby has a great potential for cruelty.
    (B) students who do not succeed in the program will have to work on a chicken farm.
    (C) students who do well will be selected for inclusion in the officers' corps.
    (D) some students will fail or flunk out of the program.
    (E) students who resent Scoresby's success will tar and feather him.

6. The writer creates ironic contrast by using

    (A) the first-person point of view.
    (B) chronological sequence of events.
    (C) similes and metaphors.
    (D) elevated diction to describe trivial subjects.
    (E) ornate language embellished with many figures of speech.

7. The phrase "so I drilled him and crammed him and crammed him and drilled him" is an example of which of the following literary devices?
   I. Metaphor
   II. Parallelism
   III. Paradox

   (A) I
   (B) II
   (C) III
   (D) I and II
   (E) I and III

8. What does Frankenstein symbolize in this passage?

   (A) The importance of creativity as well as rote learning
   (B) How our best efforts are sometimes not sufficient to ensure success
   (C) The monster the narrator has created by pushing Scoresby past his abilities
   (D) How inspiration often comes from unlikely sources
   (E) How you can create something new and better by cobbling together spare parts

9. Which of the following literary techniques is dominant in this passage?
   I. Humor
   II. Satire
   III. Irony

   (A) I
   (B) II
   (C) III
   (D) I and III
   (E) II and III

10. The rhetorical style of this passage is best described as

   (A) cheerfully optimistic.
   (B) gently satirical.
   (C) cloyingly sentimental.
   (D) coolly objective.
   (E) conversational vernacular.

Answers and Explanations

1. **The correct answer is (C).** In the context of the passage, the simile "as serene as a graven image" (paragraph 1) is used as a metaphor for Scoresby's total lack of intelligence and potential. Scoresby is a "woodenhead," as stupid as a block of wood.

2. **The correct answer is (B).** The author creates a humorous tone by describing Scoresby giving answers "veritably miraculous for stupidity and ignorance." The overstatement is funny in a gently mocking way. Therefore, choice (C), *sarcasm*, is too strong.

3. **The correct answer is (A).** Scoresby's behavior arouses compassion in the narrator because the narrator feels that Scoresby cannot possibly succeed without help. This is plain in the following passage: "Here was a woodenhead whom I had put in the way of glittering promotions and prodigious responsibilities, but one thing could happen: he and his responsibilities would all go to ruin together at the first opportunity." There is no support for either choice (B) or choice (C).

4. **The correct answer is (E).** The simile "drilled him like a galley slave" in the first paragraph implies that the narrator worked Scoresby brutally hard. This simile is an allusion to the image of convicts or slaves of ancient and medieval times who were condemned to row ships.

5. **The correct answer is (D).** In the context of the passage, the phrases "flung over" and "plucked" (paragraph 1) are used to mean that some students will fail or flunk out of the program. Both phrases are slang.

6. **The correct answer is (D).** The writer creates ironic contrast by using elevated diction to describe trivial subjects. This is especially clear in the conclusion: "Better men grow old and gray in the service before they climb to a sublimity like that."

7. **The correct answer is (B).** The phrase "so I drilled him and crammed him and crammed him and drilled him" is an example of parallelism. The nouns have the same grammatical form.

8. **The correct answer is (C).** Frankenstein symbolizes the monster that the narrator has created by pushing Scoresby past his abilities. This passage is especially confusing because the author (Mark Twain) has the narrator make a common mistake: Frankenstein was the *creator* of the monster, *not* the monster itself. If you have not already read the novel that provides the source of this commonplace allusion, you may wish to: It's *Frankenstein* by Mary Shelley.

9. **The correct answer is (D).** Humor and irony are the dominant literary techniques in this passage. Twain creates humor through language and word play. For example, Twain uses exaggeration in the following passage: "Now of course the thing that would expose him and kill him at last was mathematics. I resolved to make his death as easy as I could..." It is highly ironic that such a foolish person as Scoresby could succeed so wildly.

10. **The correct answer is (E).** The rhetorical style of this passage is best described as conversational vernacular. The first-person narrator helps create the conversational tone. Twain uses many colloquial terms, such as "be flung over," "cram," "got plucked," and "woodenhead." These are all vernacular.

SAMPLE PASSAGE 2

There were two orchards belonging to the old house. One, that we called the "wild" orchard, lay beyond the vegetable garden: it was planted with bitter cherries and damsons and transparent yellow plums. For some reason it lay under a cloud; we never played there, we did not even trouble to pick up the fallen fruit; and there, every Monday morning, to the round open space in the middle, the servant girl and washerwoman carried the wet linen—Grandmother's nightdresses, Father's striped shirts, the hired man's cotton trousers and the servant girl's "dreadfully vulgar" salmon-pink flannelette drawers that jiggled and slapped in horrid familiarity.

But the other orchard, far away and hidden from the house, lay at the foot of a little hill and stretched right over the edge of the paddocks—to the clumps of wattles bobbing yellow in the bright sun and the blue gums with their streaming sickle-shaped levees. There, under the fruit trees, the grass grew so thick and coarse that it tangled and knotted in your shoes as you walked, and even on the hottest day it was damp to touch when you stopped and parted it this way and that, looking for windfalls—the apples marked with a bird's beak, the big bruised pears, the quinces, so good to eat with a pinch of salt, but so delicious to smell that you could not bite for sniffling.

One year the orchard had its Forbidden Tree. It was an apple tree discovered by Father and a friend during an after-dinner prowl one Sunday afternoon.

"Great Scott!" said the friend, lighting upon it with every appearance of admiring astonishment: "Isn't that a—?" And a rich, splendid name settled like an unknown bird on the tree.

"Yes, I believe it is," said Father lightly. He knew nothing whatever about the names of fruit trees.

1. You can infer from context that "damsons" must be

   (A)   a type of fruit.
   (B)   a type of apple.
   (C)   wild grasses.
   (D)   bitter, blighted fruits.
   (E)   especially delicious cherries.

2. As used in this passage, what does the word "drawers" mean?

   (A)   Closet
   (B)   Nightclothes
   (C)   Fancy dresses
   (D)   A type of dancing
   (E)   Underpants

3. The writer uses the phrase "horrid familiarity" in relation to the servant girl's drawers to suggest

   (A)   that she is repulsed by the sight and feeling of wet clothing.
   (B)   the drudgery of laundry day.
   (C)   the difficulty women experienced in the past.
   (D)   the servant girl's unwillingness to know her place in society and keep to it.
   (E)   the wide social gulf between the narrator's family and their domestic help.

4. The ideas in the first two paragraphs are developed primarily according to

   (A) process analysis.
   (B) cause and effect.
   (C) comparison and contrast.
   (D) problem solution.
   (E) chronological order.

5. The imagery suggests that the second orchard most likely symbolizes

   (A) purgatory or the underworld.
   (B) the Garden of Eden.
   (C) societal repression.
   (D) the disastrous results of unrestrained growth.
   (E) a jungle.

6. If the images and symbolism carry through the story, you can predict that

   (A) the narrator will get lost in the second orchard.
   (B) something dreadful will occur in the second orchard.
   (C) the narrator will fall in love in the first orchard.
   (D) the narrator will experience an awakening from innocence to experience.
   (E) the narrator will cut down the Forbidden Tree.

7. Throughout the passage, the imagery suggests

   (A) great lushness.
   (B) deprivation and despair.
   (C) unrestrained affluence and luxury.
   (D) the unexpressed terrors of childhood.
   (E) a life free from worry or doubt.

8. The writer uses the simile "And a rich splendid name settled like an unknown bird on the tree" to suggest that

   (A) the narrator is embarrassed by her father's ignorance.
   (B) knowing technical names for aspects of nature detracts from appreciating its beauty.
   (C) the friend is an arrogant braggart.
   (D) the tree is home to many varieties of birds.
   (E) the tree is very valuable.

9. The phrase "bird's beak, the big bruised pears..." is an example of

   (A) irony.
   (B) alliteration.
   (C) a figure of speech.
   (D) an allusion.
   (E) a metaphor.

10. The best title for this excerpt would be

    (A) My Father and his Garden.
    (B) The Garden.
    (C) The Apple Tree.
    (D) The Snake.
    (E) Good and Evil.

Answers and Explanations

1. **The correct answer is (A).** You can infer from context that "damsons" must be a type of fruit. You can find the information in this clause: "...it [the orchard] was planted with bitter cherries and damsons and transparent yellow plums." "Bitter cherries" and "transparent yellow plums" suggest that the middle word must relate to fruit as well. Choice (B) is too specific to be correct. That the cherries are "bitter" is not sufficient to assume that the damsons are as well, so choice (D) is wrong. Therefore, the same must be true of choice (E).

2. **The correct answer is (E).** As used in this passage, the word "drawers" means *underpants.* They have long legs, like shorts, which "jiggled and slapped in horrid familiarity." They cannot be a *closet,* choice (A); *fancy dresses,* choice (C); or a *type of dancing,* choice (D), since they must be a type of "wet linen."

3. **The correct answer is (E).** The writer uses the phrase "horrid familiarity" in relation to the servant girl's drawers to suggest the wide social gulf between the narrator's family and their domestic help. The phrase hints that the servant girl refuses to obey the accepted social convention of her day and class.

4. **The correct answer is (C).** The ideas in the first two paragraphs are developed primarily by comparison and contrast. The first orchard is compared and contrasted to the second one. The transitional phrase "But the other orchard..." signals the contrast.

5. **The correct answer is (B).** The imagery suggests that the second orchard most likely symbolizes the Garden of Eden. You can infer this from the lush growth and the Forbidden Tree, clearly symbolizing the story of Adam and Eve.

6. **The correct answer is (D).** If the images and symbolism carry through the story, you can predict that the narrator will experience an awakening from innocence to experience. This prediction is a logical extension of the symbolism of the Garden of Eden and the Forbidden Tree. This interpretation also fits with the friend's comment about the tree's great rarity and value.

7. **The correct answer is (A).** Throughout the passage, the imagery suggests great lushness. Examples include "clumps of wattles bobbing yellow in the bright sun and the blue gums with their streaming sickle-shaped levees," "the grass grew so thick and coarse that it tangled and knotted in your shoes as you walked," and "so delicious to smell that you could not bite for sniffling." Notice that the images appeal to several senses, including touch and smell as well as sight.

8. **The correct answer is (E).** The writer uses the simile "And a rich splendid name settled like an unknown bird on the tree" to suggest that the tree is very valuable. The word "rich" carries this overtone.

9. **The correct answer is (B).** The phrase "bird's beak, the big bruised pears..." is an example of alliteration. Recall that alliteration is the repetition of initial consonant sounds in several words in a sentence or line of poetry. Writers use alliteration to create musical effects, link related ideas, stress certain words, or mimic specific sounds.

10. **The correct answer is (C).** The best title for this excerpt would be "The Apple Tree." "My Father and his Garden," choice (A), is too narrow because it does not take into consideration the Garden of Eden symbolism. Since the focus is on the tree rather than the two orchards, you can eliminate choice (B). Choices (D) and (E) extend the imagery too far. You cannot predict that the story will head in that direction.

Strategies for Success on the Essay Questions

You'll recall from Part I of this book and the sample AP English Literature and Composition exams you've taken that the essay section of the AP exam in literature consists of three questions:

- a poem or pair of poems to analyze.

- a close reading of a prose passage. This might be part of a novel, an essay, or a short story, for example. (In rare cases, an entire short story will be included for analysis.)

- an open-ended literary response question. A list of suggested literary texts is provided on the test, but you are free to choose any well-respected work of literature that applies to the specific question. Students usually choose a novel, a play, a biography, or an autobiography.

You are given 2 hours to complete all three essays, which gives you about 40 minutes per essay. While you're free to decide how to spend your time, logic dictates that you divide your time equally among all three essays since each of them receives the same amount of credit.

ROAD MAP

- *Overall Essay Guidelines*
- *Writing an Essay on Poetry*
- *The Basic Poetry Analysis Question*
- *Five-Step Method to a High Score*
- *Sample Questions*

OVERALL ESSAY GUIDELINES

While each of the three essays requires you to write on a different topic and focus on different elements, all three essays demand the same writing and thinking skills. The following hints can help you boost your scores.

TOP TEN HINTS FOR HIGH-SCORING ESSAYS

1. **Analyze the question.** Before you do anything else, make sure that you understand exactly what is required of you. Rephrase the question in your own words to make sure that you comprehend it and grasp any subtle points.

    It's often the little words that trip up test takers. Watch especially for "how" and "why" embedded in the writing prompts. These crucial little words are frequently misread by hurried test takers, and such a slip can result in a completely misdirected essay.

NOTE
You must write all three essays.

2. **Answer the question.** *Follow directions exactly, and do exactly what you're asked to do.* Be sure to address every single part of the question. No matter how impressive your writing is, you will not receive any credit if you don't answer the question. For example, if the question calls for you to write about the author's attitude but you write about figures of speech and never mention the author's attitude, you're sunk. If the question calls for you to write about a play or a novel, you'll receive no credit for writing about a short story—no matter how brilliant your analysis may be. You will receive only partial credit if you answer part of the question. If you grasp no other point from this book, make it this point: directly answer the question you're given, and follow the directions exactly.

3. **Use your time well.** There's no rule that you have to write the essays in order. If you blank on question 1 (the poetry essay), immediately move on to question 2 or 3 and get started. You don't have the time to sit thinking about a question for 10 minutes.

4. **Lead with your strength.** If you've been earning your best scores on the open-ended questions, begin there. Doing a good job on the first essay you write will increase your confidence for tackling the other two essays.

5. **Start writing.** It's natural to start your essay at the beginning with the introduction, but if you're stuck for an opening, don't waste time agonizing. Instead, start where you can, with the body paragraphs. While it's vital that essays are well organized and logical, it's equally vital that you get all three essays written in the 2 hours you have. The best essay in the world won't get you any points if you don't get it down on paper within the time limit.

6. **Keep writing.** If you get stuck, skip some lines and keep on going. If you can't keep on writing, take a few deep breaths and gather your wits. If you really blank and can't write, move on to the next question. Staring at the paper only wastes time. You will likely have the time to return to the essay you didn't finish, but even if you don't, at least you wrote another essay in the time you would have wasted feeling panic settling in.

7. **Write neatly.** If you're writing is illegible, the scorer won't be able to read your paper. If it's merely messy, your scorer might misread a crucial point. And as much as we don't like to admit it, neat papers *do* predispose scorers to smile more kindly. If you suspect that your handwriting is hard to read, print neatly and carefully.

   Special note to Lefties: Avoid erasable pens, because the ink tends to smear as you drag your hand across the page.

8. **Be focused, serious, and mature.** Some students take the AP test for themselves and their future; others take it for their parents or to be with their friends. Other unfortunate students are forced into it, kicking and screaming. If you didn't want to take the class and the test in the first place, this isn't the time to throw the test to prove a point. As an AP scorer, I've read too many essays that reveal the students' determination to go down in flames to prove they never should have been forced into the class. If you are in this dreadful position, prove the other point: you *can* do it.

9. **Proofread.** This can be one of the most important steps in any paper, for no matter how valid your points, how dear your examples, if you have made a great many careless writing errors, you will lose credit. While your essay will be evaluated holistically (on the total impression it makes), errors can distract your reader and reduce the effectiveness of your arguments. Try to let your essay sit for a few moments. Look over the short answers or another essay, and then go back to the essay refreshed. Always make sure that you have time to proofread, and be as careful as you can to read what is there, not what you *think* is there.

10. **Deal with panic.** You can psyche yourself up or down—it's all in your head. Convince yourself that you can succeed by working carefully and resolutely. If you start losing it, pause for a second to calm yourself and then keep soldiering on.

Always remember that scorers reward you for what you do well. They're not looking for perfection. After all, you have only 40 minutes in which to write each essay. Do the very best you can, but don't obsess about making your essay flawless.

WRITING AN ESSAY ON POETRY

On past exams, Question 1 has always concerned poetry. It's logical, then, to assume that the pattern will continue and your first essay will be an analysis of a poem. You will have the poem in front of you as you answer the question. As a result, you will be expected to make close reference to the poem and quote specific lines and words to make your point clearly. The poem will very likely be unfamiliar to you, since the test committee makes an effort to select poems that are not usually taught. You may have read something else by the same author, however.

THE BASIC POETRY ANALYSIS QUESTION

When you first start writing practice AP poetry questions, they may appear to be very different from each other. In fact, every poetry question is simply a variation on the same basic form: *analyze how the poet uses one or more poetic elements to reveal his or her meaning*. Often, "meaning" will be stated as "theme" or "attitude toward the subject of the poem." The poetic elements can include the following:

- allusions (references to well-known people, places, works of art, etc.)

- diction (word choice)

- figures of speech (metaphors, similes, personification, hyperbole, etc.)

- form (sonnet, ode, ballad, free verse, villanelle, epic, etc.)

- imagery

- language

- narrative pace

- point of view

- rhythm

- rhyme

- structure

- syntax

- tone

Each of these elements is explained in detail in Part VI: Glossary of Literary Terms.

Study these typical poetry questions:

Model Poetry Question 1:

Read the following poem carefully. Then, in a well-organized essay, discuss how the speaker uses figures of speech to convey meaning in the poem.

[You *must* describe how figures of speech create the theme. You have no choice here: you must isolate similes, metaphors, personification, oxymorons, and so on and analyze how the poet uses them to express the poem's theme.]

Model Poetry Question 2:

The following poem was written by a sixteenth-century woman. Read the poem closely and carefully, and then write an essay in which you examine how the poem's tone reveals the poet's opinion of education.

[You must link the poem's tone to the poet's opinion of education.]

Model Poetry Question 3:

Read the following poem carefully, paying close attention to the diction. Then write a well-organized essay in which you explain how the poet describes not just a day at the beach but also the true meaning of the experience to him.

[You must link the topic—a day at the beach—to the theme—what the day at the beach symbolizes or represents to the poet.]

Model Poetry Question 4:

Read the following poem carefully. Then write a well-organized essay in which you explain how the poet uses literary elements such as structure, diction, and imagery to reveal the speaker's reaction to the experience described in the poem.

[The key phrase "such as" reveals that you can consider any literary elements you wish, but you'd be wise to include at least two of the three literary elements listed.]

Model Poetry Question 5:

The following poem was written by a contemporary South African writer. Read the poem carefully. Then write an essay in which you explain how the poet uses diction, imagery, and language to express the speaker's complex attitude toward religion.

[You must consider diction, imagery, and language and show how they reveal the poet's attitude toward faith.]

FIVE-STEP METHOD TO A HIGH SCORE

1. Read the question completely and restate in your own words to make sure you clearly understand what you must write. For example, do you have to consider *all* the literary devices listed or just a few from the list? Look for the key phrase "such as" so you know how many of the literary elements you must describe.

2. Read the poem all the way through, at least twice. As you read, use the punctuation to help create meaning. Pause where the poet wants you to pause—at commas—and stop at periods rather than at the end of each line. Paraphrase the poem to make sure you understand what the speaker is saying. Use your paraphrase to get ideas for your essay.

3. Plan before you write. Create a quick jotted outline, take a few notes, or make a diagram showing the order in which you'll present your points.

4. As you write, make frequent and specific references to the poem. Quote words, phrases, and lines to support your point.

5. Always leave a few minutes to proofread and check your essay.

SAMPLE POETRY QUESTIONS AND MODEL RESPONSES

SAMPLE 1

Read the following poem carefully. Then, in a well-organized essay, discuss how the speaker uses tone and form to convey meaning in the poem.

Sonnet 130

1 My mistress' eyes are nothing like the sun;
Coral is far more red than her lips' red;
If snow be white, why then her breasts are dun;
If hairs be wires, black wires grow on her head.

5 I have seen roses damasked, red and white,
But no such roses see I in her cheeks;
And in some perfumes is there more delight
Than in the breath that from my mistress reeks.
I love to hear her speak; yet well I know

10 That music hath a far more pleasing sound:
I grant I never saw a goddess go;
My mistress, when she walks, treads on the ground.
And yet, by heaven, I think my love as rare
As any she belied with false compare.
　　　—William Shakespeare

Response 1

In "Sonnet 130" by William Shakespeare, two different tones are expressed. The first, which makes up the first twelve lines of the sonnet, is sarcastic and witty. The second, which concludes the work, is more serious.

In the first twelve lines of the poem, the speaker describes his mistress in a sarcastic manner. He creates a visual representation through such phrases as "My mistress' eyes are nothing like the sun" and "Coral is far more red than her lips red." But these descriptions in no way indicate whether or not he loves her, as the second part of the poem reveals.

In the final two lines, we see the speaker's true feelings for his mistress. Although this woman does not have any of the traditional attributes mentioned in the Elizabethan love sonnet, she has something that he obviously values more—something in her manner and personality that he finds attractive.

The tone changes from sarcastic to serious as the poem progresses, although his feelings for his mistress remain the same throughout. Love is not always based on physical attraction; it goes deeper, within the heart, mind, and soul.

Evaluation

The topic paragraph gets right to the point by clearly stating the shift in tone involved here. However, the writer does not address the second half of the question: how the poet "uses tone and form to convey meaning in the poem." *All* parts of the question must be addressed in the topic paragraph in order to answer the question completely. The omission of form is most serious, as it is central to the poem's effect.

The second paragraph begins to establish the writer's meaning, but a great deal more can be done with examples to make that meaning clear. The writer should take us step by step through the poem to show clearly how the tone is sarcastic. The transition in the final line of the second paragraph is good, as it leads logically into paragraph 3.

Paragraph 3, like paragraph 2, needs more specific examples to make the writer's point. Again, examples must be taken from the poem and fully explained to show how the tone changes. This must be tied in with theme in this specific instance to make the author's point.

The concluding lines do establish the tone of the work, but the author failed to prove the complete thesis clearly in the body of the essay.

Remember that the essay rubric is calibrated from 9–0, even though the final score you receive is calibrated from 5–1. The model essay under discussion here would receive a score of 3–4 on the AP scale. Although the writer obviously understood the poem, the issue of the relationship of form and content is ignored. Further, there aren't enough specific examples to prove the point convincingly.

Response 2

The tone of the first twelve lines of Shakespeare's "Sonnet 130" contrast sharply with the tone of the final two, and this difference establishes the theme of the entire work. In presenting his theme this way, Shakespeare is working within the convention of the English sonnet, in which the "turn," or point, is presented in the final couplet.

The first twelve lines of the poem parody the form and content of the typical love sonnet, as the woman fails to measure up to any of the traditional emblems of love and devotion. Thus, her eyes, the time-honored windows of the soul, lack the clear radiance of the sun, and her lips, the deep, rosy tint of coral. "My mistress' eyes are nothing like the sun," the poet playfully notes in line 1, and we learn in line 2 that "Coral is far more red than her lips' red." Her skin is mottled and dark, her hair, coarse wires. If that's not bad enough, she has bad breath ("And in some perfumes is there more delight/Than in the breath that from my mistress reeks") and has a voice that is far from melodious ("I love to hear her speak; yet well I know/That music hath a far more pleasing sound.") Lines 11–12 reveal that his beloved "treads on the ground" rather that ethereally floating above it as a goddess should.

The tone is playful and mocking, as Shakespeare inverts all the accepted tools of the love sonneteer's trade to construct a series of false analogies. The tone of the final two lines, however, differs sharply. As mentioned earlier, the final couplet of an English sonnet frequently serves to sum up the meaning of the preceding twelve lines and establish the author's theme. Such is the case here, for the couplet's tone and meaning differ markedly from the rest of the sonnet. These two lines are serious, not light and playful, as the author declares his love for the lady he has just pilloried at the stake of false comparison. He wrote this poem, he says in the couplet, to parody her tendency to compare their love to objects and, in so doing, establish false analogies. Their love is a rare and serious thing, he states, not to be diminished through "false compare."

The sonnet form is well suited to this difference in tone, as the couplet in the end allows Shakespeare the opportunity to sum up the first twelve lines and establish the theme. Here, he abjures the parody of the first twelve lines to declare his love firmly and seriously. In so doing, he both mocks and embraces the poetic conventions of his day.

Evaluation

This example answers the question fully with style and grace. The introduction addresses all parts of the question—tone, form and theme—and demonstrates a sophisticated use of language.

In paragraphs 2 and 3, the writer uses specific examples to describe the theme and its relationship to the poem. Note especially how smoothly the writer weaves in specific quotes from the sonnet to prove the thesis. The writer clearly demonstrates familiarity with the conventions of the English (also called "Elizabethan" or "Shakespearean" sonnet) comparison. The conclusion to the third paragraph is clear, succinct, and effective: "He wrote this poem, he says in the couplet, to parody her tendency to compare their love to objects and, in so doing, establish false analogies. Their love is a rare and serious thing, he states, not to be diminished through 'false compare.' "

The conclusion is brief but adds a graceful and intelligent note, pulling together all aspects of the question. This well-written essay fully answers the question by using specific examples, vivid word choice, and sophisticated syntax. As a result, it would earn a very high score, 8–9, on the AP exam.

SAMPLE 2

The following poem was written by the German author Heinrich Heine. Read the poem carefully and then write an essay in which you analyze how formal elements such as figures of speech, rhyme, and parallelism reveal the speaker's attitude toward love.

The Lotus Flower

1   The lotus flower is troubled
        At the sun's resplended light;
    With sunken head and sadly
        She dreamily waits for the night.

5   The moon appears as her wooer,
        She wakes at his fond embrace;
    For him she kindly uncovers
        Her sweetly flowering face.

    She blooms and glows and glistens,
10   And mutely gazes above;
    She weeps and exhales and trembles
        With love and the sorrows of love.

Response 1

Heinrich Heine uses many literary elements in "The Lotus Flower" to make his point. These include figures of speech, rhyme, and parallelism. He uses these literary elements to tell us what he thinks about love.

In this poem, he compares the lotus flower to love. This comparison is a metaphor because it compares two things that are not alike. The lotus flower hates the sun but loves the moon. This is strange because most flowers like the sun but maybe lotus flowers are different. This is all shown in the second stanza.

The poem has rhyme, too. In stanza 1, *light* and *night* rhyme; in stanza 2, *embrace* and *face* rhyme; and in stanza 3, *above* and *love* rhyme. The rhyme makes the poem flow more smoothly. This makes it easier to read and more poetic. That is why "The Lotus Flower" is considered a lyric poem.

There is a lot of parallel structure in the last stanza. The verbs *blooms, glows, glistens* in line 9 are parallel. The verbs *weeps, exhales, trembles* in line 11 are parallel.

Readers can conclude from figures of speech, rhyme, and parallelism that Heine thought a lot about love. He thought that love was beautiful, like a flower. I think that he has a point.

Evaluation

The opening is flat, dull, and uninviting. The string of simple sentences, combined with the monotonous diction, fail to engage the reader. More seriously, however, the writer does not make the point: what is the speaker's attitude toward love? Without a clear thesis, it will be difficult for this writer to stay on track and prove anything.

The second paragraph misses the point: the poet compares the lotus flower to a woman in love, not to love itself. Further, the second sentence—"This is strange because most flowers like the sun but maybe lotus flowers are different"—has nothing to do with the topic. The writer does not cite lines to make the point. A closer reading of the poem would have revealed the misunderstanding.

While the writer describes the rhyme scheme accurately, nothing is done with the information. For a detail to be effective, it must be linked to meaning—in this case, "how formal elements such as... rhyme...reveal the speaker's attitude toward love." Readers do not learn from this paragraph why Heine used rhyme, its function in the poem, or its importance to the theme.

Focus for a second on the last line of the third paragraph: "That is why 'The Lotus Flower' is considered a lyric poem." Although this sentence is true, it has nothing to do with the topic. Therefore, it must be deleted. Be very careful here: include ONLY the details and examples that make your point. Even if the detail or statement is true, it must be omitted if it is off topic.

The writer accurately identifies the parallel structure but again does nothing with this information. Therefore, it does not serve any purpose in the essay.

Finally, the conclusion shows an incomplete reading of the poem. The speaker did think love was beautiful, but he also thought that it was painful. Evaluating the paper as a whole, it would earn no more than 2–3 on the scoring rubric.

Response 2

Does love bring pain or pleasure—or perhaps some combination of the two emotions? Poets through the ages have explored love's mingling of delight and despair, as Heinrich Heine does in "The Lotus Flower." In this poem, Heine uses an extended metaphor, rhyme, parallelism, and personification to reveal his belief that love —while beautiful—is inevitably marred by sorrow.

"The Lotus Flower" is built around an extended metaphor, in which the lotus flower is compared to a woman's love. During the course of the poem, the lotus flower "wakes" (line 6) and then "blooms and glows and glistens" (line 9) as a result of love. The lotus flower's awakening is caused by the moon, which appears at night as her lover. This is revealed in the second stanza: "The moon appears as her wooer,/She wakes at his fond embrace;/For him she kindly uncovers/Her sweetly flowering face."

The rhyme scheme reinforces the poem's lyric quality and the speaker's attitude toward love. In stanza 1, *light* and *night* rhyme; in stanza 2, *embrace* and *face* rhyme; and in stanza 3, *above* and *love* rhyme. The last rhyme, linking "love" to "above," especially shows the power of love to transform everyday existence into magnificence.

The lotus flower is personified as beautiful yet shy and fragile: "She weeps and exhales and trembles/With love..." By personifying the lotus flower as timid, beautiful, and sensitive, the poet suggests that love embodies these same traits. From this personification, readers can infer that love's sorrow derives in part from its fragility. This is reinforced by the parallel structure in the last stanza. The parallel verbs *blooms, glows, glistens* in line 9 and *weeps, exhales, trembles* in line 11 also suggest the two sides of love: its joy (line 9) and its sorrow (line 11).

The conventional flower imagery and the flower's positive response to the moon's adoration suggest that Heine had an idealized view of love as a radiant, transforming experience. However, the last line suggests that he strongly recognized the sorrows that often accompany love's splendor: pleasure and pain; delight and despair.

Evaluation

The essay is extremely effective because the writer skillfully interweaves several "formal elements" to "reveal the speaker's attitude toward love." Note how the writer opens with a question to spark the reader's interest. In addition, the writer skillfully uses alliteration in the topic sentence to set a graceful tone: "Does love bring pain or pleasure—or perhaps some combination of the two emotions?" To make sure that the AP readers recognize that the technique is deliberate, the writer repeats it in the second sentence with "d" this time: "Poets through the ages have explored love's mingling of delight and despair..." The last line of the introduction makes the writer's point clearly and succinctly.

The writer covers "figures of speech" in the first paragraph by focusing on the poem's key element: the extended metaphor. The writer wisely leads off with this element because the entire poem is structured around it. Pay close attention to the way the writer cites specific details from the poem to make the point.

Next, the writer discusses rhyme. This paragraph is especially effective because it takes the discussion one step higher by linking rhyme to meaning, as shown in this line: "The last rhyme, linking 'love' to 'above,' especially shows the power of love to transform everyday existence into magnificence."

The writer adds personification, not listed in the directions but allowed because of the phrase "such as" in the prompt. Remember that when you see the phrase "such as," you can use all or some of the literary elements listed. In addition, you can bring in additional ones. If the phrase "such as" isn't included, you *must* treat the elements listed in the prompt. Personification was an excellent choice in this instance because it is a central element in the poem. Again, the writer links the literary element to the theme, thus answering the question. The writer then draws in parallelism (citing specific examples) to focus on the theme: "The parallel verbs *blooms, glows, glistens* in line 9 and *weeps, exhales, trembles* in line 11 also suggest the two sides of love: its joy (line 9) and its sorrow (line 11)."

The conclusion is very effective because it makes the writer's point and ties together all the points made earlier in the essay. The final phrase—"pleasure and pain; delight and despair"—echoes the introduction, further unifying the essay. This well-written essay fully answers the question by using specific examples of literary elements to explain the theme. As a result, the essay would earn an 8–9 on the AP scale.

SAMPLE 3

Carefully read the following poem by medieval poet Francesco Petrarch. As you read, focus on the language. Then write a well-organized essay in which you analyze how the poem's allegory expresses the speaker's complex feelings. You may also wish to include figures of speech such as oxymorons, similes, and allusions in your discussion.

The White Doe

1 A pure-white doe in an emerald glade
   Appeared to me, with two antlers of gold,
   Between two streams, under a laurel's shade,
   At sunrise, in the season's bitter cold.

5 Her sight was so suavely merciless
   That I left work to follow her at leisure,
   Like the miser who was looking for his treasure
   Sweetens with that delight his bitterness.
   Around her lovely neck, "Do not touch me"

10 Was written with topaz and diamond stone,
   "My Caesar's will has been to make me free."
   Already toward noon had climbed the sun,
   My weary eyes were not sated to see,
   When I fell in the stream and she was gone.

Response

In the "The White Doe," the speaker describes his conflicted feelings toward the woman he loves. This is accomplished largely through a number of poetic techniques, including imagery, figures of speech, and allegory.

The imagery in the opening stanza suggests that the doe is meant to symbolize a woman who occupies a central role in the speaker's imagination—if not his life. The word "appeared" in line 2 suggests a nonliteral reading of "doe." In addition, the imagery of the "pure-white doe" in line 1 connotes innocence and purity, qualities the speaker would logically associate with a woman he idolizes. The "antlers of gold" (line 2) reinforce this inference of her value. However, the antlers paradoxically suggest pain as well as beauty because antlers can gore as well as adorn.

The poem includes several references to time, such as "At sunrise in the season's bitter cold" (line 4) and "Already toward noon had climbed the sun" (line 12). The first reference to time occurs in the first stanza, the second in the last stanza. The spacing of these references to time suggests that they symbolize stages in the speaker's relationship with the woman the doe represents. The season is likely "bitter cold" because he is not yet sure that he has her love; the "noon" suggests the blazing heat of this love. He describes his years of loving the woman as a day in which he follows a perfect white doe.

The poem's oxymorons express the poet's opposing feelings for his ideal woman. They also convey his uncertainty about how to evaluate his feelings, which suggests a mind at war with itself. For example, the oxymoron "suavely merciless" (line 5) suggests that the woman is simultaneously unforgiving and cruel as well as appealing and graceful. The oxymoron prepares for the simile and paradox in lines 7–8: "Like the miser who was looking for his treasure/Sweetens with that delight his bitterness." A miser is associated with bitterness because a miser is always hoarding treasure and is never satisfied with what he gets. The speaker links his love for the woman with a miser's "love" of treasure. He can never get enough of her love, no matter how much he has. This leads to a paradox: the delight he gets from having her love is "sweetened" with the bitterness of knowing he can never have as much as he desires.

The fourth stanza suggests that a powerful man has taken the woman for his own and prevented her from having other relationships. The sonnet ends with a sudden change in the final line: the doe vanishes. The speaker's desire for her is never fulfilled. The entire poem is an allegory, dramatizing the speaker's experience with his lady.

Evaluation

This is an excellent response because it weaves together all the elements in the question to analyze the speaker's conflicted feelings toward the woman he loves. It shows a close reading of the poem and keen understanding of its unstated meaning. This is shown especially in the writer's awareness that the doe symbolizes the woman and the underlying allegory.

Note the specific textual references, such as the oxymoron "suavely merciless" in line 5, the simile and paradox in lines 7–8, and the sudden change of direction in the final line. This is an especially challenging poem, but the writer covers all the essential elements and even adds some original insights. As a result, the essay would earn an 8–9 on the AP scale.

PRACTICE POETRY ANALYSIS QUESTIONS

Use the following simulated test questions to practice what you learned in this lesson.

SAMPLE 1

In the following poem, Sir Walter Ralegh gives advice to his son. Read the poem carefully. Then write a well-organized essay in which you evaluate the speaker's advice to his son. Consider literary elements such as imagery, figures of speech, diction, form, and wit in your analysis.

Sir Walter Ralegh to His Son

> Three things there be that prosper up apace
> And flourish, whilst they grow asunder far,
> But on a day, they meet all in one place,
> And when they meet, they one another mar;
> And they be these: the wood, the weed, the wag,
> The wood is that which makes the gallow tree;
> The weed is that which strings the hangman's bag;
> The wag, my pretty knave, betokenth thee.
> Mark well, dear boy, whilst these assemble not,
> Green springs the tree, hemp grows, the wag is wild,
> But when they meet, it makes the timber rot;
> It frets the halter, and it chokes the child.
> Then bless thee, and beware, and let us pray
> We part not with thee at this meeting day.

SAMPLE 2

Read the following poem carefully. Then write a well-organized essay in which you explain how literary elements such as mood and point of view reveal the speaker's response to the old fable he describes.

The Lorelei

> I cannot explain the sadness
> That's fallen on my breast.
> An old, old fable haunts me,
> And will not let me rest.
>
> The air grows cold in the twilight,
> And softly the Rhine flows on;
> The peak of a mountain sparkles
> Beneath the setting sun.
>
> More lovely than a vision,
> A girl sits high up there;
> Her golden jewelry glistens,
> She combs her golden hair.
>
> With a comb of gold she combs it,
> And sings an evensong;
> The wonderful melody reaches
> A boat, as it sails along.

The boatman hears, with an anguish
More wild than was ever known;
He's blind to the rocks around him;
His eyes are for her alone.

—At last the waves devoured
The boat, and the boatman's cry;
And this she did with her singing,
The golden Lorelei.

SAMPLE 3

Read the following poem carefully. Then write a well-organized essay in which you discuss how the speaker uses poetic devices such as diction, imagery, meter, rhythm, rhyme, and figurative language to convey meaning in the poem.

Pied Beauty

1 Glory be to God for dappled things—
    For skies of couple-color as a brindled cow;
    For rose-moles all in stipple upon trout that swim;
    Fresh-firecoal chestnut-falls; finches' wings;

5 Landscape plotted and pieced—fold, fallow, and plough;
    And all trades, their gear and tackle and trim.

    All things counter, original, spare, strange;
    Whatever is fickle, freckled (who knows how?)
    With swift, slow; sweet, sour; adazzle, dim;

10 He fathers-forth whose beauty is past change:
    Praise him.
         —Gerard Manley Hopkins

WRITING AN ESSAY ON A PROSE PASSAGE

On past exams, question 2 has usually required test takers to read a short story, essay, or other prose passage and write an analysis of it. In nearly all cases, the passage will be fiction. Working from past practices, assume that you'll be faced with just such a topic when you turn to the second essay question. However, there have been tests in which the first and second essay questions were switched. This occurred on the 1996 exam, for example, when essay question 1 required students to write on a prose passage and question 2 asked them to write on poetry.

It's a safe bet that question 1 and question 2 will require literary analysis, one on poetry and the other on prose. Only the AP text preparation committee knows the specific order on the test that you will take.

THE BASIC PROSE ANALYSIS QUESTION

This prose analysis question is very similar to the poetry question, in that you will

1. be asked to analyze literary techniques.

2. have the literary passage in front of you to use as reference.

3. be expected to make references to the text as you write.

The basic form looks like this: *Write an essay analyzing how the author uses literary techniques to... (reveal meaning, describe the main character, recreate an experience, describe an attitude, etc.)*

You will be required to include some of the following literary techniques in your essay:

- contrast

- detail

- diction

- figurative language

- imagery

- pacing

- point of view

- repetition

- structure

- style (a combination of all these elements, also including sentence length and variety, punctuation, and parallelism)

- syntax

- tone

Even if these literary techniques are not identified by name in the question, be sure to address several of them in your response. Otherwise, you are not writing literary analysis—you'll produce little more than plot summary.

Study these examples:

Model Prose Analysis Question 1

Carefully read the following passage by William Hazlitt, which comes from a series of articles he wrote. Then write a well-organized essay in which you show some of the ways the author recreates the experience of the dinner party. You might wish to consider such literary techniques as diction, mood, and imagery.

[You have two tasks here: Describe what happens at the dinner party and then analyze how the author uses elements of style to create this effect. You must include literary elements in your analysis, but the words "you might wish to consider" tell you that you have some latitude in your choice of topics. However, I strongly suggest that you include at least two of the three literary techniques included in the prompt: diction, mood, and imagery.]

Model Prose Analysis Question 2

Carefully read the following passage from Alan Paton's novel Cry, the Beloved Country, *a novel about South Africa. Then, in a well-organized essay, analyze how changes in point of view and style reveal the author's complex attitude toward his homeland. In your analysis, consider such elements as pacing, imagery, diction, and figures of speech.*

[You have four tasks here:

1. Identify shifts in point of view and style.

2. Identify the author's complex attitude toward South Africa.

3. Analyze how shifts in point of view and style reflect the author's feelings.

4. Include literary elements in your analysis, but the words "such as" tell you that you have a choice. To be on the safe side, discuss at least three of the four literary elements included in the prompt: pacing, imagery, diction, or figures of speech..]

Model Prose Analysis Question 3

In the following passage from Michael Chabon's novel The Amazing Adventures of Kavalier and Clay *(2000), the narrator describes an emotional experience. Read the excerpt carefully. Then, in a well-organized essay, show how Chabon conveys the emotional impact to the reader. Consider such literary techniques as diction, syntax, and tone.*

[You have three tasks here:

1. Identify the emotional experience.

2. Explain how the writer creates this emotional experience.

3. Include literary elements in your analysis, but the words "consider such" tell you that you have a choice. To be on the safe side, discuss at least two of the three literary elements included in the prompt: diction, syntax, or tone.]

Model Prose Analysis Question 4

Carefully read the following diary entry by Samuel Pepys. Then, in a well-organized essay, explain what you learn about the writer and the times in which he lived from his literary style. You may emphasize whatever literary devices you choose (e.g., tone, detail, and sentence structure).

[You have three tasks here:

1. Explain what you learn about the writer and his era.

2. Identify the writer's literary style.

3. Link the writer and his life to his style.

As always, include literary elements in your analysis, but these directions clearly give you freedom of choice. When you're given such latitude, try not to use the vague word "style" in your analysis. Instead, be precise by focusing on specific elements of style, such as diction (word choice), sentence length and structure, and figures of speech.]

Model Prose Analysis Question 5

Carefully read the following passage from Ralph Ellison's novel Invisible Man. *As you read, note the author's style and purpose. Then write an essay in which you identify the author's attitude toward society. In your analysis, include such elements as diction, point of view, and figures of speech.*

[You have three tasks here:

1. Identify the author's style and purpose.

2. Figure out the author's attitude toward society.

3. Analyze the excerpt to determine how the author reveals his attitude toward society.

Be sure to include the literary elements mentioned here: diction, point of view, and figures of speech.]

FIVE-STEP METHOD TO A HIGH SCORE

1. As you did with the poetry prompt, read the prose question completely and restate it in your own words to make sure you clearly understand what you must write. For example, do you have to consider *all* the literary devices listed or just a few from the list? Look for the key phrase "such as" so you know how many of the literary elements you must describe.

2. Read the passage all the way through, at least twice. Each time you read, focus on one specific element. Always begin with meaning, including purpose and theme. Summarize the passage so you know that you got the gist. Then select one literary element at a time to identify, always starting with any that are named in the prompt. Jot down examples of literary elements that will help you prove your point.

3. Plan before you write. While you don't want to waste your time pondering small points, it's important to know where you're going before you begin. Otherwise, your essay will flounder all over the place. Create a quick jotted outline, take a few notes, or make a diagram showing the order in which you'll present your points.

4. As you write, make frequent and specific references to the excerpt. Quote words, phrases, and lines to support your point. NEVER include a detail that's off the point just to prove that you know it. Unnecessary details will cost you points, not win you any. For example, don't say "In *Portrait of the Artist as a Young Man*, James Joyce used the stream of consciousness technique" if this detail has nothing to do with the thesis.

5. Be sure to proofread your essay. You'll be surprised how many errors you can catch when re-reading your essay.

SAMPLE PROSE PASSAGE ESSAY QUESTIONS AND MODEL RESPONSES

SAMPLE 1

In the following passage from Willa Cather's short story "A Wagner Matinee," the narrator, Clark, describes taking his aunt Georgiana to a Wagner concert. Carefully read the passage. In a well-organized essay, show how Cather uses literary techniques to convey the impact of the experience on the narrator's aunt.

The second half of the program consisted of four numbers from the *Ring*, and closed with Siegfried's funeral march. My aunt [Georgiana] wept quietly, but almost continuously, as a shallow vessel overflows in a rainstorm. From time to time her dim eyes looked up at the lights which studded the ceiling, burning softly under their dull glass globes; doubtless they were stars in truth to her. I was still perplexed as to what measure of musical comprehension was left to her, she who had heard nothing but the singing of Gospel Hymns at Methodist services in the square schoolhouse on Section Thirteen for so many years. I was wholly unable to gauge how much of it had been dissolved in soapsuds, or worked into bread, or milked into the bottom of a pail.

The deluge of sound poured on and on; I never knew what she found in the shining current of it; I never knew how far it bore her, or past what happy islands. From the trembling in her face I could well believe that before the last numbers she had been carried out where the myriad graves are, into the gray, nameless burying ground of the sea; or into some world of death vaster yet, where, from the beginning of the world, hope had lain down with hope and dream with dream and, renouncing, slept.

The concert was over; the people filed out of the hall chattering and laughing, glad to relax and find the living level again, but my kinswoman made no effort to rise. The harpist slipped its green felt cover over his instrument; the flute-players shook the water from their mouthpieces; the men of the orchestra went out one by one, leaving the stage to the chairs and music stands, empty as a winter cornfield.

I spoke to my aunt. She burst into tears and sobbed pleadingly, "I don't want to go, Clark, I don't want to go."

I understood. For her, just outside the door of the concert hall, lay the black pond with the cattle-tracked bluffs; the tall, unpainted house, with weather-curled boards; naked as a tower, the crook-backed ash seedlings where the dish-cloths hung to dry; the gaunt, molting turkeys picking up refuse about the kitchen door.

Response 1

In this excerpt from her short story "A Wagner Matinee," Cather uses literary techniques to convey the impact of the experience on the narrator's aunt. The narrator's aunt really liked music so the narrator brought her to a concert. It was a Wagner concert. It made Georgiana cry because it was so sad.

In the first paragraph, the author used style to show how the music effected Aunt Georgiana. This is very difficult style. There are many long words and long sentences, which make the passage confusing. It is also a sad style. Georgiana cries all through the music "as a shallow vessel overflows in a rainstorm." She's crying so much that she's overflowing with tears. This could be because she is listening to a funeral march. That kind of music always makes people feel sad. I like happy music better.

In the second paragraph, the author uses detail to convey the impact of the experience on the narrator's aunt. The music has a "shining current" and takes her to "happy islands." This tells us that she now likes the music a lot. But then details about "graves" and "burying grounds" show the music gets sad again. The music is so sad, boring, and long that she falls asleep.

In the third paragraph, she wakes up when the concert ends. People are talking as they leave and the musicians make noise putting their instruments away. She doesn't want to get up. She starts crying because she is so sad. The concert hall is in a bad area and she is afraid of leaving. There's a "black pond" and broken-down houses. She is afraid to go back there and wants to stay with Clark. He must have a lot of money if he can take her to concerts.

We can see through all these literary techniques that the music really had an emotional impact on Clark's aunt. Music is a very powerful force.

Evaluation

This essay is empty of content and shows serious misreadings of the passage. First, the music did not make Georgiana cry because it was so sad; rather, it made her cry because it was so beautiful. Its great beauty unlocked her appreciation of music, long dead because of her mind-numbing life on the prairie. The writer's statement about the music shows a fundamental misunderstanding of the excerpt and the author's purpose.

The statement "In the first paragraph, the author used style to show how the music effected Aunt Georgiana" makes no sense. What "style"? How? (And the word the writer wants is "affected" rather than "effected.") That the style is "difficult" has nothing to with the thesis, "how Cather uses literary techniques to convey the impact of the experience on the narrator's aunt." Further, a writer's *style* can never be sad; only *tone* can be sad. The writer also misses the symbolism of the "funeral march": it represents her own living death, entombed on the prairie in abject poverty. The final two sentences—"That kind of music always makes people feel sad. I like happy music better"—are completely off the topic.

The next paragraph also shows misreadings. The music is not "so sad, boring, and long that she falls asleep"; rather, it touches her soul and awakens her dormant appreciation for beauty. In the next paragraph, she can't wake up because she was never asleep. She does start crying because she is so sad but not because "the concert hall is in a bad area and she is afraid of leaving" or because "There's a black pond and broken-down houses." She is crying because she realizes what she has missed all these years. She doesn't want to go back to her home because it is bereft of beauty, not because it is dangerous. Further, there's no proof that Clark does or does not have money.

The combination of serious misreadings and lack of proof makes this a weak paper. It would earn a 2 on the AP scale.

Response 2

For most people, a concert is a pleasant evening's entertainment, not a life-changing experience. But as Georgiana's anguished cry at the end of the concert reveals, this particular concert has touched her soul deeply. Readers can infer from her tears that she has had an epiphany, a moment of realization. The beautiful music has touched her soul and unlocked all the pain that she has been suffering for many years on the farm. Cather uses figures of speech, imagery, and syntax to convey the impact of the music on Georgiana.

The opening metaphor suggests how deeply the music has affected Georgiana, for she weeps "almost continuously, as a shallow vessel overflows in a rainstorm." She is a "shallow vessel" because she has been so deeply scarred by years of deprivation that her emotions have atrophied. Her appreciation of beauty has been stunted by years of ugliness. Rather than sitting in glorious concert halls, she has been imprisoned in "[a] tall, unpainted house, with weather-curled boards; naked as a tower." The metaphor suggests her life is stripped to its bare essentials for survival. Instead of hearing the swelling opulence of opera, she has heard "Gospel Hymns at Methodist services." It's no wonder that the glass globes in the concert hall ceiling appear to her as "stars." This celestial imagery suggests that the music is heavenly to Georgiana. The homely images that close the first paragraph contrast the glorious music to the dull life Georgiana lives, her musical appreciation "dissolved in soapsuds, or worked into bread, or milked into the bottom of a pail."

The metaphor that opens the second paragraph compares the music to a waterfall. The river of sound carries her far away, to the very essence of life and death. By using only two long sentences in the second paragraph, Cather captures the flow of the music and the entire scope of Georgiana's life. This syntax conveys the emotional impact of the music on Georgiana: just as a deluge cannot be stopped, so the flow of the past cannot be dammed once it has broken free. The repetition in the final clause ("hope...hope," "dream...dream") reinforces the two main elements in Georgiana's life, her loss of hope and dreams on the prairie.

Cather uses the same syntax in the last paragraphs. The long sentence suggests that Georgiana is trying to stretch out the experience so she doesn't have to return to reality so soon. The simile "empty as a winter cornfield" suggests how desolate her life will be back at home now that she has regained her appreciation of music. The program closes with "Siegfried's funeral march," which suggests that the concert is Georgiana's own funeral. By awakening her to the beauty she has missed all these years, Clark has doomed her to a life among the living dead, with "gaunt, molting turkeys picking up refuse about the kitchen door." Cather uses such literary techniques as figures of speech, imagery, and syntax to convey the impact of the concert on the narrator's aunt Georgiana.

Evaluation

This essay succeeds so well because it answers the question by using specific examples. In addition, the writer seamlessly interweaves the different literary techniques, placing them where they fit in the essay and thus best proving the point.

The first two sentences directly answer the question. The writer has a rich command of language, revealed in the first paragraph by the use of the word "epiphany" to describe Georgiana's moment of realization. This is effective because it directly answers the thesis: "impact of the concert on the narrator's aunt Georgiana." The sentence "The beautiful music has touched her soul and unlocked all the pain that she has been suffering for many years on the farm" nails the thesis firmly.

In the following paragraphs, the writer describes how Cather uses figures of speech, imagery, and syntax to convey the impact of the music on Georgiana. Note the "opening metaphor" (a figure of speech) and "celestial imagery." The writer pulls all the examples together to make the point.

The writer details the metaphor that opens the second paragraph, seamlessly linking this to the syntax. It's all used to show the emotional impact of the music on Georgiana. The argument is sophisticated because it takes into account sentence length and repetition as well as metaphors and imagery. The same method is used in the conclusion to reinforce and conclude the essay.

This is an excellent paper, clearly a 9 on the AP scale.

SAMPLE 2

Read the following short story by Edgar Allan Poe. Then write a well-organized essay analyzing how the author uses literary techniques to characterize the narrator.

I married early, and was happy to find in my wife a disposition not uncongenial with my own. Observing my partiality for domestic pets, she lost no opportunity of procuring those of the most agreeable kind. We had birds, gold-fish, a fine dog, rabbits, a small monkey, and a cat...

Pluto—this was the cat's name—was my favorite pet and playmate. I alone fed him, and he attended me wherever I went about the house. It was even with difficulty that I could prevent him from following me through the streets.

Our friendship lasted, in this manner, for several years, during which my general temperament and character—through the instrumentality of the Fiend Intemperance— had (I blush to confess it) experienced a radical alteration for the worse. I grew, day by day, more moody, more irritable, more regardless of the feelings of others. I suffered myself to use intemperate language to my wife. At length, I even offered her personal violence. My pets, of course, were made to feel the change in my disposition. I not only neglected, but ill-used them. For Pluto, however, I still retained sufficient regard to restrain me from maltreating him, as I made no scruple of maltreating the rabbits, the monkey, or even the dog, when, by accident, or through affection, they came in my way. But my disease grew upon me—for what disease is like Alcohol!—and at length even Pluto, who was now becoming old, and consequently somewhat peevish—even Pluto began to experience the effects of my ill temper.

One night, returning home, much intoxicated, from one of my haunts about town, I fancied that the cat avoided my presence. I seized him; when, in his fright at my violence, he inflicted a slight wound upon my hand with his teeth. The fury of a demon instantly possessed me. I knew myself no longer. My original soul seemed, at once, to take its flight from my body; and a more than fiendish malevolence, gin-nurtured, thrilled every fiber of my frame. I took from my waistcoat-pocket a penknife, opened it, grasped the poor beast by the throat, and deliberately cut one of its eyes from the socket! I blush, I burn, I shudder, while I pen the damnable atrocity . . .

In the meantime the cat slowly recovered. The socket of the lost eye presented, it is true, a frightful appearance, but he no longer appeared to suffer any pain. He went about the house as usual, but, as might be expected, fled in extreme terror at my approach. I had so much of my old heart left, as to be at first grieved by this evident dislike on the part of a creature which had once so loved me. But this feeling soon gave place to irritation. And then came, as if to my final and irrevocable overthrow, the spirit of PERVERSENESS. Of this spirit philosophy takes no account. Yet I am not more sure that my soul lives, than I am that perverseness is one of the primitive impulses of the human heart—one of the indivisible primary faculties, or sentiments, which give direction to the character of Man. Who has not, a hundred times, found himself committing a vile or a stupid action, for no other reason than because he knows he should not? Have we not a perpetual inclination, in the teeth of our best judgment, to violate that which is Law, merely because we understand it to be such? This spirit of perverseness, I say, came to my final overthrow. It was this unfathomable longing of the soul to vex itself—to offer violence to its won nature—to do wrong for the wrong's sake only—that urged me to continue and finally to consummate the injury I had inflicted upon the unoffending brute. One morning, in cold blood, I slipped a noose about its neck with the tears streaming from my eyes, and with the bitterest remorse at my heart;—hung it because I knew that it had loved me, and because I felt it had given me no reason of offense;—hung it because I knew that in so doing I was committing a sin—a deadly sin that would so jeopardize my immortal soul as to place it—if such a thing were possible—even beyond the reach of the infinite mercy of the Most Merciful and Most Terrible God.

Response 1

In the excerpt of a short story by Edgar Allan Poe, Poe uses literary techniques to characterize the narrator. The narrator is nuts. He kills a cat because he has the spirit of perverseness.

The narrator got married when he was young. He and his wife were very much alike. They both liked house pets. As a result, they get a lot of pets, including birds, gold-fish, a fine dog, rabbits, a small monkey, and a cat. The narrator liked the cat best and he named him "Pluto." Only the narrator fed the cat so the cat followed him all around the house. The cat even wanted to walk with him outside. They were very close. I could prevent him from following me through the streets.

The narrator and the cat got along real well for a few years but then the narrator was taken over by a monster, the "Fiend Intemperance." He cursed his wife and even hit her. He hurt his pets, too. As he got sicker and sicker, the narrator even began beating on the cat. This is strange because he liked the cat best of all, maybe even better than he liked his wife. When he was drunk one night, the narrator was taken over by an even more evil monster and he cut the cat's eye out! This is so gross.

At first, the narrator feels real bad but soon "the spirit of PERVERSENESS" takes him over and he hangs the cat. He knows that he's done something really terrible. Poe uses literary techniques to characterize the narrator. The narrator is really crazy to do such an awful thing to a cat.

Evaluation

The bland restatement of the thesis is adequate but not inspiring. Writing in this pedestrian manner would earn a score in the 5–6 range. However, the diction of the second sentence—"The narrator is nuts"—is too informal for the audience and purpose. When you're writing an AP essay, use diction appropriate to your readers. Instead of "nuts," for example, use "insane," "mad," or "psychotic." The third sentence has a misplaced modifier: *Who* has "the spirit of perverseness," the cat or the narrator? The writer's most serious omission is not isolating literary techniques to describe. Simply saying that "Poe uses literary techniques" won't cut it; rather, the writer must name specific techniques to describe. There are none here.

The rest of the paper has no substance because it's plot summary rather than analysis. Further, the writer misses the reason why the narrator changed. It's because he became an alcoholic, which is what he means by the phrase "Fiend Intemperance." The writer misunderstands this to mean he is taken over by a monster movie creature.

This paper would receive a score of 1–2 because it does not prove (or even address) the thesis.

Response 2

What drives a person into madness? In this excerpt from an Edgar Allan Poe short story, it's alcohol. In this terrifying story, readers are trapped along with the narrator in his hellish descent into perverse violence and viciousness. Poe creates the narrator's descent into insanity through point of view, diction, syntax, and tone.

Point of view is especially crucial in this story because it bridges the distance between the reader and narrator. By choosing the first-person point of view, Poe allows readers to view events through the narrator's eyes as the narrator traces his spiral into lunacy. As he spirals from kindness and normalcy into cruelty and debauchery, we are right there with him. This helps us experience the narrator's tragic decline more immediately than if Poe had chosen the omniscient or third-person limited point of view. This is especially clear when the narrator tries to explain his "spirit of perverseness" that makes him murder his beloved cat. By hearing his own words, readers get a more vivid description of the narrator's changing character.

Readers learn a great deal about the narrator from the words and sentences he uses. At first, the narrator uses elevated diction and elegantly formed sentences. Phrases such as "disposition not uncongenial with my own," "partiality for domestic pets," and "procuring those of the most agreeable kind" create the verbal portrait of a rational man in a happy marriage. This impression is reinforced by the description of a household filled with everyday, normal pets, including "birds, gold-fish, a fine dog, rabbits, a small monkey, and a cat." The sentences are relatively short and well formed. The diction and syntax create a rational tone. As a result, the narrator emerges as sane and balanced. However, as the story progresses and his madness builds, the narrator's words and sentences break down.

As he gets more and more out of control, the words become shrill. For example, the narrator describes his "fiendish malevolence, gin-nurtured" that leads to his "damnable atrocity." In addition, the syntax changes, as the sentences get longer and longer. They build to a climax in the last sentence: "One morning, in cold blood, I slipped a noose about its neck with the tears streaming from my eyes, and with the bitterest remorse at my heart;—hung it because I knew that it had loved me, and because I felt it had given me no reason of offense;—hung it because I knew that in so doing I was committing a sin—a deadly sin that would so jeopardize my immortal soul as to place it—if such a thing were possible—even beyond the reach of the infinite mercy of the Most Merciful and Most Terrible God." Poe uses dashes to suggest that the narrator is speaking very rapidly and running out of breath. The repeated phrases "hung it" reinforces the horror of his act, hanging a cat whose only sin was loving him. The overheated words, very long sentence, and repetition create an hysterical tone as the narrator slowly goes mad.

It's not enough to *tell* readers that someone is going crazy; for a story to be really effective, the writer has to *show* the character's madness. Poe uses the literary techniques of point of view, diction, syntax, and tone to give readers a terrifying glimpse into a madman's mind. While it's not a pretty place to be, it *is* a fascinating ride.

Evaluation

By focusing on four elements of style—point of view, diction, syntax, and tone—the writer is able to analyze how Poe uses literary techniques to characterize the narrator. As a general rule, you're on stable ground with the "magic three," any three literary elements. However, since the diction and syntax help create the tone, the writer decided to analyze that literary element as well. In this instance, it was a good bet to add the fourth element because it fits so neatly with the other three.

This opening is especially effective because it gets the reader's attention while simultaneously suggesting the topic of the essay. You can always rephrase the question to open an essay, but you'll get a higher grade if you craft a more creative opening. In this instance, the writer uses a question. Here are the basic ways to begin an AP essay:

- *restate the question* in your own words

- use a *question* that pertains to the thesis

- use a *quotation* that relates to the thesis

- use an *anecdote* (a brief story) that illustrates the point you're going to make

In general, stay away from jokes or humor of any kind unless you are very adept at using it. Humor is very tricky to write because it depends so heavily on audience. What one person thinks is funny, another person is just as likely to find offensive.

The second paragraph skillfully explains how Poe uses point of view to characterize the narrator. This is most apparent in these sentences: "As he spirals from kindness and normalcy into cruelty and debauchery, we are right there with him. This helps us experience the narrator's tragic decline more immediately than if Poe had chosen the omniscient or third-person limited point of view." The writer adds some specific details from the story to drive home the point.

The third paragraph explicates diction, syntax, and tone. Again, the writer uses specific examples to illustrate the points. The writer uses comparison and contrast to show how the narrator acts before and after madness strikes. This technique allows the writer to fully describe his change in character and the literary techniques Poe uses to create it. The sentence "However, as the story progresses and his madness builds, the narrator's words and sentences break down" serves as an effective transition between the "before" and "after."

The writer's analysis of the final sentence is especially effective because the writer notes Poe's use of diction and repetition as well as length. This combines to create the "hysterical" tone that the writer accurately describes.

This paper would earn a 9 on the AP scale for its close textual analysis, ability to marshal evidence to prove a thesis, and elegant writing style.

SAMPLE 3

Carefully read the following passage by Rebecca Harding Davis, which comes from a novel she wrote. Then write a well-organized essay in which you show some of the ways the author recreates the experience of life in the iron mills. You might wish to consider such literary techniques as imagery, figures of speech, and diction, for example.

A cloudy day: do you know what that is in a town of iron-works? The sky sank down before dawn, muddy, flat, immovable. The air is thick, clammy with the breath of crowded human beings. It stifles me. I open the window, and, looking out, can scarcely see through the rain the grocer's shop opposite.

The idiosyncrasy of this town is smoke. It rolls suddenly in slow folds from the great chimneys of the iron-foundries, and settles down in black, slimy pools on the muddy streets. Smoke on the wharves, smoke on the dingy boats, on the yellow river,—clinging in a coating of greasy soot to the house-front, the two faded poplars, the faces of the passers-by. The long train of mules, dragging masses of pig-iron through the narrow street, have a foul vapor hanging to their reeking sides. Here, inside, is a little broken figure of an angel pointing upward from the mantel-shelf; but even its wings are covered with smoke, clotted and black. Smoke everywhere! A dirty canary chirps desolately in a cage beside me. Its dreams of green fields and sunshine is a very old dream, —almost worn out, I think.

From the back-window I can see a narrow brick-yard sloping down to the river-side, strewed with rain-butts and rubs. The river, dull and tawny-colored, drags itself sluggishly along, tired of the heavy weight of boats and coal-barges. What wonder? Masses of men, with dull, besotted faces bent to the ground, sharpened here and there by pain or cunning: skin and muscle and flesh begrimed with smoke and ashes; stooping all night over boiling caldrons of metal, laired by day in dens of drunkenness and infamy; breathing from infancy to death an air saturated with fog and grease and soot, vileness for soul and body. What do you make of a case like that, amateur psychologist? You call it an altogether serious thing to be alive: to these men it is a drunken jest, a joke,—horrible to angels perhaps, to them commonplace enough. My fancy about the river was an idle one: it is no type of such a life. What if it be stagnant and slimy here? It knows beyond there waits for it odorous sunlight, —quaint old gardens, dusky with soft, green foliage of apple-trees, and flushing crimson with roses, —air, and fields, and mountains. The future of the Welsh puddler [one who refines metal] passing just now is not so pleasant. To be stowed away, after his grimy work is done, in a hole in the muddy graveyard, and after that, —*not* air, nor green fields, nor curious roses.

Response

From the first image of a "muddy, flat, immovable" sky to the last image of being buried in "a hole in the muddy graveyard," Rebecca Harding Davis paints a grim picture of life for workers in the iron mills. Through images, figures of speech, and syntax, the author describes a brutally hard life in a filthy, polluted town. Her language is so vivid that readers feel themselves a part of this tragically dead-end life.

The "thick, clammy" air, stale with "the breath of crowded human beings," plunges readers into a stifling world marked by lost hopes and lives. The air is so polluted that the narrator cannot even see the grocery shop across the street. The images of the thick black smoke that fills the town appeals to different senses. We see it roll "suddenly in slow folds" and "settle down in black, slimy pools on the muddy streets." We feel it "clinging in a coating of greasy soot to the house-front" and smell its "foul vapor" hanging to the reeking sides of a long train of mules. Symbolically, the smoke covers even the "little broken figure of an angel," extinguishing all hope of beauty or salvation.

In the next paragraph, the author personifies the river as a living thing, dragging itself "sluggishly along, tired of the heavy weight of boats and coal-barges." This figure of speech drags down the reader, too, with the weariness of endless toil and filth. Describing the men as "bent to the ground" makes them seem like animals, an image that is reinforced by the vision of them "laired by day in dens of drunkenness and infamy." By using the noun "lair" as a verb, the author suggests the men are mere brutes, animals living in dens. The people are as "stagnant and slimy" as the river, going nowhere, covered by layers and layers of muck and filth.

The images in the ending are especially grim, as the Welsh mill worker is denied salvation even in death. Instead of passing on to a glorious heaven of "odorous sunlight,—quaint old gardens, dusky with soft, green foliage of apple-trees, and flushing crimson with roses," he will be "stowed away" in a hole in the ground. No air, green fields, or flowers for him. Rebecca Harding Davis recreates the experience of life in the iron mills through many literary techniques, including imagery, figures of speech, and diction. She succeeds in plunging readers into a suffocating world of toil, filth, and hopelessness.

Evaluation

The writer opens with specific images from the selection to prove the thesis: "Rebecca Harding Davis paints a grim picture of life for workers in the iron mills." This is right on target with the task, to "show some of the ways the author recreates the experience of life in the iron mills." The writer uses all three literary elements listed in the prompt (imagery, figures of speech, and diction), although the words "You might wish to consider such literary techniques as..." and "for example" give you leeway to select other literary techniques. This writer decides to play it safe, a very smart thing to do on an AP test.

The following paragraphs of the essay are filled with specific details that directly answer the thesis. Isolating details that target each individual sense (sight, touch, and smell) show a close, thoughtful analysis. The passage on symbolism is also quite perceptive. Also notice how the writer weaves in personification, a type of figure of speech. This directly addresses "figures of speech" mentioned in the introduction. The writer's discussion of the word "laired" is astute and again shows a close reading of the passage and a deep understanding of the author's style and purpose.

This essay would earn a 9 on the AP scale for its organization, insights, and use of supporting detail.

PRACTICE PROSE ANALYSIS QUESTIONS

Use the following simulated test questions to practice what you learned in this lesson.

SAMPLE 1

In the following passage, the narrator describes a terrible thing he did. Read the excerpt carefully. Then, in a well-organized essay, analyze how changes in perspective and style reflect the narrator's complex attitude toward his deed. In your analysis, include such literary elements as point of view, tone, and detail.

One day my wife accompanied me, upon some household errand, into the cellar of the old building which our poverty compelled us to inhabit. The cat followed me down the steep stairs, and, nearly throwing me headlong, exasperated me to madness. Uplifting an ax, and forgetting in my wrath the childish dread which had hitherto stayed my hand, I aimed a blow at the animal, which, of course, would have proved instantly fatal had it descended as I wished. But this blow was arrested by the hand of my wife. Goaded by the interference into a rage more than demoniacal, I withdrew my arm from her grasp and buried the ax in her brain. She fell dead upon the spot without a groan.

This hideous murder accomplished, I set myself forthwith, and with entire deliberation, to the task of concealing the body. I knew that I could not remove it from the house, either by day or by night, without the risk of being observed by the neighbors. Many projects entered my mind. At one period I thought of cutting the corpse into minute fragments, and destroying them by fire. At another, I resolved to dig a grave for it in the floor of the cellar. Again, I deliberated about casting it in the well in the yard—about packing it in a box, as if merchandise, with the usual arrangements, and so getting a porter to take it from the house. Finally I hit upon what I considered a far better expedient than either of these. I determined to wall it up in the cellar, as the monks of the Middle Ages are recorded to have walled up their victims.

For a purpose such as this the cellar was well adapted. Its walls were loosely constructed, and had lately been plastered throughout with a rough plaster, which the dampness of the atmosphere had prevented from hardening. Moreover, in one of the walls was a projection, caused by a false chimney, or fireplace, that had been filled up and made to resemble the rest of the cellar. I made no doubt that I could readily displace the bricks at this point, insert the corpse, and wall the whole up as before, so that no eye could detect any thing suspicious.

And in this calculation I was not deceived. By means of a crowbar I easily dislodged the bricks, and, having carefully deposited the body against the inner wall, I propped it in that position, while with little trouble I relaid the whole structure as it originally stood. Having procured mortar, sand, and hair, with every possible precaution, I prepared a plaster which could not be distinguished from the old, and with this I very carefully went over the new brick-work. When I had finished, I felt satisfied that all was right. The wall did not present the slightest appearance of having been disturbed. The rubbish on the floor was picked up with the minutest care. I looked around triumphantly, and said to myself: "Here at least, then, my labor has not been in vain."

My next step was to look for the beast which had been the cause of so much wretchedness; for I had, at length, firmly resolved to put it to death. Had I been able to meet with it at the moment, there could have been no doubt of its fate; but it appeared that the crafty animal had been alarmed at the violence of my previous anger, and forbore to present itself in my present mood. It is impossible to describe or to imagine the deep, the blissful sense of relief which the absence of the detested creature occasioned in my bosom. It did not make its appearance during the night; and thus for one night, at least, since its introduction into the house, I soundly and tranquilly slept; aye, slept even with the burden of murder upon my soul.

The second and the third day passed, and still my tormentor came not. Once again I breathed as a freeman. The monster, in terror, had fled the premises for ever! I should behold it no more! My happiness was supreme! The guilt of my dark deed disturbed me but little. Some few inquiries had been made, but these had been readily answered. Even a search had been instituted—but of course nothing was to be discovered. I looked upon my future felicity as secured.

Upon the fourth day of the assassination, a party of the police came, very unexpectedly, into the house, and proceeded again to make rigorous investigation of the premises. Secure, however, in the inscrutability of my place of concealment, I felt no embarrassment whatever. The officers bade me accompany them in their search. They left no nook or corner unexplored. At length, for the third or fourth time, they descended to the cellar. I quivered not in a muscle. My heart beat calmly as that of one who slumbers in innocence. I walked the cellar from end to end. I folded my arms upon my bosom, and roamed easily to and fro. The police were thoroughly satisfied and prepared to depart. The glee at my heart was too strong to be restrained. I burned to say if but one word, by way of triumph, and to render doubly sure their assurance of my guiltlessness.

"Gentlemen," I said at last, as the party ascended the steps, "I delight to have allayed your suspicions. I wish you all health and a little more courtesy. By the bye, gentlemen, this—this is a very well-constructed house," (in the rabid desire to say something easily, I scarcely knew what I uttered at all)—"I may say an excellently well-constructed house. These walls—are you going, gentlemen?—these walls are solidly put together"; and here, through the mere frenzy of bravado, I rapped heavily with a cane which I held in my hand, upon that very portion of the brickwork behind which stood the corpse of the wife of my bosom.

But may God shield and deliver me from the fangs of the Arch-Fiend! No sooner had the reverberation of my blows sunk into silence, than I was answered by a voice from within the tomb!—by a cry, at first muffled and broken, like the sobbing of a child, and then quickly swelling into one long, loud, and continuous scream, utterly anomalous and inhuman—a howl—a wailing shriek, half of horror and half of triumph, such as might have arisen only out of hell, conjointly from the throats of the damned in their agony and of the demons that exult in the damnation.

Of my own thoughts it is folly to speak. Swooning, I staggered to the opposite wall. For one instant the party on the stairs remained motionless, through extremity of terror and awe. In the next a dozen stout arms were toiling at the wall. It fell bodily. The corpse, already greatly decayed and clotted with gore, stood erect before the eyes of the spectators. Upon its head, with red extended mouth and solitary eye of fire, sat the hideous beast whose craft had seduced me into murder, and whose informing voice had consigned me to the hangman. I had walled the monster up within the tomb.

SAMPLE 2

Carefully read the following excerpt from a short story by Nathaniel Hawthorne. As you read, note the author's style and purpose. Then write an essay in which you identify the author's attitude toward science. In your analysis, include such elements as diction, point of view, and figures of speech.

In the latter part of the last century there lived a man of science, an eminent proficient in every branch of natural philosophy, who not long before our story opens had made experience of a spiritual affinity more attractive than any chemical one. He had left his laboratory to the care of an assistant, cleared his fine countenance from the furnace smoke, washed the stain of acids from his fingers, and persuaded a beautiful woman to become his wife. We know not whether Aylmer possessed this degree of faith in man's ultimate control over Nature. He had devoted himself, however, too unreservedly to scientific studies ever to be weaned from them by any second passion. His love for his young wife might prove the stronger of the two; but it could only be by intertwining itself with his love of science, and uniting the strength of the latter to his own.

Such a union accordingly took place, and was attended with truly remarkable consequences and a deeply impressive moral. One day, very soon after their marriage, Aylmer sat gazing at his wife with a trouble in his countenance that grew stronger until he spoke.

"Georgiana," said he, "has it never occurred to you that the mark upon your cheek might be removed?"

"No, indeed," said she, smiling; but perceiving the seriousness of his manner, she blushed deeply. "To tell you the truth it has been so often called a charm that I was simple enough to imagine it might be so."

"Ah, upon another face perhaps it might," replied her husband; "but never on yours. No, dearest Georgiana, you came so nearly perfect from the hand of Nature that this slightest possible defect, which we hesitate whether to term a defect or a beauty, shocks me, as being the visible mark of earthly imperfection."

"Shocks you, my husband!" cried Georgiana, deeply hurt; at first reddening with momentary anger, but then bursting into tears. "Then why did you take me from my mother's side? You cannot love what shocks you!"

To explain this conversation it must be mentioned that in the center of Georgiana's left cheek there was a singular mark, deeply interwoven, as it were, with the texture and substance of her face. Its shape bore not a little similarity to the human hand, though of the smallest pygmy size. Georgiana's lovers were wont to say that some fairy at her birth hour had laid her tiny hand upon the infant's cheek, and left this impress there in token of the magic endowments that were to give her such sway over all hearts. Masculine observers, if the birthmark did not heighten their admiration, contented themselves with wishing it away, that the world might possess one living specimen of ideal loveliness without the semblance of a flaw. After his marriage—for he thought little or nothing of the matter before,—Aylmer discovered that this was the case with himself.

Had she been less beautiful,—if Envy's self could have found aught else to sneer at,—he might have felt his affection heightened by the prettiness of this mimic hand, now vaguely portrayed, now lost, now stealing forth again and glimmering to and fro with every pulse of emotion that throbbed within her heart; but seeing her otherwise so perfect, he found this one defect grow more and more intolerable with every moment of their united lives. It was the fatal flaw of humanity which Nature, in one shape or another, stamps ineffaceably on all her productions, either to imply that they are temporary and finite, or that their perfection must be wrought by toil and pain. The crimson hand expressed the ineludible grip in which mortality clutches the highest and purest of earthly mould, degrading them into kindred with the lowest, and even with the very brutes, like whom their visible frames return to dust. In this manner, selecting it as the symbol of his wife's liability to sin, sorrow, decay, and death, Aylmer's somber imagination was not long in rendering the birthmark a frightful object, causing him more trouble and horror than ever Georgiana's beauty, whether of soul or sense, had given him delight . . .

WRITING AN OPEN-ENDED LITERARY RESPONSE

On past exams, question 3 has always been the "open-ended" question in which students are presented with a prompt but allowed to choose the literary work to answer it. When I distributed question 1, question 2, and question 3 to a wide variety of students to elicit responses, nearly everyone choose to respond to question 3. We can assume, therefore, that the question is perceived to be the least onerous of the three essays you must write. Do not be mislead into assuming that this automatically makes it the "easiest" question to answer, however.

THE BASIC OPEN-ENDED QUESTION

Virtually all open-ended questions focus on *content,* what the work is about. This is likely because the poetry question and prose question focus on style as well as meaning.

The open-ended question focuses on one of these topics:

- theme (the meaning)

- relationship of a part (specific incident) to the whole (entire literary work)

- characterization

- setting

- point of view

Each of these elements is explained in detail in Part VI: Glossary of Literary Terms.

You will be provided with a list of appropriate literary works, but you are free to choose any work of recognized literary merit. *Always* play it safe by selecting a novel or play that you know will be acceptable to your audience. Stay away from literary works (no matter how famous or notorious) that might offend your readers. Your goal is to earn a high score, not to shock or antagonize your readers.

Study these examples:

Model Open-Ended Question 1

Choose a major character from any work of recognized literary merit and show how that character is unable to adjust successfully to his or her environment. Describe the reasons for the character's maladjustment and what happens as a result.

[You must show how a character cannot adjust to his or her surroundings. Explain the reason the character is alienated and the results of it.]

Model Open-Ended Question 2

First chapters are often important in establishing the personality of a main character. Select any novel of recognized literary worth that you have read and show how this is true.

[You must explain how the first chapter in a novel sets forth the a main character's personality.]

Model Open-Ended Question 3

In some novels or full-length plays, the historical and/or social background is so important to the theme and plot that the work could not have been set in any other time or place. Show how this is true in any novel or play that you have read.

[You must explain how the setting affects the plot and theme.]

Model Open-Ended Question 4

Some first chapters set forth all the themes of the novel as well as establish characters and setting. Show how this is true in any novel you have read. Trace the themes and show how they are introduced in the first chapter.

[You must explain how the first chapter introduces all the major themes. You can bring in aspects of character and setting as well.]

Model Open-Ended Question 5

The final chapter of a novel is sometimes a letdown for the reader for a variety of reasons. Select a novel or play of recognized literary value and show how the ending does not live up to the promise of the beginning.

[You must analyze the conclusion to explain how it is unsuccessful.]

FIVE-STEP METHOD TO A HIGH SCORE

1. Several weeks before the exam, choose several novels and plays from different eras to review thoroughly. For example, *Pride and Prejudice* concerns the themes of society, family, and appearance vs. reality; *The Scarlet Letter* has sin, guilt, and retribution. Both novels offer sharp contrasts in tone, writing style, and symbolism as well so you're prepared for a wide variety of questions. Also become very familiar with a tragedy such as *Macbeth, Hamlet,* or *King Lear* as well as a contemporary novel such as *The Song of Solomon, The Joy Luck Club,* or *Things Fall Apart*. Reread the literary work and your notes; do not rely on prepackaged study guides and notes. The scorers are all teachers who have read these notes. They recognize "insights" and comments lifted from study guides.

2. Be sure to select a literary work that really fits the question. Simply because the novel or play is on the list or covered in your AP class does not mean that it will fit the particular question you're now answering. An average essay on a work that fits the question will earn a higher score than a brilliant essay on an ill-fitting or outright inappropriate literary work.

3. Plan before you write. Create a quick jotted outline, take a few notes, or make a diagram showing the order in which you'll present your points.

4. As you write, quote *relevant* words, phrases, and lines to support your point. Quotes thrown in just to prove that you memorized some lines will not get you any extra points; in fact, they might cost you credit as padding, irrelevance, or dead wood. *Be very sure that you are writing analysis rather than mere plot summary.*

5. Proofread your essay carefully to catch mistakes in grammar, usage, mechanics, and details.

RECOMMENDED BOOKS

The following literary works have been listed on past AP tests as "recommended" for question 3. As you choose a handful of novels and plays to review for the test, I strongly recommend that you select books from this list or a similar one.

NOTE
Do NOT waste your time preparing essays, poems, or short stories, since this question requires a "novel or play." (The play can be in verse, however, such as any play by Shakespeare.)

The Adventures of Huckleberry Finn
The Age of Innocence
All My Sons
All the Pretty Horses
Anna Karenina
Antigone
As I Lay Dying
The Awakening
The Birthday Party
Beloved
Billy Budd
Bless Me, Ultima
Candide
Catch-22
Ceremony
The Color Purple
Crime and Punishment
The Crucible
Cry, the Beloved Country

David Copperfield (or any novel by
  Dickens)
Delta Wedding
Dinner at the Homesick Restaurant
A Doll's House (or any play by Ibsen)
Dr. Faustus
Emma
An Enemy of the People
Equus
A Farewell to Arms
The Glass Menagerie
The Great Gatsby
Gulliver's Travels
Hamlet
Heart of Darkness
The Iceman Cometh
Invisible Man
Jane Eyre
Jasmine

The Joy Luck Club
Jude the Obscure (or any novel by
   Hardy)
King Lear
A Lesson Before Dying
Lord Jim
Macbeth
The Mayor of Casterbridge
A Member of the Wedding
Moby Dick
Mrs. Dalloway
Native Speaker
The Oresteia (or any Greek tragedy)
Othello
Our Town
The Piano Lesson
A Portrait of the Artist as a Young Man
The Portrait of a Lady
Praisesong for the Widow

Pride and Prejudice
Pnin
A Raisin in the Sun
Saint Joan (or any play by George
   Bernard Shaw)
The Scarlet Letter
The Shipping News
Song of Solomon
Sons and Lovers
The Sound and the Fury
The Stone Angel
Sula
Their Eyes Were Watching God
Things Fall Apart
The Turn of the Screw
Waiting for Godot
The Warden
Wuthering Heights
1984

SAMPLE OPEN-ENDED QUESTIONS AND MODEL RESPONSES

SAMPLE 1

"Failure in human relationships results when one avoids the normal responsibilities of one's position in life." Show how this is true for any one character from any work of recognized literary value that you have read. You may select a novel from the list below or another novel or play of significant literary merit. (See list on page 103)

Response 1

People fail in their relationships when they avoid the responsibilities of their particular position in life. In *The Glass Menagerie*, Tom Wingfield, a young man frustrated by life and its difficulties, gives us a perfect example of this unfortunate situation.

Tom's expected responsibility is to support his mother and sister because his father deserted the family. In the thirties, when this story takes place, women had little chance of finding work outside the home. Amanda, the mother, had tried to obtain work selling magazine subscriptions over the telephone, and the little bit of money that she was able to make went to send her handicapped daughter to secretarial school. Tom had a job in a warehouse and did the best he could to sustain the family. The problem began when Amanda began to criticize everything Tom did, including his eating habits, his smoking, and his movie-going. Her constant carping created a great deal of friction between them, as he began to resent her and their relationship deteriorated. Amanda told Tom that he was responsible for the family until his sister Laura was married, but Tom wanted no part in finding his sister a suitable husband. He avoided fulfilling his responsibilities by deserting the family and joining the Merchant Marines.

While it is obvious that Amanda's nature did not help her relationship with her son, if Tom would have attempted to resolve their difficulties, perhaps things could have turned out differently. However, as a result of not providing for the family and fulfilling his expected responsibilities, Tom's relationship with his mother failed.

Evaluation

The first sentence is well written, a clear restatement of the thesis. While it could be made more interesting through the use of a quote or a brief anecdote from the work, it nonetheless gets to the point and alerts the reader to the topic.

The second sentence can be improved: the author's name is missing, and the description of Tom is too general. Be specific in describing the topic of your AP essay. In this instance, the writer should have mentioned Tom's desire for freedom versus the necessity of supporting his mother and sister. The topic paragraph needs at least one more sentence to flesh it out. As a rule of thumb, every paragraph needs at least three sentences to be complete. These include a topic sentence, a body sentence, and a clincher sentence, for a paragraph is an essay in miniature. You'll want to include more than three sentences to provide specific examples of the points you wish to make. One possible solution for this topic paragraph is to move up the first sentence of paragraph 2 ("Tom's expected responsibility") and write a new topic sentence for paragraph 2.

If the first sentence of paragraph 2 is going to remain in the paragraph, it has to be more closely related to the sentence that follows. As it stands, the style is choppy and weak. The third sentence of paragraph 2 has a lot of good specific detail, but it could be improved by adding the name of the daughter, Laura, to parallel the inclusion of the name of the mother, Amanda. Sentence 4 ("Tom had a job in a warehouse . . . ") can be improved.

Where did he work? Did he really do his best to support the family? A great deal more detail can be added here to make the point more clearly. Sentence 5 ("The problem began . . . ") is not totally correct. Actually, the problem began much earlier, when Tom's desire to be a poet was thwarted by the family's need. There is no doubt that Amanda's constant carping created a rift between them, but Tom already bitterly resented the lot he had been appointed in life. To suggest otherwise is to miss the nuances in the play. The remainder of paragraph 2 is too vague and only partially incorrect. It is not true that "Tom wanted no part in finding his sister a suitable husband," for Tom did indeed bring home his friend, Jim (ironically a young man Laura had long admired), as a possible suitor. Again, the writer misreads the play.

The first sentence of paragraph 3 must be rewritten, for its meaning is not proven in the essay. The writer offers no proof that either of the characters could have healed the breach. The last sentence is fine.

This paper would receive a 4–5 on the AP grading scale. The basic outline is good, but the essay lacks specific details and includes some inaccurate statements.

Response 2

When a person avoids the normal responsibilities of his or her position in life, human relationships will likely collapse. This is true of Macbeth in William Shakespeare's play, *Macbeth*. In the beginning of the play, Macbeth is a loyal warrior to his king, Duncan, but as the play progresses he shuns his responsibilities and thus fails in human relationships.

As King Duncan's kinsman, Macbeth is one of the most trusted generals. His reputation was burnished by his many loyal and brave acts during battle. When Macbeth upholds his reputation by fighting bravely for the king against the traitorous Thane of Cawdor's armies, Duncan rewards him with the title of the defeated Thane of Cawdor. This shows how Duncan is a fair and decent King, rewarding his men justly and generously for their bravery. It also shows how Macbeth fights with distinction in the beginning of the play, fulfilling the expected responsibilities as a loyal thane. But all this changes right after the battle, when Macbeth encounters three witches.

As they journey home from battle, Macbeth and his friend Banquo come upon three weird sisters. The witches tell Macbeth that he shall have a glorious future as Thane of Cawdor (he does not yet know he is to receive the title) and eventually King. Intrigued, Macbeth continues on his journey home to learn that he has indeed been given the title of the disloyal thane. This sparks his ambition, and he first begins thinking about killing the King to hasten any chance he may have to become King himself. He tells his wife, Lady Macbeth, what has happened, and she fans his ambition, plotting how to kill Duncan. They accomplish the heinous deed that night, stabbing the good and generous King and planting the daggers on his guards. Macbeth has clearly deviated from his normal responsibilities as a loyal servant to his King, for killing one's king is treacherous indeed. From this point on, the play describes the destruction of all of Macbeth's relationships.

All suspected enemies are killed to help Macbeth maintain his shaky power base. Macbeth even has his close friend Banquo murdered, for the witches had prophesied that Banquo's heirs would become king. He had intended to kill both Banquo and his son, Fleance, but Fleance escapes the murderers during the fray. He also murders Macduff's family in Act IV, scene 2, for the loyal Macduff, another of Duncan's original soldiers, organized the rebellion against the now power-crazed Macbeth. The scene where Macbeth's soldiers murder Macduff's family—all the little "chickens"—shows us again how far Macbeth has moved away from his responsibility, how fully he has failed in human relationships.

Macbeth's denial of his normal responsibilities as a loyal soldier to the good King Duncan results in the destruction of all human relationships. By the end of the play he has become a murderous tyrant, devoid of all humanness. Fortunately, few people cause as much devastation as Macbeth did when he shattered individual families and left Scotland in ruins. However, irresponsible people can still cause havoc and sorrow when they avoid their expected responsibilities.

Evaluation

The introduction divides the answer into two parts: Macbeth's loyalty to the good King Duncan in the beginning of the play and his later denial of his proper role as kinsman and thane.

This structure is maintained throughout the essay, as paragraph 2 discusses the first point and paragraph 3, the second point. The student explains Macbeth's behavior during battle and describes how the good King rewards him. This is crucial, for it must be shown that Macbeth is slaying a good king and thus committing a heinous deed. The setting aside of normal responsibilities would make no sense if Macbeth were killing an evil person—witness Macduff's actions in the end of the play. The final part of this paragraph is especially good, as the writer specifically says "This shows how . . . " Include phrases such as "This proves...," "This illustrates...," and "This is an example of..." to keep yourself on topic.

In paragraph 3, the writer does a very good job of showing that in killing the king, Macbeth has violated the duties of any subject, much less a sworn supporter. The sentence "Macbeth has clearly deviated from his normal responsibilities as a loyal servant to his King..." is especially good, for it ties up the rest of the paragraph and makes the point. The final sentence explains that the rest of the essay will show how all of Macbeth's relationships are destroyed.

The student proves the rest of the thesis by showing how Macbeth's relationships with Banquo, Fleance, and Macduff are destroyed when Macbeth sets aside his normal and expected human responsibilities. The reference to "chickens"—recalling Macduff's impassioned speech upon hearing of the murder of his family—is an effective specific detail. The final sentence restates the topic and makes the point clear.

This is a excellent essay, well organized and supported with specific detail. It would earn an 8–9 on the AP scale.

Response 3

Achilles, a character in Homer's *Iliad,* avoids his responsibilities and thus fails in human relationships. Achilles' duty is to lead the Achaeans into battle against the Trojans, but he lets his personal feelings interfere with his duty as a soldier.

Achilles withdraws from the battlefield in anger, furious with the Commander-in-Chief of the Achaean army, the greedy Agamemnon, who has threatened to take his mistress, Briseis, away from him. Achilles is maddened by Agamemnon's insolence, and despite his reverence for honor, retires from the battlefield. To placate Achilles' wounded pride, Agamemnon offers an apology, but Achilles will not accept it. Achilles' wounded pride and deep frustration with Agamemnon leads him to avoid his responsibility to the Achaean Army and leads to his failure in human relationships. He has an obligation to his fellow Achaeans, who greatly respect him and would honor him if he would return to battle. But he refuses to honor his responsibilities as a leader of men and remains apart from his fellows.

One consequence of his withdrawal is the death of his dearest friend, Patroclus. Standing on the sidelines and watching the enemy advance, Achilles asks Patroclus to fight in his place, but Patroclus is not a warrior—he is Achilles' squire. Although he is inexperienced as a warrior, he feels it is his duty to honor Achilles' request. He goes to war in Achilles' armor and in the heat of battle is slain by Hector, a Trojan hero. This shows a failure on Achilles' part, for he had set aside his duty and forced another to take his place.

After Patroclus is killed, even greater fighting and vast destruction take place. An especially fierce battle erupts around Patroclus' corpse, for the Trojans have taken it and the Achaeans are determined to recover it themselves. The Achaeans want Achilles to join in the Trojan War to recover Patroclus' corpse, which they hope will in some way alleviate Achilles' guilt for causing the death of his best friend. Hector instructs his Trojan allies to enter the conflict over the body, and the Trojans force back the Achaeans. Hippothus, a respected Achaean warrior, is slain. The ground runs red with blood.

Death and destruction follow Achilles' refusal to honor his responsibility to serve in battle. When he does finally join the battle, much destruction has already ensued, and his closest friend has been killed.

Evaluation

This response is an 8–9 on the AP scoring scale, because it clearly proves the thesis that Achilles avoids responsibility and thus fails in human relationships. There is a good deal of clear, specific detail, and the style is mature and graceful. Note the variety of sentences, from the simple "Death and destruction follow Achilles' refusal to honor his responsibility to serve in battle" (5th paragraph) to two compound sentences in the first paragraph. Note how artfully the complex sentences have been crafted, with a variety of punctuation and stylistic devices. The writer has been especially successful in compressing a great deal of information into each sentence while retaining clarity and stylistic variation. We see this in the beginning of the second paragraph, where Agamemnon is both identified and characterized as the writer makes the point. The sentences exhibit an elegant agility as well. The dash in the second sentence of the third paragraph, for example, effectively shows a dramatic change in thought. The images are vivid, such as the startlingly effective "The ground runs red with blood" in the fourth paragraph. It is also impressive to see how thoroughly the writer has studied and understood the work, keeping the characters and their relationships clear.

SAMPLE 2

A sharp insight can change a person's life for better or worse. Using any recognized work of literary merit, show how this assertion is true. You may select a novel from the list below or another novel or play of significant literary merit. (See list on page 103)

Response 1

In some novels, there are characters who experience a sharp insight into the world around them that can alter their lives for better or worse. In Erich Maria Remarque's *All Quiet on the Western Front,* a young German soldier named Paul Baumer is hurled into harsh surroundings and experiences just such an insight. Paul has many realizations that change his life.

Paul first begins to realize that any hope for a normal life is doomed after a few months of feeling cold, hungry, and afraid. He begins to wonder what he would do with his life should peace be declared that very day. He understands that the education he has received in high school has left him unprepared for life. By being subjected to the nightmares associated with war, Paul suddenly realizes that he is too mature to re-enter school and too old to become apprenticed in any skill. Readers can see from Paul's sudden realization that he is in a precarious position. He has missed all the fun and excitement associated with a normal high school life. He feels alienated and worried because the war has destroyed all his aspirations.

While on leave, Paul realizes that he no longer feels comfortable in his own home. He has an awkward feeling about himself; he is aware that it is he, not the home, who has changed drastically. The hastened maturity that he has undergone has caused him to drift away from his former way of life, and he has unwillingly become isolated from all that he was because of these changes. Suddenly, he feels alienated.

There is another instance when he realizes a sudden change. He is temporarily stationed at a prison camp where he takes a long look at the other prisoners, who are Russians. He suddenly realizes that these men are really human beings just like his countrymen, his friends, but due to the decisions of their leaders, these people like him have become enemies. Paul unexpectedly realizes that they could just as easily have become friends if the leaders had decided so. This insight shows how confused Paul is, for he does not understand why he is fighting a war. He can see no difference between himself and the Russian prisoners and is baffled that a simple word of command could set up barriers between people.

Paul Baumer has several sharp realizations during his experiences in World War I. He was forced to mature too soon in order to cope with the blood, death, and constant bombardment.

Evaluation

The essay is seriously off-base because it does not answer the question: the prompt required the writer to select *one* sharp insight and show how it "can change a person's life for better or worse." What is it that Paul realizes? What clear insight does he have that alters his life? Without this clear statement of purpose, the rest of the paper skirts around the issue, ending up showing a handful of insights but not answering the question. Therefore, this essay describes several insights but does not show how they changed Paul's life. Readers can infer that these experiences changed his life for the worse, but readers shouldn't have to do any inferring; the thesis must be stated up front and proven through specific details.

This paper could not receive more than a 2–3 on the AP scale.

Response 2

Sometimes a character in a story experiences a sharp insight that changes his life. In Erich Maria Remarque's *All Quiet on the Western Front,* a young German soldier named Paul Baumer is hurled into the devastation of World War I and experiences just such an epiphany. Paul's experiences lead him to realize suddenly that he is part of a "lost generation," cut off from any future because of his war-time experiences. As a result of this realization, Paul gives up all hope for the future. His realization destroys his life.

When he enlists in the German Army during World War I, 19-year-old Paul is not at all prepared for the hardships and extreme hatred of the enemy that a soldier must have in order to kill. After a few weeks on the battlefield, Paul understands that his life as a child has come to an end, and he wishes that he could return to the simple life he had previously experienced. He expresses this as he says, "I am little more than a child; in my wardrobe still hangs short, boy's trousers—it is such a little time ago, why is it over?" Paul begins to understand that the war has robbed him of his childhood. His life-changing insight comes shortly thereafter.

After Paul intentionally kills someone for the first time, the complete desolation of his situation bursts forth. He whispers to the dead soldier, "I will fight against this war which has struck us both down; from you, taken life—and from me—? Life also. There is no hope of ever getting out of this." This shattering realization causes Paul to lose sight of his dreams of fame and glory, and he no longer wants to be involved in fighting and death. But he is compelled to continue—"We are insensible, dead men who through some trick, some dreadful magic, are still able to run and kill." As a result of this epiphany, Paul realizes that his life no longer has worth. This causes his death on a day "so quiet and still on the Western Front."

Paul Baumer experiences the sharp insight that war has robbed him of any hope for a normal life. As a result, he becomes lost, alienated from all that he once loved—friends, family, and home. He has suddenly realized that he is a member of a confused, frightened, and wandering society, living out an unthinkable nightmare.

Evaluation

This paper is right on target, as the writer identifies the "sharp insight" that Paul experiences (the realization that he is part of a "lost generation") and how it changed his life "for better or worse": "As a result of this realization, Paul gives up all hope for the future. His realization destroys his life."

Notice how the student writer makes the point and links ideas with transitions. For example, at the end of paragraph 2, the student writes, "Paul begins to understand that that war has robbed him of his childhood. His life-changing insight comes shortly thereafter." Paragraph 3 describes the "sharp insight," the discussion directed by the topic sentence: "After Paul intentionally kills someone for the first time, the complete desolation of his situation bursts forth." The quotes from the novel are effective not because they are precise but because they directly make the point. Remember: peppering your writing with direct quotes and other examples is only effective when every quote and example directly contributes to your point. Otherwise, they are mere space-fillers. The final lines of paragraph 3 sum up the point and directly answer the question. The conclusion is equally good, again because it proves the writer's thesis.

This is an excellent, well-organized essay that is supported with specific detail. It would earn an 8–9 on the AP scale.

SAMPLE 3

At the end of some novels, readers feel like saying, "That's just right. That's how it should have ended." At the end of other novels, however, readers are left with a sense of incompleteness or dissatisfaction. Choose a novel and show by specific reference why the ending was or was not satisfactory to you. You may select a novel from the list below or another novel or play of significant literary merit. (See list on page 103)

Response

At the close of a novel, the reader expects to be left with a sense of completeness and satisfaction. As we close the book, we should feel like saying, "That's just right. That's how it should have ended." In *A Portrait of the Artist as a Young Man* by James Joyce, readers get this feeling because Stephen Dedalus' decision to leave Ireland and become a writer follows logically from his personality and experiences.

The book's title is the first clue readers have about the ending. Stephen *will* become an artist, no matter what burdens stand in his way. The second clue is Stephen Dedalus' name: "Stephen" is a Christian martyr; "Dedalus" refers to the famous story of the Greek youth who flew too close to the sun and perished. These clues foreshadow the ending: Stephen must forge a new path for himself—even if he risks becoming a martyr or perishing from his boldness.

It is clear from the beginning of the novel that Stephen is very different from his peers. While he obeys his parents and the rules of the Catholic church, he has an unusual sensitivity to aesthetics. Simple sentences in a spelling book strike him as poetry. He wishes to experiment and create beauty, but the Catholic church and his class-bound family place strict restraints on him. Stephen is told that magistrates and priests are the most intelligent figures and artists matter for little. A priest tries to turn him to a career in the church, asking him: "Have you ever felt that you had a vocation?" Stephen rejects this path, even turning away from the priests as they pass him on the bridge. Stephen feels that he must fulfill his destiny as the "great artificer" whose name he bears. Girls tempt him, but he turns away. His friends playing in the water beckon him, but he remains resolute.

Ultimately, Stephen makes the bold decision to become an artist. The novel ends in spring, the traditional time of rebirth, as Stephen declares that he "will not serve" Ireland. He will leave his homeland, a country that is a "pig eating its young." Abroad, he will discover an art that lets his spirit "express itself in unfettered freedom." Stephen understands that as an artist, his true father is Dedalus who will help him pursue the art he was born to create. "Old father, old artificer, stand now and ever in good stead," Stephen says as he announces his mission to "forge in the smithy of my soul the uncreated conscience of my race." The ending leaves readers feeling satisfied because Stephen Dedalus was destined to become an artist.

Evaluation

The writer stays right on target by providing specific details that prove that the ending perfectly fits what came before. Here's how the essay looks when reduced to its bare bones:

Thesis: The ending is satisfactory. ("In *A Portrait of the Artist as a Young Man* by James Joyce, readers get this feeling because Stephen Dedalus' decision to leave Ireland and become a writer follows logically from his personality and experiences.")

Details: Book's title
Main character's name
Sensitive to aesthetics
Rejects priesthood
Rejects all friends (girls as well as boys)
Rejects homeland
Embraces art

This is an excellent, well-organized essay that is supported with specific detail. It would earn an 8–9 on the AP scale.

PRACTICE OPEN-ENDED LITERARY RESPONSE QUESTIONS

Use the following simulated test questions to practice what you learned in this lesson.

SAMPLE 1

Writer Michael Dorris argues, "Books, important as they can and should be, are after all but a part of the much larger context that informs them. They illuminate our experiences but at the same time our experience sheds light back upon their ideas and theories. A book converts less than it nudges us toward what we otherwise already think. The existence of characters who are distasteful or complicated merely reflect the world as it is." Choose a play or novel in which a character is distasteful or complicated and show how the character reflects qualities of the "real" world. Analyze the character and show how he or she is rooted in reality. You may select a novel from the list below or another novel or play of significant literary merit. (*See list on page 103*)

SAMPLE 2

People make adjustments with varying degrees of success to certain factors in their environment. These factors may be their physical surroundings, other people, or the customs and traditions of the society in which they live. Choose a novel or play in which a person was or was not successful in adjusting to their surroundings. Analyze what the adjustment reveals about the person as well as his or her culture. You may select a novel from the list below or another novel or play of significant literary merit. (*See list on page 103*)

SAMPLE 3

English novelist E.M. Forster once said, "If I had to choose between betraying my country and betraying my friend, I hope I should have the guts to betray my country." Choose a novel or play of significant literary merit in which a character was faced with just this choice. Describe whether the character betrayed his or her country or friends, and analyze why the character made this choice. Then explain whether you agree or disagree with the character's decision and why. You may select a novel from the list below or another novel or play of significant literary merit. (*See list on page 103*)

SAMPLE 4

In literature as in life, some characters are forced by circumstances, other people, or other forces to compromise their principles. Other characters, in contrast, are able to withstand the pressure to betray their most deeply held beliefs. Choose a play or novel in which a character believed strongly in a principle. Show how the character stayed true to these beliefs or betrayed them. Analyze the causes and effects of the character's decision. You may select a novel from the list below or another novel or play of significant literary merit. (*See list on page 103*)

Additional Practice Tests

GENERAL DIRECTIONS FOR THE PRACTICE TESTS

These tests were constructed to be representative of what you will encounter on the AP English Literature and Composition exam. Take the test in a quiet room without distractions, following all directions carefully and observing all time limits. Try to get as close as possible to actual test conditions, and take the test in one sitting. The more carefully you match test conditions, the more accurate your results will be and the better able you will be to evaluate your strengths and weaknesses.

ROAD MAP

- *General Directions for the Practice Tests*
- *Practice Test 1*
- *Answers and Explanations*
- *Practice Test 2*
- *Answers and Explanations*
- *Practice Test 3*
- *Answers and Explanations*
- *Practice Test 4*
- *Answers and Explanations*

PRACTICE TEST 1: ENGLISH LITERATURE AND COMPOSITION

SECTION I: MULTIPLE-CHOICE QUESTIONS

Time—1 hour

> **Directions:** This section contains selections from two passages of prose and two poems with questions on their content, style, form, and purpose. Read each selection closely and carefully. Then choose the best answer from the five choices.

Questions 1–14. Read the following selection carefully before you mark your answers.

THE wrath of God is like great waters that are dammed for the present; they increase more and more and rise higher and higher, till an outlet is given; and the longer the stream is stopped, the more rapid and mighty is its course when once it is let loose. 'Tis true that judgment against your evil work has not been executed hitherto; the floods of God's vengeance have been withheld; but your guilt in the meantime is constantly increasing, and you are every day treasuring up more wrath; the waters are continually rising and waxing more and more mighty; and there is nothing but the mere pleasure of God that holds the waters back, that are unwilling to be stopped, and press hard to go forward. If God should only withdraw his hand from the floodgate, it would immediately fly open, and the fiery floods of the fierceness and wrath of God would rush forth with inconceivable fury, and would come upon you with omnipotent power; and if your strength were ten thousand times greater than it is, yea, ten thousand times greater than the strength of the stoutest, sturdiest devil in hell, it would be nothing to withstand or endure it.

The bow of God's wrath is bent, and the arrow made ready on the string, and justice bends the arrow at your heart and strains the bow, and it is nothing but the mere pleasure of God, and that of an angry God, without any promise or obligation at all, that keeps the arrow one moment from being made drunk with your blood.

The God that holds you over the pit of hell much as one holds a spider or some loathsome insect over the fire, abhors you, and is dreadfully provoked; his wrath toward you burns like fire; he looks upon you as worthy of nothing else but to be cast into the fire; he is of purer eyes than to bear to have you in his sight; you are ten thousand times so abominable in his eyes as the most hateful and venomous serpent is in ours. You have offended him infinitely more than ever a stubborn rebel did his prince; and yet it is nothing but his hand that holds you from falling into the fire every moment. 'Tis ascribed to nothing else, that you did not go to hell the last night; that you were suffered to awake again in this world after you closed your eyes to sleep and there is no other reason to be given why you have not dropped into hell since you arose in the morning, but that God's hand has held you up. There is no other reason to be given why you have not gone to hell since you have sat here in the house of God, provoking his pure eyes by your sinful wicked manner of attending his solemn worship. Yea, there is nothing else that is to be given as a reason why you don't this very moment drop down into hell.

O sinner! Consider the fearful danger you are in. 'Tis a great furnace of wrath, a wide and bottomless pit, full of the fire of wrath, that you are held over in the hand of that God whose wrath is provoked and incensed as much against you as against many of the damned in hell. You hang by a slender thread with the flames of divine wrath flashing about it.

1. What two things are being compared in the simile in the first sentence?

   (A) God's anger to the devil wrecking havoc on earth
   (B) God's anger to His hand
   (C) God's anger to an uncontrolled floodthat is temporarily being held back
   (D) The devil to humanity's evilness
   (E) The stoutest, sturdiest devil in hell to God

2. According to the author, God is angry because

   (A) people continue to sin and have not repented of their sins.
   (B) a great flood has destroyed all of His accomplishments.
   (C) God's bow is bent.
   (D) people are drinking blood.
   (E) insects and serpents are infesting the land.

3. What poetic techniques does the author use in this passage to convey his main idea? "...floodgate, it would immediately fly open, and the fiery floods of the fierceness and wrath of God would rush forth with inconceivable fury ..."

   (A) Paradox and irony
   (B) Assonance and understatement
   (C) Alliteration and imagery
   (D) Hyperbole and inversion
   (E) Similes and metaphors

4. What figure or figures of speech does the author use in the second paragraph?
   I. Metaphor
   II. Personification
   III. Irony

   (A) I
   (B) II
   (C) I and II
   (D) III
   (E) I and III

5. All of the following are used as metaphorical images in the selection EXCEPT

   (A) spidersand other horrible bugs.
   (B) snakes.
   (C) obstinate rebels.
   (D) fire and water.
   (E) toads and flies.

6. The effect of the imagery is to

   (A) strike fear in people's hearts.
   (B) reassure people that to err is human, but to forgive is divine.
   (C) remind people that they have been led astray by false leaders.
   (D) convince people that their lives are worthless.
   (E) convey the essence of goodness.

7. In the last paragraph, the author

   (A) introduces a new topic.
   (B) makes his point that sin can be washed away.
   (C) directly addresses God.
   (D) compares and contrasts the past and the present.
   (E) summarizes his previous points to reinforce his message.

8. On which of God's characteristics does the author focus?

   (A) His mercy
   (B) His anger
   (C) His kindness
   (D) His goodness
   (E) His determination

9. The subject of the selection is

   (A) hatred.
   (B) love.
   (C) guilt.
   (D) sin.
   (E) fury.

10. The tone of this selection is best described as

    (A) rational.
    (B) weary.
    (C) annoyed.
    (D) apathetic.
    (E) enraged.

11. The author's purpose is most likely to

    (A) convince his readers to live a virtuous life or risk eternal damnation.
    (B) accept the author of the selection as the one true leader.
    (C) reject religion in favor of hard work and abstinence.
    (D) terrify his readers so they never misbehave again.
    (E) entertain his readers.

12. The author's style is best described as

    (A) natural and direct.
    (B) conversational.
    (C) marked by short sentences and colloquial language.
    (D) spare and simple.
    (E) ornate and embellished with many figures of speech.

13. This selection is most likely an excerpt from a(n)

    (A) biography.
    (B) autobiography.
    (C) short story.
    (D) sermon.
    (E) prayer.

Questions 14–33. Read the following selection carefully before you mark your answers.

1

From harmony, from heavenly harmony
This universal frame began;
When Nature underneath a heap
Of jarring atoms lay,
And could not heave her head,
The tuneful voice was heard from high,
"Arise, ye more than dead."
Then cold and hot and moist and dry
In order to their stations leap,
And Music's power obey.
From harmony, from heavenly harmony
This universal frame began:
From harmony to harmony.
Through all the compass of the notes it ran,
The diapason[1] closing full in Man.

2

What passion cannot Music raise and quell?
When Jubal[2] struck the chorded shell,
His listening brethren stood around,
And, wondering, on their faces fell
To worship that celestial sound.
Less than a god they thought there could not dwell
Within the hollow of that shell
That spoke so sweetly, and so well.
What passion cannot Music raise and quell?

3

The trumpet's loud clangor
Excites us to arms
With shrill notes of anger
And mortal alarms.
The double double double beat
Of the thundering drum
Cries, "Hark! the foes come:
Charge, charge, 'tis too late to retreat."

---

[1] the entire range of notes on a musical scale
[2] inventor of the lyre and pipe

4

The soft complaining flute
In dying notes discovers
The woes of hopeless lovers,
Whose dirge is whispered by the warbling lute.

5

Sharp violins proclaim
Their jealous pangs and desperation.
Fury, frantic indignation,
Depth of pains and heights of passion,
For the fair, disdainful dame.

6

But Oh! What art can teach,
What human voice can reach
The sacred organ's praise?
Notes inspiring holy love,
Notes that wing their heavenly ways
To mend the choirs above.

7

Orpheus could lead the savage race,
And trees unrooted left their place,
Sequactious of the lyre:
But bright Cecilia raised the wonder higher:
When to her organ vocal breath was given,
And angel heard, and straight appeared
Mistaking earth for heaven.

GRAND CHORUS

As from the power of sacred lays
The spheres began to move.
And sung the great Creator's praise
To all the blessed above;
So when the last and dreadful hour
This crumbling pageant shall devour,
The trumpet shall be heard on high,
The dead shall live, the living die,
And Music shall untune the sky.

14. As used in line 2, the phrase *universal frame* most nearly means

   (A)   the structure of musical instruments.
   (B)   an orchestra.
   (C)   the structure of the universe.
   (D)   the human body.
   (E)   the ubiquitous appreciation of music.

15. What figure of speech does the poet use in lines 3–5 to capture the chaos that preceded the creation of the universe?
    I. Personification
    II. Onomatopoeia
    III. Parallelism

    (A) I
    (B) II
    (C) III
    (D) I and II
    (E) I and III

16. "Cold and hot and moist and dry" in line 8 are an allusion to the

    (A) four different emotions that music can evoke in listeners: anger, passion, admiration, and love.
    (B) four elements that comprise the universe: earth, fire, water, and air.
    (C) four seasons: winter, spring, summer, and fall.
    (D) four main types of instruments in an orchestra: the strings, brass, woodwind, and drums.
    (E) four main types of music people enjoy: classical, jazz, western, and rock.

17. The word *harmony* dominates the first stanza. The poet uses the word *harmony* to refer to

    (A) musical sweetness and symmetry.
    (B) unity and cohesion.
    (C) synthesis out of individuality.
    (D) the power of music to sway even the hardest heart.
    (E) the centrality of music to the human experience.

18. Line 16 represents the poem's

    (A) topic, its subject.
    (B) main "character."
    (C) paradox.
    (D) rhetorical question.
    (E) theme, its focal point.

19. In line 16, the poet uses alliteration in the phrase "celestial sound" for all the following reasons EXCEPT to

    (A) create musical effects.
    (B) link related ideas.
    (C) stress certain words.
    (D) make a reference to a well-known song.
    (E) mimic specific sounds.

20. The second stanza consists mainly of rhymed couplets to suggest the

    (A) sweet harmony being described.
    (B) different instruments in an orchestra.
    (C) power of music to transform reality.
    (D) gods of music.
    (E) passion that music evokes.

21. In the third stanza, the poet makes the flute and lute seem to come alive by using

    (A) alliteration.
    (B) personification.
    (C) symbolism.
    (D) similes and metaphors.
    (E) allusions.

22. As used in line 34, the word *discovers* most nearly means

    (A) withholds.
    (B) hides.
    (C) obscures.
    (D) reveals.
    (E) treasures.

23. The third and fourth stanzas show a marked contrast in

    (A) topic.
    (B) mood.
    (C) style.
    (D) technique.
    (E) form.

24. According to the poet, what represents the "depth of pain and the height of passion"?

    (A) Women
    (B) The violin
    (C) The flute
    (D) The lute
    (E) Hopeless lovers

25. What passion does the poet associate with the organ?

    (A) Love
    (B) Hate
    (C) Religious devotion
    (D) Jealously
    (E) Anger

26. Stanzas three through six represent the

    (A) three gods of music.
    (B) four main reasons why the world needs music.
    (C) four main kinds of instruments in an orchestra.
    (D) four passions that music can advance and subdue.
    (E) five different types of rhyme.

27. You can infer from the context that Orpheus (line 48) is an allusion to

    (A) a type of rare and valuable tree.
    (B) Saint Cecilia, the patron saint of music.
    (C) angels.
    (D) a barbarous race of people.
    (E) a poet and musician who could charm creatures through his music.

28. The angel's mistake in confusing earth for heaven suggests that

    (A) the universe has no music.
    (B) music has the power to transform reality.
    (C) the poet believes we create our heaven on earth.
    (D) the angel thrives on music.
    (E) music is an emotional as well as an intellectual experience.

29. Which musical instrument does the poet think is most heavenly?

    (A) The violin
    (B) The flute
    (C) The organ
    (D) The lyre
    (E) The human voice

30. Why will music "untune the sky" in the "last and dreadful hour"?

    (A) When the world ends on the Biblical Judgment Day, there will no longer be harmony.
    (B) When the world ends on the Biblical Judgment Day, all music will cease.
    (C) Unharmonious music will cause the world to cease revolving on its axis.
    (D) The modern decline in music is causing a decline in civility.
    (E) It is a paradox that the world needs music to survive.

31. Which stanzas in this ode have a regular pattern of rhyme?

    (A) 1
    (B) 1 and 2
    (C) 1 and 3
    (D) 6 and 7
    (E) None of the above

32. The diction in this poem is best described as

    (A) colloquial.
    (B) idiomatic.
    (C) elevated and stately.
    (D) vernacular and conversational.
    (E) dignified but commonplace.

33. The rhyme scheme in the first and last stanzas suggests the

    (A) emergence of harmony out of chaos and the return of chaos.
    (B) outburst of harmony from chaos.
    (C) continued chaos of the universe.
    (D) unending harmony of the universe.
    (E) power of music to create consistency.

Questions 34–44. Read the following selection carefully before you mark your answers.

Terminus

1 It is time to be old,
To take in sail:—
The god of bounds,
Who sets to seas a shore,

5 Came to me in his fatal rounds,
And said: 'No more!
No farther shoot
Thy broad ambitious branches, and thy root.
Fancy departs: no more invent;

10 Contract thy firmament
To compass of a tent.
There's not enough for this and that,
Make thy option which of two;
Economize the failing river,

15 Not the less revere the Giver,
Leave the many and hold the few.
Timely wise accept the terms,
Soften the fall with wary foot;
A little while

20 Still plan and smile,
And, —fault of novel germs,—
Mature the unfallen fruit.
Curse, if thou wilt, thy sires,
Bad husbands of their fires,

25 Who, when they gave thee breath,
Failed to bequeath
The needful sinew stark as once,
The Baresark marrow to thy bones,
But left a legacy of ebbing veins,

30 Inconstant heat and nerveless reins,—
Amid the Muses, left thee deaf and dumb,
Amid the gladiators, halt and numb.
As the bird trims her to the gale,
I trim myself to the storm of time,

35 I man the rudder, reef the sail,
Obey the voice at eve obeyed at prime:
'Lowly faithful, banish fear,
Right onward drive unharmed;
The port, well worth the cruise, is near,

40 And every wave is charmed.'

34. At what time in the speaker's life is the poem set?

    (A) At the beginning of his life
    (B) When he is still a young child
    (C) When he is middle-aged
    (D) Near the end of his life
    (E) After he has died

35. In line 2, the metaphor "to take in sail" is best interpreted as

    (A) tying up all his business matters to prepare for his death.
    (B) putting his boat in dry-dock for the winter.
    (C) stocking nonperishable goods and preparing his home for a fierce storm.
    (D) gathering his friends and family around him one last time.
    (E) earning more money.

36. What advice does the god of boundaries give the speaker?

    (A) Do not garden any longer.
    (B) Do not harm any more animals.
    (C) Help preserve the environment, especially trees.
    (D) Go camping with the people you cherish.
    (E) Make ready for the end of your life.

37. What figure of speech does the poet use in line 27 to create musical effects and link related ideas?

    (A) Alliteration
    (B) Assonance
    (C) Paradox
    (D) Hyperbole
    (E) Understatement

38. Throughout the poem, the imagery suggests that

    (A) we should rail against nature and human limitations.
    (B) human life has natural, inescapable boundaries.
    (C) people get increasingly bitter as they realize how little control they have over their fate.
    (D) the ocean and human life are inextricably entwined.
    (E) we all need a guide to help us maneuver our way through life successfully.

39. The tone or mood of this poem is best characterized as

    (A) sour.
    (B) caustic.
    (C) resigned.
    (D) upbeat.
    (E) buoyant.

40. What does the poem's tone reveal about the speaker's outlook?

    (A) The speaker accepts his fate.
    (B) The speaker rails against the unfair way he has been treated.
    (C) The speaker's ambition is undimmed, and he continues to strive for success.
    (D) The speaker rejects that which he cannot understand.
    (E) The speaker has been rendered deaf and dumb by events outside his control.

41. Which of the following literary devices does the author use to unify the poem?

    (A) Repetition of key words
    (B) Personification
    (C) Irony
    (D) Imagery
    (E) Aphorisms

42. What literary device does the poet use in the final stanza to convey his theme?

   (A) A literary allusion
   (B) An extended metaphor
   (C) Dramatic irony
   (D) A flashback
   (E) Foreshadowing

43. The "port" in line 39 is a symbol of

   (A) life.
   (B) failure.
   (C) despair.
   (D) gloom.
   (E) death.

44. In Roman mythology, Terminus is the guardian of boundaries. The author used "Terminus" as the title of this poem to suggest that

   (A) we are never constrained by boundaries, whether they are artificial or manmade.
   (B) we must respect our heritage.
   (C) our lives are bounded by forces outside of our control, and we must respect these barriers.
   (D) everyone needs a guardian angel.
   (E) death is the final frontier.

Questions 45–53. Read the following selection carefully before you mark your answers.

When I finished my last prison term twelve years ago, I never dreamed I would go back. But not long ago I found myself looking up at the famous San Quentin tower as I followed an escort guard though the main gates. I should have been overjoyed since this time I was a free man, the writer of a film which would require a month of location-shooting there. But being there had a disquieting effect on me. I was confused. I knew that I would be able to leave every night after filming, but the enclosed walls, the barbed wire, and the guards in the towers shouldering their carbines made old feelings erupt in me. While my mind told me I was free, my spirit snarled as if I were a prisoner again, and I couldn't shake the feeling. Emotionally, I could not convince myself that I was not going to be subjected once more to horrible indignities, that I would not have to live through it all again. Each morning when the guards checked my shoulder bag and clanked shut the iron door behind me, the old convict in me rose up full of hatred and rage for the guards, the walls, the terrible indecency of the place. I was still the same man who had entered there freely, a man full of love for his family and his life. But another self from the past reawakened, an imprisoned self, seething with the desire for vengeance on all things not imprisoned.

As I followed the guard, passing with the crew and actors from one compound to another, a hollow feeling of disbelief possessed me and I was struck dumb. The grounds were impeccably planted and groomed, serene as a cemetery. Streamlined circles of flowers and swatches of smooth lawn rolled to trimmed green margins of pruned shrubbery, perfectly laid out against the limestone and red brick cellblocks. But I knew that when you penetrated beyond this pretty landscaping, past the offices, also with their bouquets of flowers, past the cellblock's thick walls, there thrived America's worst nightmare. There the green, concealing surface lifted from the bubbling swamp, a monster about to arise from its dark depths. There writhed scaly demons, their claws and fangs primed for secret and unspeakable brutalities.

45. The writer chose the first-person point of view to

    (A) create a distance between the narrator and his audience.
    (B) give his writing an immediacy and increase reader identification.
    (C) establish his credentials for describing the scene.
    (D) allow readers to see the scene from a number of vantage points.
    (E) afford him the opportunity to describe how others react to the situation.

46. The writer finding himself back at San Quentin as a film maker rather than as a prisoner is an example of

    (A) irony.
    (B) humor.
    (C) satire.
    (D) caricature.
    (E) understatement.

47. What figure or figures of speech does the writer use to convey his emotions in this sentence: "While my mind told me I was free, my spirit snarled as if I were a prisoner again, and I couldn't shake the feeling."
    I. Personification
    II. Alliteration
    III. Hyperbole

    (A) I
    (B) II
    (C) I and II
    (D) II and III
    (E) III

48. Read this sentence: "As I followed the guard, passing with the crew and actors from one compound to another, a hollow feeling of disbelief possessed me..." What literary technique does the writer use to reinforce his feelings of disassociation?

    (A) A tense shift
    (B) The active voice
    (C) The passive voice
    (D) Metaphor
    (E) Exaggeration

49. In the second paragraph, the primary effect of using long sentences with numerous prepositional phrases is to

    (A) suggest the long journey the narrator has made from prisoner to successful, law-abiding citizen.
    (B) describe the setting in precise detail so readers can visualize it.
    (C) lead in to his horror story.
    (D) establish a suitably grave tone.
    (E) soothe the reader into a sensitive frame of mind.

50. The last paragraph describes a shift from the beautiful exterior of the prison to the terrifying cellblocks to suggest

    (A) prisoners are not treated well, even in one of America's best prisons.
    (B) the appearance of a prison can help inmates deal with their incarceration.
    (C) most prisons are well maintained.
    (D) people who care about their jobs do better than those who are apathetic.
    (E) the sharp contrast between appearance and reality.

51. The "monsters" and "demons" in the last paragraph are best interpreted as

    (A) real beasts kept under the prison.
    (B) the prisoners and the suffering they endure.
    (C) our collective guilt about the dreadful conditions in San Quentin.
    (D) prisoners about to break out of San Quentin.
    (E) the ultimate failure of his career as a film maker.

52. The tone of this passage is best described as

    (A) neutral.
    (B) eerie.
    (C) grim.
    (D) lightly ironic.
    (E) serious.

53. Which of the following literary devices does the writer NOT use to convey his main idea?

    (A) Imagery
    (B) Similes
    (C) Hyperbole
    (D) Symbolism
    (E) Alliteration

SECTION II: ESSAY QUESTIONS

Time—2 hours

Question 1
Suggested Time: 40 minutes

Directions: In his *Preface to The House of the Seven Gables* (1851), Hawthorne explained some differences between the romance and the novel. Read the following excerpt from Nathaniel Hawthorne's essay. Then select any novel that you have read that you believe fits his definition of a "romance." Isolate at least two examples of how the work functions as a romance and show how they are evident in the literary work.

When a writer calls his work a Romance, it need hardly be observed that he wishes to claim a certain latitude, both to its fashion and material, which he would not have felt himself entitled to assume, had he professed to be writing a Novel. The latter form of composition is presumed to aim at a very minute fidelity, not merely to the possible, but to the probable and ordinary course of man's experience. The former—while, as a work of art, it must rigidly subject itself to laws, and while it sins unpardonably, so far as it may swerve aside from the truth of the human heart—has fairly a right to present that truth under the circumstances, to a great extent, of the writer's own choosing or creation. If he think fit, also, he may so manage his atmospherical medium as to bring out or mellow the lights and deepen and enrich the shadows of the picture. He will be wise, no doubt, to make a very moderate use of the privileges here stated, and, especially, to mingle the Marvellous rather as a slight, delicate, and evanescent flavor, than as any portion of the actual substance of the dish offered to the public.

Question 2
Suggested Time: 40 minutes

Directions: Carefully read the following poem by Edmund Spenser. Then write a well-organized essay in which you discuss the poem's use of literary devices to express the poet's view of immortality. You may wish to consider some or all of the following literary devices in your analysis: word play, symbolism, syntax, alliteration, rhyme, and imagery.

Sonnet 75

1   One day I wrote her name upon the strand,
    But came the waves and washed it way;
    Again I wrote it with a second hand,
    But came the tide, and made my pains his prey,

5   "Vain man," said she, "that dost in vain assay,
    A mortal thing so to immortalize,
    For I myself shall like to this decay,
    And eek my name be wiped out likewise."
    "Not so," quod I, "let baser things devise

10 To die in dust, but you shall live by fame:
    My verse your virtues rare shall eternize,
    And in the heavens write your glorious name.
    Where whenas death shall all the world subdue,
    Our love shall live, and later life renew."

Question 3
Suggested Time: 40 minutes

Directions: All literary characters face problems; indeed, conflict propels the plot of any literary work. But how should people solve the problems they face as part of society? Is it better to enlist aid to right a wrong or to battle injustice on your own? Select a major character from any work of recognized literary merit and show what problem society faces and how the character deals with the conflict that arises. Be sure to include specific examples from the work under discussion to make your point. If you wish, you may select a literary work from the following list:

Madame Bovary	Ethan Frome
Vanity Fair	Moby Dick
Lord Jim	Catch-22
Fahrenheit 451	The Scarlet Letter
The Turn of the Screw	David Copperfield
Native Son	Invisible Man
Like Water for Chocolate	The Great Gatsby
The Sun Also Rises	Nicholas Nickleby
Cry, the Beloved Country	Julius Caesar
Othello	Romeo and Juliet
Jane Eyre	Our Town
Pride and Prejudice	The Sound and the Fury

QUICK-SCORE ANSWERS

1. C		19. D		37. A	
2. A		20. A		38. B	
3. C		21. B		39. C	
4. C		22. D		40. A	
5. E		23. B		41. D	
6. A		24. B		42. B	
7. E		25. A		43. E	
8. B		26. D		44. C	
9. D		27. E		45. B	
10. E		28. B		46. A	
11. A		29. C		47. C	
12. E		30. A		48. C	
13. D		31. E		49. A	
14. C		32. C		50. E	
15. A		33. A		51. B	
16. B		34. D		52. C	
17. A		35. A		53. C	
18. E		36. E			

COMPUTING YOUR SCORE

You can use the following worksheet to compute an approximate score on the practice test. Since it is difficult to be objective about your own writing and since you are not a trained ETS scorer or English teacher, you may wish to ask a friend who has already taken the test (and earned a score of 4 or 5) to score your three essays.

Recognize that your score can only be an approximation (at best), as you are scoring yourself against yourself. In the actual AP English Literature and Composition Exam, you will be scored against every other student who takes the test as well.

Section I: Multiple-Choice Questions

	_____	number of correct answers
−	_____	.25 × number of wrong answers
=	_____	raw score
	_____	raw score
×	_____	1.25
=	_____	scaled score (out of a possible 67.5)

Section II: Essays

_____	essay 1 (0–9)
_____	essay 2 (0–9)
_____	essay 3 (0–9)
× _____	3.055
= _____	scaled score (out of a possible 82.5)

Scaled Score

_____	multiple-choice scaled score
+ _____	essay scaled score
= _____	final scaled score (out of a possible 150)

AP Score Conversion Chart

Scaled Score	Likely AP Score
150–100	5
99–86	4
85–67	3
66–0	1 or 2

ANSWERS AND EXPLANATIONS

SECTION I: MULTIPLE-CHOICE QUESTIONS

1. **The correct answer is (C).** In the simile in the first sentence, the speaker says, "the wrath of God is like great waters that are dammed for the present." God's anger—his "wrath"—is like an uncontrolled flood—"great waters."

2. **The correct answer is (A).** According to the speaker, God is angry because people continue to sin and have not repented of their sins. You can infer this from the phrases "judgment against your evil work," "provoking his pure eyes by your sinful wicked manner of attending his solemn worship," and "O sinner!"

3. **The correct answer is (C).** The speaker uses alliteration and imagery in this passage to convey his main idea. Recall that *alliteration* is the repetition of initial consonant sounds in several words in a sentence or line of poetry. Writers use alliteration to create musical effects, link related ideas, stress certain words, or mimic specific sounds. Alliteration is shown in the words *floodgate, fly, fiery, floods, fierceness, forth,* and *fury.* The images of destruction by flooding convey the speaker's idea that God is furious at humanity's continued sinning.

4. **The correct answer is (C).** In the second paragraph, the speaker uses metaphors and personification. The metaphors compare God's anger to a bow and arrow ("The bow of God's wrath is bent, and the arrow made ready on the string, and justice bends the arrow at your heart and strains the bow."). The personification gives human traits to an arrow, "being made drunk with your blood."

5. **The correct answer is (E).** The speaker creates metaphorical images with spiders and other horrible bugs,choice (A), when he says, "The God that holds you over the pit of hell much as one holds a spider or some loathsome insect over the fire." He uses snakes, choice (B), when he says: "so abominable in his eyes as the most hateful and venomous serpent is in ours." Choice (C) is used in this line: "You have offended him infinitely more than ever a stubborn rebel did his prince." Choice (D) is shown in the first paragraph: "THE wrath of God is like great waters that are dammed for the present." The metaphor of fire is included in choice (A), cited previously in this passage. Only choice (E) is not included as metaphors or images.

6. **The correct answer is (A).** The effect of the imagery is to strike fear in the readers' hearts. The speaker heaps images of hellfire and damnation to convince his listeners to repent. This is the opposite of choice (B). It has nothing to do with choice (C). Choices (D) and (E) offers only part of the answer.

7. **The correct answer is (E).** In the last paragraph, the speaker summarizes his previous points to reinforce his message when he directly addresses his listeners ("O sinner! Consider the fearful danger you are in.") in an attempt to get them to realize the danger they face if they do not atone for their sins. He uses metaphors and images that continue the theme of hell: " 'Tis a great furnace of wrath, a wide and bottomless pit, full of the fire of wrath." He also reiterates his point that God is furious at humanity's sinning: "...you are held over in the hand of that God whose wrath is provoked and incensed as much against you as against many of the damned in hell."

8. **The correct answer is (B).** The speaker focuses on God's anger. This is shown through his repeated references to God's wrath. For instance, study this typical example: "THE wrath of God is like great waters that are dammed for the present."

9. **The correct answer is (D).** The subject of the poem is sin. You can infer this from lines such as "There is no other reason to be given why you have not gone to hell since

you have sat here in the house of God, provoking his pure eyes by your sinful wicked manner of attending his solemn worship." Do not confuse this with *hatred,* choice (A); *guilt,* choice (C); or *fury,* choice (E). All these emotions are present in the selection, but the focus is on sin.

10. **The correct answer is (E).** The tone of this selection is best described as *enraged.* You can infer this from the images of anger, fury, and wrath.

11. **The correct answer is (A).** The author's purpose is most likely to convince his listeners to live a virtuous life or risk eternal damnation. As listeners consider the "fearful danger they are in," they are being offered the opportunity to repent. Choice (D) is a close second, but choice (A) is closer to his overall purpose.

12. **The correct answer is (E).** The speaker's style is best described as ornate and embellished with many figures of speech. He uses many metaphors, similes, alliteration, and other poetic techniques to convey his point. In addition, the sentences are long and ornate, so choices (A), (B), (C), and (D) cannot be correct.

13. **The correct answer is (D).** This selection is most likely an excerpt from a sermon. This is shown by the topic—God, sin, and repentance—as well as the heavy religious imagery. You can also infer the form by the author's tone and use of direct address ("O sinner! Consider the fearful danger you are in.").

14. **The correct answer is (C).** As used in line 2, the phrase *universal frame* most nearly means the structure of the universe. You can infer this from the context, especially the references to "Nature" and "jarring atoms." Choices (A), (B), and (E) cannot be correct because the poet does not refer to music until the second stanza. There is no support for choice (D).

15. **The correct answer is (A).** In lines 3–5, the poet uses *personification* to capture the chaos that preceded the creation of the universe. Nature is referred to as a living being unable to "heave her head."

16. **The correct answer is (B).** "Cold and hot and moist and dry" in line 8 are an allusion to earth, fire, water, and air, the four elements that comprise the universe, according to the ancient Greeks. Each of these elements "in order to their stations leap" as they combine to create the universe, as described in stanzas 1 and 2.

17. **The correct answer is (A).** The word *harmony* dominates the first stanza. The poet uses the word to refer to musical sweetness and symmetry. This is especially evident in lines 11–13, as the poet describes how the celestial bodies (spheres) were put into motion by angelic song. The motion of the spheres was believed to create harmonious music, a hymn of praise sung by the created. This divine music was not audible to human ears.

18. **The correct answer is (E).** Line 16 represents the poem's theme, its focal point. The poem dramatizes the ancient idea of the universe as a harmony created out of the warring element of chaos.

19. **The correct answer is (D).** In line 16, the poet uses alliteration in the phrase "celestial sound" for all the following reasons EXCEPT to make a reference to a well-known song. No specific song is named or even referred to in this poem. Recall that *alliteration* is the repetition of initial consonant sounds in several words in a sentence or line of poetry. Writers use alliteration to create musical effects, link related ideas, stress certain words, or mimic specific sounds.

20. **The correct answer is (A).** The second stanza consists mainly of rhymed couplets to suggest the sweet harmony being described here. Poets often match the form of their composition to its function, as is the case here. Notice that the rest of the poem is not

comprised of rhymed couplets; on the contrary, each stanza has a different rhyme scheme. The lack of rhyme in the first and last stanzas suggests chaos, for example.

21. **The correct answer is (B).** In the third stanza, the poet makes the flute and lute seem to come alive by using personification. *Personification* is giving human traits to nonhuman things. For example, "The book begged to be read."

22. **The correct answer is (D).** As used in line 34, the word *discovers* most nearly means "reveals." The flute's last notes show the "woes of hopeless lovers." This is the opposite of choices (A), (B), and (C). Choice (E) does not make sense in context.

23. **The correct answer is (B).** The third and fourth stanzas show a marked contrast in *mood*. The third stanza has an exciting mood, while the fourth stanza is depressed and sad.

24. **The correct answer is (B).** According to the poet, the violin represents the "depth of pain and the height of passion." You can figure this out from reading the following lines from the fifth stanza: "Sharp violins proclaim/Their jealous pangs and desperation..."

25. **The correct answer is (A).** The poet associates the passion of love with the organ. Again, this is shown directly in context: "The sacred organ's praise?/Notes inspiring holy love."

26. **The correct answer is (D).** Stanzas 3 through 6 represent the four passions that music can advance and subdue. They are as follows:
    Stanza 3: the excitement and fear of war
    Stanza 4: hopeless love
    Stanza 5: passionate love
    Stanza 6: holy love

27. **The correct answer is (E).** You can infer from the context that Orpheus (line 48) is an allusion to a poet and musician who could charm creatures through his music. This is shown in the following line: "Orpheus could lead the savage race." It's a good idea to review Greek and Roman myths to prepare for the AP exam, as many writers make allusions to these classic stories.

28. **The correct answer is (B).** The angel's mistake in confusing earth for heaven suggests that music has the power to transform reality. The earthly music is so glorious, the poet suggests, that the angel assumes that earth must be heaven.

29. **The correct answer is (C).** The poet thinks the organ is most heavenly. You can infer this from stanza 6.

30. **The correct answer is (A).** When the world ends on the Biblical Judgment Day, there will no longer be harmony. As a result, music "untune the sky" in the "last and dreadful hour." Choice (B) represents an exaggeration of the content. Choice (C) confuses cause and effect. There is no support for choice (D). Indeed, since the poem was written in the seventeenth century, this choice shows a serious misreading. Choice (E) makes no sense.

31. **The correct answer is (E).** None of the stanzas in this ode has a regular pattern of rhyme. Each stanza has a different rhyme scheme. As explained later, in this way the poet matches the form of each stanza to his theme.

32. **The correct answer is (C).** The diction in this poem is best described as *elevated and stately*. The poet uses eloquent language to convey his theme.

33. **The correct answer is (A).** The rhyme scheme in the first and last stanzas suggests the emergence of harmony out of chaos and the return of chaos. The irregular rhyme captures the chaos. Choices (B) and (C) are only part of the answer. Choice (D) cannot

be correct because of the chaos described in the beginning. Choice (E) reverses cause and effect. Music is not creating consistency; the universe creates it own harmony.

34. **The correct answer is (D).** "Terminus" is set near the end of the speaker's life. The poem is a calm, dignified, realistic statement of an old man accepting his age and fast-approaching death. The first line—"It is time to be old"— can be cited to support this. Lines 39–40—"The port, well worth the cruise, is near,/And every wave is charmed"—also illustrate this.

35. **The correct answer is (A).** In line 2, the metaphor "to take in sail" is best interpreted as the speaker tying up all his business matters to prepare for his death. When you "take in sail," you prepare to bring your vessel into harbor. In this case, harbor represents death, the end of life's voyage.

36. **The correct answer is (E).** The god of boundaries advises the speaker to make ready for the end of his life. This is shown in these lines: "...[He] Came to me in his fatal rounds,/And said: 'No more!/No farther shoot/Thy broad ambitious branches, and thy root./Fancy departs: no more invent;/Contract thy firmament/To compass of a tent....'" The word "fatal" suggests death; the phrase "No more!" shows that the speaker is to cease his earthly activities.

37. **The correct answer is (A).** In line 27, the poet uses *alliteration* to create musical effects and link related ideas. Recall that *alliteration* is the repetition of initial consonants in a line of poetry or prose. In line 27, the letter "s" is repeated in the words *sinew* and *stark*. Choice (B) is wrong because *assonance* is the repetition of vowel sounds preceded and followed by different consonant sounds, as in *tide* and *mine*. Choice (C) is wrong because a *paradox* is a seeming contradiction. Choice (D) is wrong because hyperbole is *exaggeration* for literary effect. Finally, choice (E) is wrong because *understatement* is saying less than is actually meant, generally in an ironic way.

38. **The correct answer is (B).** Throughout the poem, the imagery suggests that human life has natural, inescapable boundaries. You can infer this from the following lines: "Timely wise accept the terms,/Soften the fall with wary foot;/A little while/Still plan and smile..." The speaker's calm acceptance of his demise argues against choice (A). The same is true of choice (C). Choices (D) and (E) do not speak to the imagery's larger meaning in the context of the poem.

39. **The correct answer is (C).** The tone or mood of this poem is best characterized as *resigned*. The speaker accepts his fate, as shown in lines such as these from the final stanza: "As the bird trims her to the gale,/I trim myself to the storm of time,/I man the rudder, reef the sail,/Obey the voice at eve obeyed at prime:/'Lowly faithful, banish fear..." Choices (D) and (E) are too strong. The speaker accepts his fate but does not eagerly embrace it.

40. **The correct answer is (A).** The poem's tone reveals that the speaker accepts his fate, as explained in item 39. This is the direct opposite of choices (B), (C), and (D). Choice (E) is a misreading of the imagery in line 31 ("Amid the Muses, left thee deaf and dumb").

41. **The correct answer is (D).** The author uses *imagery* to unify the poem. The images of life as a voyage are introduced in lines 1 and 2 ("It is time to be old,/To take in sail:") and are summarized at the end of the poem ("I man the rudder, reef the sail,/...The port, well worth the cruise, is near,/And every wave is charmed"). Choice (A) is incorrect because *key words* are not repeated; rather, key *images* are. Choice (B) is wrong because there is no *personification*. Choice (C) is wrong because there is no *irony:* the images and ideas are straightforward. Finally, while some of the lines are memorable,

they are not *aphorisms* (brief, pithy statements that convey important truths or lessons), choice (E).

42. **The correct answer is (B).** In the final stanza, the poet uses an *extended metaphor* to convey his theme. The metaphor concerns the comparison between sailing and living. There is no *literary allusion,* choice (A), or reference to a famous person, place, or work of art. Choice (C) is wrong because the poem is not *ironic.* Likewise, choices (D) and (E) are off the mark because these literary elements are not present in the poem.

43. **The correct answer is (E).** The "port" in line 39 is a symbol of death. Therefore, choice (A), life, cannot be correct. While death is sad, the poet does not present it as *failure,* choice (B); *despair,* choice (C); or *gloom,* choice (D). These emotions are belied by his calm acceptance of the end of his life.

44. **The correct answer is (C).** In Roman mythology, Terminus is the guardian of boundaries. The author used "Terminus" as the title of this poem to suggest that our lives are bounded by forces outside of our control, and we must respect these barriers. Everyone must die; it is inescapable. This is the direct opposite of choice (A). The poem is concerned with life and death, so choices (B) and (D) have nothing to do with the writer's point. Choice (E) is a meaningless slogan.

45. **The correct answer is (B).** The writer chose the first-person point of view to give his writing an immediacy and increase reader identification. *Point of view* is the position from which a story is told. In the *first-person point of view,* the narrator is one of the characters in the story. As a result, the narrator explains the events through his or her own eyes, using the pronouns *I* and *me.* In the *third-person limited point of view,* the narrator tells the story through the eyes of only one character, using the pronouns *he, she,* and *they.* In the *omniscient point of view,* the narrator is not a character in the story. Instead, the narrator looks through the eyes of all the characters. As a result, the narrator is all-knowing. Only the first-person point of view gives writing an immediacy and helps readers identify with the narrator. Every other point of view creates a distance by showing multiple vantage points.

46. **The correct answer is (A).** The writer finding himself back at San Quentin as a film maker rather than as a prisoner is an example of irony. *Irony* occurs when something happens that is different from what was expected. In *verbal irony,* there is a contrast between what is stated and what is suggested. In *dramatic irony,* there is a contrast between what a character believes and what the audience knows is true. In *irony of situation,* an event reverses what the readers or characters expected. Since the narrator never expected to find himself back in a federal penitentiary, yet he is indeed back, he is describing the irony of situation.

47. **The correct answer is (C).** The writer uses *personification* and *alliteration* in this sentence: "While my mind told me I was free, my spirit snarled as if I were a prisoner again, and I couldn't shake the feeling." We see personification in use of "snarled" to describe "spirit." The writer is attributing human qualities ("snarled") to a non-living entity ("spirit"). *Alliteration,* the repetition of initial consonants in a series of words, is shown in the repeated "s" of "spirit snarled." There is no *hyperbole,* exaggeration for literary effect.

48. **The correct answer is (C).** The writer uses the passive voice to reinforce his feelings of disassociation in this sentence: "As I followed the guard, passing with the crew and actors from one compound to another, a hollow feeling of disbelief possessed me..." In addition to showing time, most verbs also indicate whether the subject is performing an action or having an action performed on it. This is called verb *voice.* English has two verb voices: the *active voice* and the *passive voice.*
In the *active voice,* the subject performs the action.
Example: Angela wrote the poem.

In the *passive voice*, the action is performed upon the subject.

Example: The poem was written by Angela.

The active voice is usually preferable to the passive because it is more vigorous and concise. For example, notice that there are six words in the second example but only four words in the first. However, the passive voice has very important uses. Use the passive voice to avoid placing blame or when you don't know who performed the action. Also use the passive voice as the writer does here, to suggest weakness, lack of control, or being dissociated with events.

49. **The correct answer is (A).** In the second paragraph, the primary effect of using long sentences with numerous prepositional phrases is to suggest the long journey the narrator has made from prisoner to a successful, law-abiding citizen. By drawing out his sentences, the writer suggests that he has come a long way in his life. Choice (B) is an effect of long sentences only when they are loaded with detail. In addition, that is not the writer's *primary* effect of using long sentences here. *A lead-in to his horror story* is reading too literally, so choice (C) is wrong. The sentence length has little to do with the tone, so you can eliminate choice (D). While long sentences can be soothing, that is not the author's primary purpose, so you can eliminate choice (E).

50. **The correct answer is (E).** The last paragraph describes a shift from the beautiful exterior of the prison to the terrifying cellblocks to suggest the sharp contrast between appearance and reality. The prison *appears* to be beautiful, but it houses a terrible secret: the ugliness of the crimes the prisoners have committed and the dreadful way the prisoners are maltreated. The lovely landscaping is juxtaposed to "the terrible indecency of the place." Choice (A) is wrong because it is only partly correct: the prisoners are not treated well, even in one of America's best prisons, but this doesn't show a contrast between appearance and reality. There is no proof for choice (B). The same is true for choices (C) and (D).

51. **The correct answer is (B).** The "monsters" and "demons" in the last paragraph are best interpreted as the prisoners and the suffering they endure. There is no suggestion that real beasts are kept under the prison, so you can eliminate choice (A). While some people may feel badly about prison conditions, we cannot conclude that people share a collective guilt about the dreadful conditions in San Quentin, so choice (C) is wrong. There's no proof that the prisoners are about to break out, choice (D), or that the narrator has not been a success as a film maker, choice (E). On the contrary, just the opposite appears to be true; he appears to be very successful, as evinced by his filming at San Quentin.

52. **The correct answer is (C).** The tone of this passage is best described as *grim*. Returning to San Quentin has a disquieting effect on the narrator. This builds to terror: "Emotionally, I could not convince myself that I was not going to be subjected once more to horrible indignities, that I would not have to live through it all again. Each morning when the guards checked my shoulder bag and clanked shut the iron door behind me, the old convict in me rose up full of hatred and rage for the guards, the walls, the terrible indecency of the place. I was still the same man who had entered there freely, a man full of love for his family and his life. But another self from the past reawakened, an imprisoned self, seething with the desire for vengeance on all things not imprisoned."

53. **The correct answer is (C).** The writer uses every literary device except *hyperbole,* exaggeration for a literary effect.

SECTION II: ESSAY QUESTIONS

QUESTION 1

This question requires you to analyze a full-length literary work to show how it embodies the characteristics of a romance. For example, does the literary work contain elements that do not strictly adhere to reality?

To earn a high score on this question,

- select a recognized work of literature that does indeed contain elements of romance. Possibilities include *The Blithedale Romance, The Scarlet Letter*, and Cooper's *Leatherstocking* series, for instance. Stephen King's horror novels would also fit, as would Henry James' *The Turn of the Screw*.

- isolate specific elements of romance.

- tie these elements to Hawthorne's analysis in the excerpt from his essay, using specific examples and details drawn from the book.

The following model response would earn a top score because it fulfills the requirements of this question and the standards of good writing:

1. Introduction establishes writer's knowledge of subject.

1   On the surface, a novel and a romance seem to be the same. After all, they are both long works of fiction. Their elements—plot, characterizations, setting, and theme—are developed in detail. Novels and romances usually have one main plot and several less important subplots. However, novels and romances are not as similar as they appear. A romance, unlike a novel, is characterized by removal from reality and a certain use of the mysterious. Very often there will be a handsome hero on a shining white horse, a dastardly villain, or fair maiden in need of assistance. As a result, there may also be daring rescues and hair-breadth escapes, as well as various mysterious happenings. Nathaniel Hawthorne, one of the architects of the romance, delineated its characteristics in his famous *Preface to The House of the Seven Gables* (1851). In his essay, Hawthorne highlights

2. Specific elements to be discussed.

2   how romances, in contrast to novels, are not bound to strict realism and often have a mysterious mood. We can see this very clearly in Hawthorne's romance, *The Scarlet Letter*.

3. First topic: romances deviate from boundaries of realism.

In *The Scarlet Letter*, readers clearly see the "A" on Hester's chest and the miniature version on Pearl's chest, but is there or is

3   there not an "A" on the Reverend Dimmesdale's chest? The mystery of the "A" on the Reverend's chest is an element of a romance rather than a novel. Early on, the evil Chillingworth (Hester's husband) dances with glee when he believes he has discovered an "A" on the minister's chest. No one else sees the Reverend's chest until the end of the novel, when Dimmesdale

4. Details from the book linked to the thesis.

4   rips apart his vestment before the entire community to reveal something—but what is it? Some say they see the very semblance of an "A," identical to that displayed on the chest of his lover, Hester Prynne, all these years. Others swear that his breast is as clean as that of a newborn baby's. Is there a real A? If so, did the Reverend brand it on or has it sprung from his guilt? The matter of the A on Dimmesdale's chest is clearly not bound by realism

but rather shows "truth under the circumstances...of the writer's own choosing or creation."

The mood of *The Scarlet Letter* also reveals it to be a romance rather than a novel. In his famous *Preface to The House of the Seven Gables,* Hawthorne allowed writers of romances "a certain latitude" to interpret experience "to mingle the Marvellous

5 rather as a slight, delicate, and evanescent flavor." We see this eerie mood in the giant "A" that lights up the night sky. The spooky mood is also created by the characters' odd behavior. As he gets more and more obsessed with ferreting out the truth about Hester's lover Dimmesdale, Chillingworth's eyes glow an evil red. The product of Hester and Dimmesdale's illicit love, Pearl, is

6 a strange elfin child. Her eyes have a "freakish, evil cast" and she acts as though possessed by an "evil spirit."

Hawthorne took full advantage of the license he afforded writers of romance as he crafted *The Scarlet Letter*. The "A" appears and

7 disappears in mysterious forms, adding to the supernatural mood. The strange glow in Dimmesdale's eyes and the odd look in Pearl's eyes also contribute to the mingling of the marvelous and

8 the mysterious that distinguishes the novel from the romance.

5. Second topic: eerie mood of romances.

6. Details from the book linked to the thesis.

7. Main points summarized.

8. Thesis reiterated.

QUESTION 2

This is a typical AP question: analyze a poem to reveal how the poet creates meaning. With these questions, you are expected to use the literary techniques as tools to prove your thesis. Try these suggestions as you answer these types of literary analysis questions:

- Start by reading the poem several times through. Each time you read, look for different literary elements, such as word play or symbols. As you read, see how all the literary elements fit together to help the writer express his or her insight about life.

- Use the clear clues the poet gives you. For example, if a poem is called "Sonnet 75," assume that it follows the set format for a sonnet. It will have 14 lines and a specific rhyme scheme (the exact form depending on whether it is an Italian on Elizabethan sonnet). As you have already learned (but it bears repeating), these questions are not designed to trip you up; rather, they are crafted to test what you have learned about literary analysis in class and on your own.

- Unless you're desperately stuck for an opening gambit, don't rephrase the question in your topic sentence. Remember that the scorers are reading hundreds of essays on the same topic, so they're not likely to be impressed if the opening to your essay is just like the opening of the question in the previous fifty essays they have read. Instead, get right to your point by stating your thesis.

- Follow with specific examples drawn from the poem. Carefully relate each point to your main idea.

- Interweave all the elements together into a meaningful whole. You may treat metaphor, irony, and allusions in each paragraph, for example, examining different examples of each literary element to make your point. In general, don't separate the literary elements out, one in each paragraph, as this usually results in a choppy and redundant essay.

- Sum up by briefly reiterating your point. Don't introduce any new information in the conclusion, but reach for an insight or point that ties everything together in an intelligent and logical way.

- Be sure to proofread your essay for errors in grammar, usage, punctuation, capitalization, and spelling. You won't get clobbered for a few minor errors, but why not improve your chances of earning a top score by being letter-perfect?

The following model response would earn a top score because it fulfills the requirements of this question and the standards of good writing:

1 In Sonnet 75, Edmund Spenser shows that he views poetry as a means of achieving immortality. Form matches function as this sonnet becomes a poetic tribute that keeps the memory of a loved one alive forever. The poem shows a sharp contrast between the

2 impermanence of a name written in the sand and the immortality conferred on a loved one by recording her virtues in verse.

3 The word play of "vain" in line 5 reinforces Spenser's belief that eternal life can best be achieved through art. "Vain" means *proud of one's ability* as well as *without success*. We are so vain that we want—and expect!—to be remembered forever, yet our efforts will be in vain through conventional means such as writing our names in the sand. The waves will quickly erase our efforts, as we see in lines 2-4.

4 The sand on the beach can be read as a symbol of the sands of time, a traditional symbol for enduring fame. The poet suggests in these lines that writing in the "sands of time" will endure only if we write it as a poem. His lover "shall live by fame," notes the speaker in line 10, because his "verse your virtues rare shall eternize,/And in the heavens write your glorious name." His beautiful poem will shout her name throughout the world, reaching to heaven. And even when the entire world perishes (line 13), "Our love shall live, and later life renew."

5 The imagery reinforces the poet's belief in the achievement of immortality through poetry. The "dust" that we become when we die (line 10) is contrasted to the glory of the "heavens" (line 12). The dust symbolizes being forgotten; the heavens, being remembered through the ages. The images become more memorable through alliteration—"die in dust," "verse your virtues," and "love shall live, and later life."

6 Life is short, but art is long. Edmund Spenser suggests that if we want to be remembered past our allotted years, we consider creating art —or having someone else do it for us!

1. The thesis is directly stated.

2. The writer clearly gets the main point.

3. First literary element tied to theme.

4. Second literary element tied to theme.

5. Third literary element tied to theme.

6. Conclusion sums up main points.

QUESTION 3

This is the third type of essay question that you will encounter on the AP test: the free-choice opened-ended response.

Consider these guidelines as you answer this particular essay question:

- Be sure to define *conflict* correctly. Recall that *conflict* in literature is a struggle or fight. Conflict makes a story interesting because readers want to find out the outcome.

- Recall that there are two kinds of conflict. In an *external conflict*, characters struggle against a force outside themselves. In an *internal conflict*, characters battle a force within themselves. Novels and full-length plays often contain both external and internal conflicts.

The following model response would earn a top score because it fulfills the requirements of this question and the standards of good writing:

1. Introduction describes conflict to rephrase and answer the question.

2. Shows how character deals with conflict.

3. Traces character's solo actions.

4. Shows outcome.

5. Ties up all main ideas.

1   Together we stand; divided we fall? Perhaps, but not in all situations. Certain problems can best be solved one person at a time rather than through groupthink. By reaching out to the right person, you can successfully change the enemy's mind. You might even be able to make the enemy the one who rescues society. This is what Faber succeeds in doing in Ray Bradbury's novel *Fahrenheit 451*.

2   Faber is an old professor who lives hidden in fear from society. He has lost his teaching job after society banned books and firemen started to burn them. Faber tries to remedy the situation by reaching out to Montag, a fireman, whom he meets in a park. Faber gives Montag his telephone number, which gives the fireman the choice whether or not to contact him.

3   Montag does indeed call Faber. After the call, Faber really begins to challenge the system that would encourage book burning. Faber gives Montag a small earpiece that he designed that allows the two of them to communicate secretly. Faber begins an underground rebellion through this action. He reads Montag to sleep through the earpiece and allows him to read books, an illegal act. Faber is the fireman's guide, although the old professor remains in hiding.

4   Faber is somewhat successful in his attempt to fight the law banning books. He is the catalyst that assists Montag in his defiance. At the conclusion of the novel, Faber's whereabouts are unknown. Montag survives the destruction of the city and heads back to teach the citizens the benefits of reading. He does this with people who are very much like Faber. He has met these people in the woods. Faber prepares Montag for his journey to help redeem society.

5   Faber trains Montag to be a leader. This helps preserve culture and humanity. It also demonstrates that one person can make a difference. We can attempt to solve some of society's problems in groups, or individually. Only the person and the situation can determine whether we fly in a flock or solo.

PRACTICE TEST 2: ENGLISH LITERATURE AND COMPOSITION

SECTION I: MULTIPLE-CHOICE QUESTIONS

Time— 1 hour

Directions: This section contains selections from two passages of prose and two poems with questions on their content, style, form, and purpose. Read each selection closely and carefully. Then choose the best answer from the five choices.

Questions 1–13. Read the following selection carefully before you mark your answers.

To S. M., a Young African Painter on Seeing His Works

1   To show the lab'ring bosom's deep intent,
    And thought in living characters to paint,
    When first thy pencil did those beauties give,
    And breathing figures learnt from thee to live,

5   How did those prospects give my soul delight,
    A new creation rushing on my sight!
    Still, wondrous youth! each noble path pursue;
    On deathless glories fix thine ardent view:
    Still may the painter's and the poet's fire,

10 To aid thy pencil and thy verse conspire!
    And may the charms of each seraphic theme
    Conduct thy footsteps to immortal fame!
    High to the blissful wonders of the skies.
    Elate thy soul, and raise thy wishful eyes.

15 Thrice happy, when exalted to survey.
    That splendid city, crowned with endless day,
    Whose twice six gates on radiant hinges ring:
    Celestial Salem blooms in endless spring.
    Calm and serene thy moments glide along,

20 And may the muse inspire each future song!
    Still, with the sweets of contemplation blessed,
    May peace with balmy wings your soul invest!
    But when these shades of time are chased away,
    And darkness ends in everlasting day,

25 On what seraphic pinions shall we move,
    And view the landscapes in the realms above!
    There shall thy tongue in heavenly murmurs flow,
    And there my muse with heavenly transport glow;
    No more to tell of Damon's tender sighs,

30 Or rising radiance of Aurora's eyes;
    For nobler themes demand a nobler strain,
    And purer language on the ethereal plain.
    Cease, gentle Muse! the solemn gloom of night
    Now seals the fair creation from my sight.

1. What has S. M. done to win the poet's admiration?

   (A) Made people come alive on canvas and revealed the human soul in art
   (B) Become both a poet and a painter
   (C) Built a radiant city with twelve gates
   (D) Died after a glorious career as a painter, poet, builder—a man of the world
   (E) Become a noble Greek warrior as well as a painter

2. "Seraphic" in line 11 most nearly means

   (A) a long, flowing robe; hence, a long, involved theme.
   (B) a singer of melodious songs.
   (C) foreign, mysterious.
   (D) angelic.
   (E) colorful, vivid.

3. What hopes does the poet have for S. M.'s future?

   (A) That he will always burn with creative energy
   (B) That his work will not attain immortality because it will adversely affect his art
   (C) That his soul will shine from heaven
   (D) That he will find inspiration in Salem
   (E) That he will serve as the poet's personal Muse

4. What do "shades of time" symbolize in line 23?

   (A) Temporal, insubstantial life in heaven
   (B) Temporal, insubstantial life on earth
   (C) Temporal, insubstantial life devoid of art
   (D) The specific cares and woes of all painters, permanent and universal
   (E) The dull, dark days common to even the most talented

5. What may "darkness" symbolize in line 24?

   (A) The suffering the Roman slaves experienced each day
   (B) The blindness of the poet Homer
   (C) Death
   (D) The suffering the black slaves experienced daily
   (E) The suffering of a person who never received adequate recognition for his or her work

6. What does the poet envision for both herself and the painter?

   (A) A life of promise and hope
   (B) A life of creativity and perpetual bloom
   (C) A realm of noble companions
   (D) A better command of the resources of the temporal world
   (E) Nothing better than what they now have

7. The poet's style is marked by

   (A) metaphysical conceits.
   (B) ironic commentary.
   (C) inverted phrases.
   (D) an unusual rhyme scheme.
   (E) onomatopoeia.

8. According to the poem, what will happen to the poet and the painter in the afterlife?

   (A) They will be three times happier.
   (B) They will finally be able to move to Salem.
   (C). All people will be able to be artists.
   (D) All people will again be young and vigorous.
   (E) Their art will change.

9. What does "everlasting day" symbolize in line 24?

   (A) Heaven
   (B) Salem
   (C) Greece during the Golden Age
   (D) Africa
   (E) Eternal damnation

10. The metaphors in lines 29 and 30 are derived from

   (A) romance.
   (B) religion.
   (C) art.
   (D) mythology.
   (E) music.

11. The rhyme scheme of this poem is

   (A) abcd abcd efgh efgh.
   (B) aaab bbbc ddde.
   (C) abba cddc effg.
   (D) aa bb cc dd.
   (E) abc abc def def.

12. Which term best describes the tone of this poem?

   (A) Resigned
   (B) Formal, lofty
   (C) Angry
   (D) Despairing
   (E) Informal, relaxed

13. The theme of this poem can most precisely be stated as follows:

   (A) Artists will finally be appreciated only when they are dead.
   (B) Slaves will be released from bondage and enjoy endless creativity when they enter heaven.
   (C) Heaven is for the talented; there they can flourish and grow.
   (D) Art is the highest human attainment.
   (E) Poetry is a greater art than painting.

Questions 14–28. Read the following selection carefully before you mark your answers.

1   Petey hadn't really believed that Dad would be doing it—sending Granddad away. "Away" was what they were calling it. Not until now could he believe it of Dad.

2   But here was the blanket that Dad had that day bought for him, and in the morning he'd be going away. And this was the last evening they'd be having together. Dad was off seeing that girl he was to marry. He'd not be back till late, and they could sit up and talk.

3   It was a fine September night, with a silver moon riding high over the gully. When they'd washed up the supper dishes they went out on the shanty porch, the old man and the bit of a boy, taking their chairs. "I'll get me fiddle," said the old man, "and play ye some of the old tunes." But instead of the fiddle he brought out the blanket. It was a big, double blanket, red, with black cross stripes.

4   "Now, isn't that a fine blanket!" said the old man, smoothing it over his knees. "And isn't your father a kind man to be giving the old fellow a blanket like that to go away with? It cost something, it did—look at the wool of it! And warm it will be these cold winter nights to come. There'll be few blankets there the equal to this one!"

5   It was like Granddad to be saying that. He was trying to make it easier. He'd pretended all along it was he that was wanting to go away to the great brick building—the government place, where he'd be with so many other old fellows having the best of everything . But Petey hadn't believed Dad would really do it, until this night when he brought home the blanket.

6   "Oh, yes it's a fine blanket," said Petey, and got up and went into the shanty. He wasn't the kind to cry, and, besides, he was too old for that, being eleven. He'd just come in to fetch Granddad's fiddle.

7   The blanket slid to the floor as the old man took the fiddle and stood up. It was the last night they'd be having together. There wasn't any need to say, "Play all the old tunes." Granddad tuned up for a minute, and then said, "This one you'll like to remember."

8   The silver moon was high overhead, and there was a gentle breeze playing down the gully. He'd never be hearing Granddad play like this again. It was as well Dad was moving into that new house, away from here. He'd not want, Petey wouldn't, to sit here on the old porch of fine evenings, with Granddad gone.

9   The tune changed. "Here's something gayer." Petey sat and stared out over the gully. Dad would marry that girl. Yes, that girl who'd kissed him and slobbered over him, saying she'd try to be a good mother to him, and all . His chair creaked as he involuntarily gave his body a painful twist.

10   The tune stopped suddenly, and Granddad said: "It's a poor tune, except to be dancing to." And then: "It's a fine girl your father's going to marry. He'll be feeling young again, with a pretty wife like that. And what would an old fellow like me be doing around their house, getting in the way, an old nuisance, what with my talk of aches and pains! And then there'll be babies coming, and I'd not want to be there to hear them crying at all hours. It's best that I take myself off, like I'm doing. One more tune or two, and then we'll be going to bed to get some sleep against the morning, when I'll pack up my fine blanket and take my leave. Listen to this, will you? It's a bit sad, but a fine tune for a night like this."

11   They didn't hear the two people coming down the gully path, Dad and the pretty girl with the hard, bright face like a china doll's. But they heard her laugh, right by

the porch, and the tune stopped on a wrong, high, startled note. Dad didn't say anything, but the girl came forward and spoke to Granddad prettily: "I'll not be seeing you leave in the morning, so I came over to say good-by."

12   "It's kind of you," said Granddad, with his eyes cast down; and then, seeing the blanket at his feet, he stopped to pick it up. "And will you look at this," he said in embarrassment, "the fine blanket my son has given me to go away with!"

13   "Yes," she said, "it's a fine blanket." She felt of the wool, and repeated in surprise, "A fine blanket—I'll say it is!" She turned to Dad, and said to him coldly, "It cost something, that."

14   He cleared his throat, and said defensively, "I wanted him to have the best."

15   The girl stood there, still intent on the blanket. "It's double, too," she said reproachfully to Dad.

16   "Yes," said Granddad, "it's double—a fine blanket for an old fellow to be going away with."

17   The boy went abruptly into the shanty. He was looking for something. He could hear that girl reproaching Dad, and Dad becoming angry in his slow way. And now she was suddenly going away in a huff. As Petey came out, she turned and called back, "All the same, he doesn't need a double blanket! "And she ran up the gully path.

18   "Oh, she's right," said the boy coldly. "Here, Dad"—and he held out a pair of scissors. "Cut the blanket in two." Both of them stared at the boy, startled. "Cut it in two, I tell you, Dad!" he cried out. "And keep the other half!"

19   "That's not a bad idea," said Granddad gently. "I don't need so much of a blanket."

20   "Yes," said the boy harshly, "a single blanket's enough for an old man when he's sent away. We'll save the other half, Dad; it will come in handy later. I'll give it to you, Dad—when you're old and I'm sending you—away."

21   There was a silence, and then Dad went over to Granddad and stood before him, not speaking. But Granddad understood, for he put out a hand and laid it on Dad's shoulder. Petey was watching them. And he heard Granddad whisper, "It's all right, son—I knew you didn't mean it." And then Petey cried.

22   But it didn't matter—because they were all three crying together.

14. The word "shanty" in paragraph 3 suggests

   (A)   a broad, expansive country estate.
   (B)   a well-to-do family.
   (C)   a historic old home.
   (D)   a family living a lower-middle-class existence.
   (E)   abject poverty.

15. What is the tone of paragraphs 7 to 9?

   (A)   Revulsion
   (B)   Quiet happiness
   (C)   Peaceful contentment
   (D)   Bitter resentment
   (E)   Sadness and pain

16. The girl is described as a "china doll"

    (A) to show how down-to-earth she is.
    (B) to show how pretty she is.
    (C) to indicate her concern for Granddad, however muted it may appear on the surface.
    (D) to indicate what a poor wife she would be.
    (E) to indicate what a suitable wife she would be.

17. The term "china doll" was selected to describe the girl because

    (A) she is very pretty and uses cosmetics to the best advantage.
    (B) her "hard, bright face" reveals her true nature.
    (C) it explains why Petey and Granddad admire her.
    (D) she has very fine manners, revealed when she says goodbye to Granddad.
    (E) she is like a fragile doll.

18. How is Granddad's tone in paragraph 10 different from Petey's tone in paragraphs 19–24?

    (A) Brave resignation to bitter sarcasm
    (B) Clever subterfuge to childlike solemnity
    (C) Disguised sarcasm to cold fear
    (D) Melancholy gaiety to bewildered confusion
    (E) Open bitterness to bitter sarcasm

19. The "scissors" best represent

    (A) severing the bonds of love, duty, and respect.
    (B) severing the bonds of unpleasant duty.
    (C) cutting loose from that which is holding you back.
    (D) cutting dead weight.
    (E) assuming new freedoms and human possibility.

20. Granddad's attitude can best be described as

    (A) considerate and understanding.
    (B) carefully controlled resentment toward his son's fiance.
    (C) anxious and worried.
    (D) bitter but resigned to the treatment he is receiving.
    (E) understandably very upset.

21. What is the predominant symbol in this tale?

    (A) The fiddle
    (B) The blanket
    (C) The china doll
    (D) The moon
    (E) The scissors

22. What does that main symbol represent?

    (A) The problems of the aged in America
    (B) The enormous rise in divorce and remarriage with all its problems
    (C) The father's attempt to assuage his guilt
    (D) The difficulty of life in rural America
    (E) The importance of cutting bonds and knowing when to let go

23. As used in the story, the "blanket" connotes

    (A) warmth.
    (B) suffocation.
    (C) love.
    (D) marriage.
    (E) old age.

24. What is the author saying about old age and the difference between generations?

    (A) There really is an enormous difference among the three generations.
    (B) Old age is a golden time.
    (C) It is better to be young than old.
    (D) There is no real "generation gap": we will all be old someday.
    (E) The old are very poorly treated as a general rule.

25. What is the theme of this story?

    (A) Life was rough for this family, and however unpleasant it may be, it was necessary to hold on to good items like blankets.
    (B) The old man got exactly what was his due.
    (C) Unintentionally, we all do cruel and unpleasant things.
    (D) It can be very difficult having old people around, especially if there is a remarriage in the family.
    (E) Things have changed greatly over the past fifty years.

26. What is the overall tone of this story?

    (A) Melancholic
    (B) Cheerful
    (C) Uplifting
    (D) Sardonic
    (E) Sarcastic

27. The point of view in this story is most closely described as

    (A) first-person observer.
    (B) first-person participant.
    (C) omniscient.
    (D) editorial omniscient.
    (E) limited omniscient.

28. The best title for this story would be

    (A) "The Scissors."
    (B) "Old Age in the Country."
    (C) "Stepfamilies."
    (D) "Three Generations."
    (E) "The Blanket."

Questions 29–43. Read the following selection carefully before you mark your answers.

1   I saw him once before,
    As he passed by the door,
    And again
    The pavement stones resound,
5   As he totters o'er the ground
    With his cane.

    They say that in his prime,
    Ere the pruning-knife of Time
    Cut him down,
10 Not a better man was found
    By the Crier on his round
    Through the town.

    But now he walks the streets,
    And he looks at all he meets
15 Sad and wan,
    And he shakes his feeble head,
    That it seems as if he said,
    "They are gone."

    The mossy marbles rest
20 On the lips that he has pressed
    In their bloom,
    And the names he loved to hear
    Have been carved for many a year
    On the tomb.

25 My grandmamma has said—
    Poor old lady, she is dead
    Long ago—
    That he had a Roman nose,
    And his cheek was like a rose
30 In the snow.

    But now his nose is thin,
    And it rests upon his chin
    Like a staff,
    And a crook is in his back,
35 And a melancholy crack
    In his laugh.

    I know it is a sin
    For me to sit and grin
    At him here;
40 But the old three-cornered hat,
    And the breeches, and all that,
    Are so queer!

    And if I should live to be
    The last leaf upon the tree
45 In the spring,
    Let them smile, as I do now,
    At the old forsaken bough
    Where I cling.

29. The speaker in this poem is discussing

    (A)   a generation of old soldiers.
    (B)   his own condition.
    (C)   an old man who lives in town.
    (D)   his revered grandfather.
    (E)   a hero long dead.

30. In Line 11, the "Crier" is best interpreted as

    (A)   a newspaper.
    (B)   the local gossip.
    (C)   a snoop.
    (D)   the town courier.
    (E)   his grandmother.

31. From its context, you can deduce that "wan" (line 15) must mean

    (A)   pale and haggard.
    (B)   irate.
    (C)   degraded.
    (D)   misunderstood.
    (E)   needy.

32. You can infer that a "Roman nose" (line 28) must be

    (A) a small nose.
    (B) considered a handsome feature.
    (C) considered an unattractive characteristic.
    (D) considered very old-fashioned.
    (E) very florid.

33. What figure of speech does the poet use in lines 32–33?

    (A) Personification
    (B) Alliteration
    (C) Hyperbole
    (D) Simile
    (E) Understatement

34. The speaker in this poem

    (A) envies the respect the old man is accorded.
    (B) admires the old man's distinguished appearance.
    (C) realizes that the old man is a genuine hero.
    (D) mocks the old man for living beyond his time.
    (E) is horrified at the old man's injuries.

35. Who is the speaker in the poem?

    (A) A young man
    (B) An old woman
    (C) An old man
    (D) A great war hero
    (E) The poet

36. Throughout the poem, the imagery suggests

    (A) the inevitable strife between generations.
    (B) the lack of respect given to heroes.
    (C) the swift passage of time.
    (D) the difficulty of dealing with change.
    (E) sin and guilt.

37. The tone of this poem is best characterized as

    (A) grim.
    (B) bleak and dour.
    (C) serious.
    (D) intense.
    (E) light, even mocking.

38. The imagery in lines 40–41 suggests that the poem is set

    (A) in the mid-seventeenth century in America.
    (B) about fifty years after the Revolutionary War, in America.
    (C) in the present, in England.
    (D) during the Civil War, in America.
    (E) in the future.

39. What does the "bough" in the last stanza symbolize?

    (A) Death
    (B) Stories of the past
    (C) Our fragile reputation
    (D) Our hold on life
    (E) A cradle

40. Which of the following literary devices does the poet use to unify the poem?
    I. Rhyme
    II. Imagery
    III. Irony

    (A) I and II
    (B) I
    (C) II
    (D) I and III
    (E) III

41. By symbolizing the old man as the last leaf, the poet suggests that

    (A) life is brief and difficult to sustain.
    (B) we all get swept up in the eddies of time.
    (C) the old man is the last of his kind.
    (D) people are part of the natural order.
    (E) we can grow and change, even in the last years of our lives.

42. The best title for this poem would be

    (A) "Beware of What You Wish For."
    (B) "The Last Leaf."
    (C) "Nothing Lasts."
    (D) "The Forsaken Bough."
    (E) "The Terror of Old Age."

Questions 43–51. Read the following selection carefully before you mark your answers.

Eventually the whole business of purveying to the hospitals was, in effect, carried out by Miss Nightingale. She, alone, it seemed, whatever the contingency, knew where to lay her hands on what was wanted; she alone possessed the art of circumventing the pernicious influences of official etiquette. On one occasion 27,000 shirts arrived, sent out at her insistence by the Home Government, and were only waiting to be unpacked. But the official "Purveyor" intervened; "He could only unpack them" he said, "with an official order from the Government." Miss Nightingale pleaded in vain; the sick and the wounded lay half-naked, shivering for want of clothing; and three weeks elapsed before the Government released the shipment. A little later, on a similar occasion, Miss Nightingale ordered a Government consignment to be forcibly opened, while the "Purveyor" stood by, wringing his hands in departmental agony.

43. The use of a phrase like "she alone" gives the reader an idea of Miss Nightingale's

    (A) loneliness.
    (B) conceit.
    (C) femininity.
    (D) uniqueness.
    (E) inefficiency.

44. Describing the influence of official etiquette as "pernicious" reveals the author's awareness of the

    (A) dangers of red tape.
    (B) efficiency of command procedure.
    (C) lack of blood plasma.
    (D) women's liberation movement.
    (E) horrors of war.

45. The description of the sick and wounded as "half-naked" and "shivering" serves as

    (A) an introduction of physical detail.
    (B) weather information.
    (C) historic documentation.
    (D) a contrast to bureaucratic lack of concern.
    (E) a metaphor.

46. What does "vain" mean as used in this context: "Miss Nightingale pleaded in vain"?

    (A) With her ego held in check
    (B) In a conceited manner
    (C) In an arrogant way
    (D) Without help from anyone else
    (E) Without any success

47. The Purveyor seems concerned only with

    (A) humanity.
    (B) the ill men.
    (C) the men's needs.
    (D) departmental procedure.
    (E) Miss Nightingale's requests.

48. The tone of the phrase "departmental agony" is

    (A) ironic.
    (B) despairing.
    (C) serious.
    (D) tragic.
    (E) funny.

49. The main effect of using long sentences with multiple clauses is to

    (A) establish Miss Nightingale's determination and intelligence.
    (B) create a precise narrative setting.
    (C) suggest Miss Nightingale's long, difficult efforts to procure the supplies.
    (D) trace multiple causes and effects.
    (E) demonstrate the foolishness of officious bureaucrats.

50. In this selection, the author's tone is best communicated by his

    (A) metaphors.
    (B) similes.
    (C) onomatopoeia.
    (D) word choice.
    (E) general figurative language.

51. The author's tone reveals that his attitude toward Miss Nightingale is one of

    (A) amazement and chagrin.
    (B) admiration and respect.
    (C) prejudice and apathy.
    (D) frustration and fright.
    (E) dislike bordering on active hatred.

Question 1
Suggested Time: 40 minutes

Directions: Carefully read the following poem by Stephen Crane. Then write a well-organized essay in which you discuss how the poem's tone reveals the author's view of a Supreme Deity. You may wish to consider some or all of the following literary devices: similes, imagery, metaphors, diction, tone, symbolism, and personification.

A Man Adrift on a Slim Spar

1   A man adrift on a slim spar
     A horizon smaller than the rim of a bottle
     Tented waves rearing lashy dark points
     The near whine of froth in circles.

5   God is cold.
     The incessant raise and swing of the sea
     And growl after growl of crest
     The sinkings, green, seething, endless
     The upheaval half-completed.

10 God is cold.
     The seas are in the hollow of The Hand;
     Oceans may be turned to a spray
     Raining down through the stars
     Because of a gesture of pity toward a babe.

15 Oceans may become gray ashes,
     Die with a long moan and a roar
     Amid the tumult of the fishes
     And the cries of the ships.
     Because The Hand beckons the mice.

20 A horizon smaller than a doomed assassin's cap,
     Inky, surging tumults
     A reeling, drunken sky and no sky
     A pale hand sliding from a polished spar.
     God is cold.

25 The puff of a coat imprisoning air:
     A face kissing the water-death
     A weary slow sway of a lost hand
     And the sea, the moving sea, the sea.
     God is cold.
          —Stephen Crane

Question 2
Suggested Time: 40 minutes

Directions: As expressed in the essay that follows, what is the cost of our reliance on and interest in amassing property? Examine the premise of "Reliance on Property" and write an essay in which you show that the author's thesis does or does not hold true today.

Reliance on Property

And so the reliance on property, including the reliance on governments which protect it, is the want of self-reliance. Men have looked away from themselves and at things so long that they have come to esteem the religious, learned and civil institutions as guards of property, and they deprecate assaults on these, because they feel them to be assaults on property. They measure their esteem of each other by what each has, and not by what each is. But a cultivated man becomes ashamed of his property, out of new respect for his nature. Especially he hates what he has if he sees that it is accidental,—came to him by inheritance, or gift, or crime; then he feels that it is not having; it does not belong to him, has no root in him and merely lies there because no revolution or no robber takes it away. But that which a man is, does always by necessity acquire; and what the man acquires, is living property, which does not wait the beck of rulers, or mobs, or revolutions, or fire, or storm, or bankruptcies, but perpetually renews itself wherever the man breathes. "Thy lot or portion of life," said the Caliph Ali, "is seeking after thee; therefore be at rest from seeking after it." Our dependence on these foreign goods leads us to our slavish respect for numbers. The political parties meet in numerous conventions; the greater the concourse and with each new uproar of announcement, The delegation from Essex! The Democrats from New Hampshire! The Whigs of Maine! The young patriot feels himself stronger than before by a new thousand of eyes and arms. In like manner the reformers summon conventions and vote and resolve in multitude. Not so, O friends! Will the God deign to enter and inhabit you, but by a method precisely the reverse. It is only as a man puts off all foreign support and stands alone that I see him to be strong and to prevail. He is weaker by every recruit to his banner. Is not a man better than a town? He who knows that power is inborn, that he is weak because he has looked for good out of him and elsewhere, and, so perceiving, throws himself unhesitatingly on his thought, instantly fights himself, stands in the erect position, commands his limbs, works miracles; just as a man who stands on his feet is stronger than a man who stands on his head.

—Ralph Waldo Emerson

Question 3
Suggested Time: 40 minutes

Using any novel from the list below or any other novel of comparable quality, show how the main character is unwilling or unable to accept help from members of his community or family and is thus isolated and alone. Consider at least two elements of fiction such as theme, symbol, setting, characterization, or any other aspect of the writer's craft in your discussion.

Hamlet	*The Fixer*
Madame Bovary	*Ethan Frome*
Death of a Salesman	*Moby Dick*
Lord Jim	*Catch-22*
The Turn of the Screw	*Gulliver's Travels*
Native Son	*Invisible Man*
The Sun Also Rises	*The Color Purple*
Cry, the Beloved Country	*Julius Caesar*
Othello	*Romeo and Juliet*
Jane Eyre	*Our Town*
Pride and Prejudice	*The Sound and the Fury*

QUICK-SCORE ANSWERS

1.	A	18.	A	35.	A
2.	D	19.	A	36.	C
3.	A	20.	A	37.	E
4.	B	21.	B	38.	B
5.	D	22.	C	39.	D
6.	B	23.	C	40.	A
7.	C	24.	D	41.	C
8.	E	25.	C	42.	B
9.	A	26.	A	43.	D
10.	D	27.	C	44.	A
11.	D	28.	E	45.	D
12.	B	29.	C	46.	E
13.	B	30.	D	47	D
14.	E	31.	A	48.	A
15.	E	32.	B	49.	C
16.	B	33.	D	50.	D
17.	B	34.	D	51.	B

COMPUTING YOUR SCORE

You can use the following worksheet to compute an approximate score on the practice test. Since it is difficult to be objective about your own writing and since you are not a trained ETS scorer or English teacher, you may wish to ask a friend who has already taken the test (and earned a high score of 4 or 5) to score your three essays.

Recognize that your score can only be an approximation (at best), as you are scoring yourself against yourself. In the actual AP English Literature and Composition Exam, you will be scored against every other student who takes the test as well.

Section I: Multiple-Choice Questions

	_____	number of correct answers
−	_____	.25 × number of wrong answers
=	_____	raw score
	_____	raw score
×	_____	1.25
=	_____	scaled score (out of a possible 67.5)

Section II: Essays

_____	essay 1 (0–9)
_____	essay 2 (0–9)
_____	essay 3 (0–9)
× _____	3.055
= _____	scaled score (out of a possible 82.5)

Scaled Score

_____	multiple-choice scaled score
+ _____	essay scaled score
= _____	final scaled score (out of a possible 150)

AP Score Conversion Chart

Scaled Score	Likely AP Score
150–100	5
99–86	4
85–67	3
66–0	1 or 2

ANSWERS AND EXPLANATIONS

SECTION I: MULTIPLE-CHOICE QUESTIONS

1. **The correct answer is (A).** To win the poet's admiration, S.M. has made people come alive on canvas and revealed the human soul in art. The first two lines of the poem explain the basis for the poet's admiration of S.M. He can "show the lab'ring bosom's deep intent" (line 1), which is closest in meaning to *reveal the human soul in art*. S.M. is also able to paint "living characters" (line 2) and to "make people come alive on canvas." Choice (B) is incorrect, for the author is not saying that S.M. is both a poet and painter; rather, she refers to him as a painter and to herself as the poet, as "wondrous youth" who pursue different "noble" paths. Choice (C) is also wrong, because S.M. has not built heaven. Choice (D) is incorrect because S.M. was very much alive when the poem was written. Choice (E) is incorrect, because S.M. is a young African painter, as the title indicates. He is not a Greek warrior.

2. **The correct answer is (D).** "Seraphic" in line 11 most nearly means *angelic*. This relates the poem's discussion of heaven. The word "immortal" in line 12 ("Conduct thy footsteps to immortal fame!") is a context clue.

3. **The correct answer is (A).** The poet hopes that in the future, S. M.'s life will always burn with creative energy. This is shown in line 20: "And may the muse inspire each future song!" Choice (B) is the opposite of what the speaker hopes. She wants his work to become immortal, as shown in line 12: "Conduct thy footsteps to immortal fame!" Choice (C) is wrong because she wants his work rather than his soul to live on: "And may the charms of each seraphic theme/Conduct thy footsteps to immortal fame!" There is no textual support for choice (D) or (E).

4. **The correct answer is (B).** In line 23, the "shades of time" symbolize temporal, insubstantial life on earth. You can infer this from the second half of the quote: "But when these shades of time are chased away,/And darkness ends in everlasting day." The "everlasting day" is heaven, so "shades of time" must be earth.

5. **The correct answer is (D).** In line 24, "darkness" symbolizes the suffering the black slaves experienced daily. You can infer this from the second part of the title, "....a Young African Painter." There is no textual support for any of the other answer choices.

6. **The correct answer is (B).** For both herself and the painter, the poet envisions a life of creativity and perpetual bloom. We can see this in line 27 ("There shall thy tongue in heavenly murmurs flow"), line 28 ("And there my muse with heavenly transport glow"), line 31 ("For nobler themes demand a nobler strain"), and line 32 ("And purer language on the ethereal plain."). These lines indicate that the author envisions an eternity of creativity in heaven. Choice (D) is incorrect, for the poem's ending moves the action to heaven. Choice (C) is wrong, because the poet does not indicate that heaven will be populated with any but themselves.

7. **The correct answer is (C).** The poet's style is marked by inverted phrases. For example, "May peace with balmy wings your soul invest!" (line 22) may be restated without the inversion as "May your soul be invested with peace on balmy wings!" Choice (A) is wrong, since this poem does not contain any extended comparisons of two unlike objects. Choice (B) is incorrect, because the poet is not ironic in her

discussion. Rather, she is very serious and straightforward in her admiration of S.M.'s talent and future. Choice (D) is wrong because the rhyme scheme in this poem is commonplace, comprised of rhymed couplets, pairs of rhyming lines. Finally, choice (E) is wrong, because *onomatopoeia* is the use of words whose sounds suggest their meaning.

8. **The correct answer is (E).** The poet believes that their verse will change. This is shown in lines 31 and 32: "For nobler themes demand a nobler strain,/And purer language on the ethereal plain." Choice (A) may be true, but we cannot deduce this from the poem. Choices (B), (C), and (D) have no support in the poem.

9. **The correct answer is (A).** In line 24, "everlasting day" symbolizes heaven. This is a traditional interpretation of the image.

10. **The correct answer is (D).** The metaphors in lines 29 and 30 are derived from mythology. Damon and Aurora are figures from Roman mythology. Choice (A) is wrong, because there are no stock figures in this type of writing. Choice (B) is wrong because these are not religious figures. Choices (C) and (E) are also wrong, because these figures are not linked to these subjects.

11. **The correct answer is (D).** The rhyme scheme of this poem is aa bb cc dd. The poem is written in rhymed couplets: intent/paint (aa); give/live (bb), delight/sight (cc), and so on.

12. **The correct answer is (B).** The tone of this poem is best described as formal and lofty. The elevated, formal tone is evident in the poet's use of language. This is shown from the very start: "To show the lab'ring bosom's deep intent,/And thought in living characters to paint." It is also shown in the poem's style, including diction and poetic contractions. Choice (A) is incorrect because the poet sees a brilliant future for them both. Choice (C) is also off the mark, because the painter's skill inspires the poet's admiration and she foresees a glorious afterlife. Choices (D) and (E) are incorrect for the reasons cited above.

13. **The correct answer is (B).** The theme of this poem can most precisely be stated as follows: slaves will be released from bondage and enjoy endless creativity when they enter heaven. The poet believes that she and S.M. will be released from earthly bondage to enjoy everlasting creativity in heaven. Choice (A) is wrong, for the poet appreciates S.M. now, and he is not dead. Choice (C) is not as complete an answer as choice (B), so it is not as good a choice. There is no textual support for choices (D) or (E).

14. **The correct answer is (E).** The word "shanty" suggests abject poverty. A *shanty* is a poor hovel. The author selected the word to convey the family's poverty.

15. **The correct answer is (E).** The tone of paragraphs 7 to 9 is best described as sad and painful. Petey's sadness is shown in his desire to cry, even though he is "too old for that, being eleven." The end of the paragraph shows the pain: "He'd never be hearing Granddad play like this again. It was as well Dad was moving into that new house, away from here. He'd not want, Petey wouldn't, to sit here on the old porch of fine evenings, with Granddad gone."

16. **The correct answer is (B).** The girl is described as a "china doll" to show how pretty she was. The phrase conveys her delicate charm. Since china is very fragile, choice (A)

cannot fit. China has no emotions, so choice (C) is wrong. Choices (D) and (E) cannot be inferred from the description.

17. **The correct answer is (B).** The term "china doll" was selected to describe the girl because her "hard, bright face" reveals her true nature. "Hard and bright" are used to show that she is a cold and unfeeling person; she begrudges the double blanket for the old man, feeling a single would have been more than enough.

18. **The correct answer is (A).** In paragraph 10, Granddad's tone is brave resignation. This contrasts sharply to Petey's tone of bitter sarcasm in paragraphs 19–24. In paragraph 10, Granddad says: "And what would an old fellow like me be doing around their house, getting in the way, an old nuisance, what with my talk of aches and pains!.... It's best that I take myself off, like I'm doing." This shows that he is facing his future with courage and surrender. However, the speaker's tags on Petey's dialogue reveal his bitterness. This is shown in "said the boy *coldly*" and "said the boy *harshly*."

19. **The correct answer is (A).** The scissors symbolize cutting the bonds of love, duty, and respect. By cutting the blanket in half, Petey suggests that we do not owe any allegiance to the people who have loved us and nurtured us. This is more than *severing the bonds of unpleasant duty,* so choice (B) is incorrect. The same is true of choices (C) and (D). Petey is not only suggesting that Dad cut the "dead weight" but also that he abandon his humanity by rejecting his father. Clearly, choice (E) is opposite of the correct interpretation.

20. **The correct answer is (A).** Granddad's attitude can best be described as considerate and understanding. We must understand that Granddad is not being sarcastic in what he says; he honestly attempts to see his son's point of view.

21. **The correct answer is (B).** The predominant symbol in this tale is the blanket. It carries through the entire story, unlike the other items mentioned here.

22. **The correct answer is (C).** The blanket represents the father's attempt to assuage his guilt. By giving his father and expensive blanket, Dad can make himself feel better about sending his father to an old-age home. Choice (A) is too general to be correct. The same is true of choice (D). Choice (B) is only part of the response: Dad is sending Granddad away because Dad is remarrying, but this response omits specific mention of the blanket. Choice (E) is the opposite of the author's point. Instead, the author is suggesting that we maintain our bonds with our family members, especially through the generations.

23. **The correct answer is (C).** In the beginning of the story, the blanket connotes warmth, comfort, home, and love. In the middle of the story, the symbol takes on an ironic twist, when Dad considers cutting it in half—severing his love. By the end of the story, however, the blanket has resumed its original meaning, as Dad comes to realize how badly he has treated his father.

24. **The correct answer is (D).** Concerning old age and the difference between generations, the author suggests that there is no real "generation gap" because we will all be old someday. This is shown in the story's climax, when Petey offers to cut the blanket in half and save a portion for his own father when his time comes to be sent away. While choice (E) may be true, it is not the specific focus of this story.

25. **The correct answer is (C).** The theme of this story is "Unintentionally, we all do cruel

and unpleasant things." Dad did not understand how cruelly he was treating his father until Petey pointed it out. At that point, Dad broke down into tears.

26. **The correct answer is (A).** Despite the happy ending, the overall tone of this story is melancholy, as we feel the sad music and lonely times bred by misunderstanding and conflict.

27. **The correct answer is (C).** The point of view in this story is omniscient. *Point of view* is the position from which a story is told. In the *first-person point of view,* the narrator is one of the characters in the story. As a result, the narrator explains the events through his or her own eyes, using the pronouns *I* and *me.* In the *third-person limited point of view,* the narrator tells the story through the eyes of only one character, using the pronouns *he, she,* and *they.* In the *omniscient point of view,* the narrator is not a character in the story. Instead, the narrator looks through the eyes of all the characters. As a result, the narrator is all-knowing.

28. **The correct answer is (E).** The best title for this story would be "The Blanket." Choice (A) is too narrow, considering the small role the scissors play in the story. Conversely, choices (B), (C), and (D) are all too broad.

29. **The correct answer is (C).** The speaker in this poem is discussing an old man who lives in town. You can infer this from the following lines: "They say that in his prime,/Ere the pruning-knife of Time Cut him down,/Not a better man was found..." The old man is "feeble," and all his contemporaries "are gone." He visits their graves, the "mossy marbles," because "the names he loved to hear/Have been carved for many a year/On the tomb."

30. **The correct answer is (D).** In line 11, the "Crier" is best interpreted as the town courier. The term "Crier" is a contraction for "Town Crier." The context clearly indicates a person, so you can eliminate choice (A). Since there is no indication that the "Crier" is malicious, you can eliminate choices (B) and (C). There is no indication that the Crier is the speaker's grandmother, so choice (E) is also invalid.

31. **The correct answer is (A).** From its context, you can deduce that "wan" (line 15) must mean pale and haggard. Study these lines: "Sad and wan,/And he shakes his feeble head." Choices (C) and (D) are too big a leap in meaning. The same is true for choice (E).

32. **The correct answer is (B).** You can infer that a "Roman nose" (line 28) must be considered a handsome feature. Deduce this by looking at the rest of the stanza: "My grandmamma has said/ Poor old lady, she is dead/Long ago—/That he had a Roman nose,/And his cheek was like a rose/In the snow." It is clear from these lines that the speaker's grandmother greatly admired the old man's appearance in his youth. He was clearly a handsome man in his prime.

33. **The correct answer is (D).** In lines 32–33, the poet uses a *simile,* comparing his nose to a staff when he writes, "But now his nose is thin,/And it rests upon his chin/Like a staff." Choice (A) is wrong because *personification* is giving human qualities to nonhuman objects. Choice (B) is wrong because *alliteration* is repeating initial consonants in series of words. Choice (C) is wrong because *hyperbole* is exaggeration for literary effect. Finally, choice (E) is wrong because *understatement* is downplaying a statement, again for literary effect. Saying a flood is like a "small pond" is an example of understatement.

34. **The correct answer is (D).** The speaker in this poem mocks the old man for living beyond his time. This tone is shown in the following stanza: "I know it is a sin/For me

to sit and grin/At him here;/But the old three-cornered hat,/And the breeches, and all that,/Are so queer!"

35. **The correct answer is (A).** The speaker in the poem is a young man. This is most clearly shown in the last stanza: "And if I should live to be/The last leaf upon the tree/In the spring,/Let them smile, as I do now..." Choice (E) is <u>always</u> wrong: never confuse the poet with the speaker, no matter how closely they seem allied. The speaker/narrator is never the same as the author, even in an autobiography or an autobiographical essay.

36. **The correct answer is (C).** Throughout the poem, the imagery suggests the swift passage of time. The old man, the subject of the poem, has outlived his peers. He is depressed and dispirited, as shown in line 15 ("sad and wan"), and has a "melancholy crack/In his laugh" (line 35–36). In the last stanza, the speaker flashes forward to his own dotage: "And if I should live to be/The last leaf upon the tree" to consider how fast time flies. There's no support for choice (A), which isn't inevitable at all. While the speaker doesn't seem to have much respect for the old man—choice (B)—the imagery doesn't reinforce this notion.

37. **The correct answer is (E).** The tone of this poem is best characterized as light, even mocking. This is shown especially in the following lines: "I know it is a sin/For me to sit and grin/At him here;/But the old three-cornered hat,/And the breeches, and all that,/Are so queer!" This is the opposite of choices (A), (B), (C), and (D).

38. **The correct answer is (B).** The imagery in lines 40–41 suggests that the poem is set about fifty years after the Revolutionary War in America. You can infer this from the image of "the old three-cornered hat" and "the breeches." These fashions were popular during the Revolutionary period, immortalized in countless portraits. Since the man's clothes are clearly out of place and he is dressing as he did when he was a young man, add fifty years to the time. This results in fifty years after the Revolutionary War.

39. **The correct answer is (D).** The "bough" in the last stanza symbolizes our hold on life. Study the relevant lines: "Let them smile, as I do now,/At the old forsaken bough/Where I cling." The speaker anticipates himself clinging to life, like a leaf clinging to a bough.

40. **The correct answer is (A).** The poet uses rhyme and imagery to unify the poem. The poem has very strong rhyme (hear/year, said/dead, etc.). It is so strong that you could argue that it's intrusive. The imagery focuses on the old man's appearance, as this example shows: "But now his nose is thin,/And it rests upon his chin/Like a staff,/And a crook is in his back,/And a melancholy crack/In his laugh." There is no irony in the poem; it is a straightforward exploration of the effects of outliving your peers.

41. **The correct answer is (C).** By symbolizing the old man as the last leaf, the poet suggests that the old man is the last of his kind. He is the "last leaf" on the tree, the last of his generation. His extreme old age argues against choice (A). Choice (B) is too general to have any meaning. The same is true of choice (C). The old man has not changed, so choice (E) is clearly untrue.

42. **The correct answer is (B).** The best title for this poem would be "The Last Leaf" because it most closely fits with the poem's topic, imagery, and theme.

43. **The correct answer is (D).** The use of the phrase "she alone" gives the reader an idea of Miss Nightingale's uniqueness. The first sentence reveals that she alone is responsible for the welfare of the suffering.

44. **The correct answer is (A).** Describing the influence of official etiquette as "pernicious" reveals the author's awareness of the dangers of red tape. The incident concerning the delay in unpacking shirts already in the hospital shows the author's

feelings about "red tape," the official tendency to make things more difficult than they need be.

45. **The correct answer is (D).** The description of the sick and wounded as "half-naked" and "shivering" serves as contrast to bureaucratic lack of concern. The author underscores the same point with the example of the shirts unreleased.

46. **The correct answer is (E).** As used in this context, "vain" means *without any success.* This is shown by the fact that "three weeks elapsed before the Government released the shipment" of clothing for half-naked, shivering, and sick wounded men.

47. **The correct answer is (D).** The Purveyor seems concerned only with departmental procedure. That he could stand by and watch people suffer shows this. The final incident is another example of his disregard for people's suffering.

48. **The correct answer is (A).** The tone of the phrase "departmental agony" is ironic. The department has no agony, but the suffering men do. The author creates irony by contrasting the clerk's "agony" over having to forcibly open a Government consignment to the very real suffering of the men.

49. **The correct answer is (C).** The main effect of using long sentences with multiple clauses is to suggest Miss Nightingale's long, difficult efforts to procure the supplies. By mirroring form and content, the author reinforces the difficulty Miss Nightingale experienced. Choice (A) is not a result of the long sentences; neither is choice (E). Choices (B) and (D) do not make any sense in context.

50. **The correct answer is (D).** In this selection, the author's tone is best communicated by his word choice. The use of phrases like "half-naked" reveal the importance of word choice.

51. **The correct answer is (B).** The author's tone reveals that he admires and respects Miss Nightingale. The final example, where she circumvented official policy to make sure that the suffering men were taken care of, reveals his attitude toward her.

SECTION II: ESSAY QUESTIONS

QUESTION 1

You've seen this AP question before: you're asked to analyze a poem to reveal how the poet creates meaning. With these questions, you are expected to use the standard literary techniques as tools to prove your thesis

Try these suggestions as you answer these types of literary analysis questions:

- Start by formulating a thesis that directly answers the question. In this case, be sure to explain how the poem's tone reveals the author's view of a Supreme Deity.

- Read the poem all the way through several times until you are sure that you've figured out what the author's view of the Supreme Deity actually is. Even if everyone around you is writing furiously, take a few extra minutes to make sure that you've got an accurate interpretation that you can support with specific examples drawn from the poem.

- Don't dawdle, but don't rush in so quickly that you misread the poem and so misinterpret it. As a general rule, if you allocate 40 minutes for each essay, you can spread your time this way:

planning	5 minutes
drafting	20–25 minutes
editing, revising	10 minutes
proofreading	2–3 minutes

- Do not treat each literary element in its own paragraph. Rather, weave them together around a common theme.

- Don't feel bound to isolate each poetic element in order (line 1, line 2, line 3, and so on), but do include line references to make it easier for your reader to follow your argument.

The following model response would earn a top score because it fulfills the requirements of this question and the standards of good writing:

1. Thesis clearly stated.

1 Stephen Crane's poem "A Man Adrift on a Slim Spar" describes an omnipotent God who is nonetheless cold and indifferent to humanity. The poem's bitter tone reveals Crane's God as an unfeeling being who allows a man to die needlessly.

2. Imagery used as a supporting detail.

3. Simile used as a supporting detail.

4. Personification used as a supporting detail.

5. Metaphor used as a supporting detail.

6. Literary elements woven into a seamless whole.

On a literal level, "A Man Adrift on a Slim Spar" describes a man vainly clinging to a slender scrap of wood in the middle of the fierce ocean. The poet clearly stacks the odds against the drowning man with vivid images of hopelessness: the spar is
2 "slim" (line 1), the ocean endlessly "rearing lashy dark points"
3 (line 3). The simile in line 2—the "horizon smaller than the rim of a bottle"—reinforces the man's desperate situation. Crane
4 personifies the ocean as a living being whose froth "whine[s]... in circles" (line 4). Line 7, "And growl after growl of crest," depicts the ocean as a mad dog nipping at the man's heels, eager to devour him. The simile in line 20 ("A horizon smaller than a
5 doomed assassin's cap") shows that the man is doomed to die. The metaphor of the "reeling, drunken sky and no sky" in line 22
6 captures the unpredictable motion of the ocean, tossing the man up and down with no predictable pattern.

God is all-powerful, the poet says, able to control the seas in the hollow of His hand, to make of them what He wishes. The ocean may be transformed into a gentle "spray/Raining down through the stars" (lines 12–13) because God feels compassion toward a child, or it may become a merciless storm that brings fishes and sailors alike to their brutal ruin—all at His whim. The man adrift in the ocean 6is doomed, his "pale hand sliding from a polished
7   spar" (line 23) as his face kisses "the water-death" (line 26) and he sinks from sight.

God is not actively against this man—or any man, for that matter—the poet says; rather, He is merely "cold," indifferent to
8   the man's suffering and torment in the harsh, cold ocean of life. Crane uses the refrain "God is cold" to reinforce his theme. The simple, straightforward diction of this line drives his point home
9   coolly and crisply. The ocean is a symbol of life: vast and brutally indifferent to humanity. "A Man Adrift on a Slim Spar"
10 has a bitter and harsh tone, a result of the world's lack of concern for humanity.

7. Additional textual support makes the point.

8. Refrain used as a supporting detail.

9. Symbol used as a supporting detail.

10. Main idea nailed.

QUESTION 2

Now we turn to an analysis of a prose passage, as you've come to expect. Consider the following guidelines as you answer this particular essay question:

- Start by defining Emerson's point. What is he saying about our "Reliance on Property"? Find specific examples in the text to make sure that you understand his point.

- Then agree or disagree with Emerson's point, showing that it does or does not hold true today. Draw specific examples from the text and your own experiences to make your point.

- Stick with examples that are not only specific but also suit your audience and purpose. This is not the time to shock, titillate, or annoy. You'd be surprised how many students go out on a limb and then saw it off. Please do not be one of them.

- Consider jotting down ideas to help you focus on specific details. Since you're likely getting weary and wish the test were over already, it's tempting to take refuge in vague words, general language, meaningless clichés, and nebulous generalities. Fight the urge! Stay focused on specific details and examples. Study this chart:

Vague	Specific
car	Buick Le Sabre, Chrysler PT Cruiser, Jeep Cherokee
place	The Empire State Building, New York City; Orlando, Florida
red	scarlet, maroon, ruby, crimson, cherry, carmine, cerise
good	moral, upright, virtuous, exemplary, swell, admirable, commendable, exceptional, tractable, dutiful, compliant

The following model response would earn a top score because it fulfills the requirements of this question and the standards of good writing:

1. Emerson's point defined.

1   In "Reliance on Property," Emerson asserts that our interest in amassing property is achieved at the expense of our self, our independence, and our self-reliance. Emerson states this at the very beginning of his essay when he says: "Men have looked away from themselves that they have come to esteem the religious, learned and civil institutions as guards of property, and they deprecate assaults on these, because they feel them to be assaults on property."

2. Emerson's thesis developed.

2   Given our concern for possessions, it's no surprise that we have become fixated on amounts. This concern extends to the political as well as personal arena, Emerson argues. The more people who support us, the richer we feel we are. We gain our strength from others and not from ourselves, Emerson claims: "The young patriot feels himself stronger than before by a new thousand of eyes and arms. In like manner the reformers summon conventions and vote and resolve in multitude." Emerson argues that we can only be strong if we throw off our reliance on amounts of people and things and replace it with a reliance on ourselves. We do not derive our power from those who support us or what we own but

3. Specific examples.

3   rather from who we are. "He who knows that power is inborn, that he is weak because he has looked for good out of him and elsewhere," he concludes.

4   I agree that we have become far too materialistic. Wealthy people around the world often take the things they have for granted. Fifty percent of the people in the world have never made a phone call, but high school students often spend up to 6 hours a day on the phone or using the phone line for other purposes, such as the Internet. As of last year, only 2 percent of the world's population is on the Internet. None of my friends thinks twice about signing on line and checking their e-mail or sending an instant message to friends; however, 98 percent of the population has never done

5   any of these things. Americans seem obsessed with money and status symbols like designer jeans, expensive sneakers, and new cars. For example, the Jeep Grand Cherokee costs about $48,000. Who needs a car that costs that much, uses so much gas, and hogs the road? It can only be for status.

6   However, no man is an island. Just because people shout someone's name at a political convention does not make them the best candidate, of course. But it's the rare person who can get things done alone. It's almost impossible to bring about social change in a vacuum. Emerson notes that "the reformers summon conventions and vote and resolve in multitude" but he does not

7   note the reason: they have to. No one can get reforms passed single-handedly. It took many, many people to pass the Pure Food and Drug Act, mandate special education for the handicapped, or even lower speed limits on local roads.

8   Emerson is correct when he says that too many people define themselves by what they own—and are the poorer for it. However, Emerson is incorrect when he says "It is only as a man puts off all foreign support and stands alone that I see him to be strong and to prevail." We must work with others to change the world.

4. Agrees with first part of Emerson's thesis.

5. Specific examples.

6. Disagrees with second part of Emerson's thesis.

7. Specific examples.

8. Conclusion sums up main points.

QUESTION 3

This is the third type of essay question that you will encounter on the AP test: the free-choice opened-ended response.

Study these guidelines as you answer this particular essay question:

- As you prepare for the exam in the weeks before it, consider memorizing key lines from a handful of famous literary works. For example, memorize several lines from Hamlet's famous "To be or not to be" soliloquy or Willie Loman's "A man is not a piece of fruit" speech from Arthur Miller's *Death of a Salesman.* You can use these direct quotations as precise examples to help you prove your point.

- Try to begin your essay with an interesting quotation, anecdote, or statistic. Remember that you're working with readers' interest—and your readers have read stacks and stacks of essays on the same topic.

- Include lots and lots of detail, but always make sure that the detail is directly on the mark. Don't put in detail just to fill space.

- As you write, pause every few minutes to reread the question. This will help you stay focused on your thesis and not drift from it.

The following model response would earn a top score because it fulfills the requirements of this question and the standards of good writing:

1. Quote gets the reader's attention.

2. Introduction states the thesis.

3. Details prove thesis.

4. Excellent specific details.

5. Details about setting relate to question.

1   "Make new friends but keep the old; one is silver and the other gold." That's great advice, but unfortunately not everyone has
2   friends or is able to reach out to them in times of need. Instead, some people retreat into isolation, often with disastrous consequences. This is the case with Shakespeare's Prince of Denmark, Hamlet, in the play of the same name.

Hamlet attempts to establish contact with members of his family and community but finds that his efforts are rebuffed or
3   misunderstood. After he returns to Denmark from school to attend his father's funeral, Hamlet discovers that his mother has married his father's brother King Claudius a scant two months after his father's death. Hamlet finds himself unable to talk to his mother after she has remarried with such unseemly haste, and he distrusts King Claudius, which turns out to be very wise indeed. Hamlet's lover, Ophelia, is of no help either, because her father, Polonius, has told her to rebuff Hamlet's overtures. Thus, she returns his letters and gifts and denies him access to her.
4   Hamlet's two old friends, Rosencrantz and Guildenstern, are turncoats, accepting pay from King Claudius to spy on their friend.

5   Hamlet is also isolated in part by the play's setting: medieval Denmark. While Hamlet's mother, Queen Gertrude, attempts to discover the source of her son's depression, she does not have access to professional help. Today, someone feeling as isolated as Hamlet would be likely to see a psychiatrist, psychologist, or social worker. The setting also precludes Hamlet's confiding in a friend. Hamlet starts to speak to Horatio, but the male code of behavior of the time did not encourage such confidences. The closest Hamlet can get is telling Horatio that he is not really mad, but only pretending to be so: "I am but mad north-northwest; when the wind is southerly, I know a hawk from a handsaw," Hamlet says.

However, Hamlet never tells his friend the true extent of his depression.

6   Part of the reason for Hamlet's isolation lies in his own character. Shakespeare characterizes Hamlet as the "melancholy Dane." Readers are lead to believe that he was always of an inward nature, even though he is very popular with the "distracted masses," his subjects in the kingdom. In his famous "to be or not to be" soliloquy, Hamlet explores the full extent of his isolation. Hamlet is so cut off from help that he actually considers suicide. Pointing an unsheathed dagger at his chest, Hamlet says:

6. Details about characterization relate to question.

To be, or not be to, that is the question:

Whether 'tis nobler in the mind to suffer

7   The slings and arrows of outrageous fortune,

Or to take arms against a sea of troubles,

And by opposing end them. (III, I)

7. Direct quote proves the point.

Hamlet is stopped by a consideration of the afterlife: will he be damned by killing himself? Hamlet concludes that he cannot kill himself because he cannot risk eternal damnation.

8. Writer claims only what can be proven.

We cannot conclude that Hamlet would recover more quickly
8   from his father's assassination and his uncle's and mother's betrayal if he had been able to reach out to his friends, Horatio, Rosencrantz, and Guildenstern, or his beloved, Ophelia. We can
9   conclude, however, that Hamlet is unwilling and unable to accept help from members of his community and family and is thus
10   isolated and alone. Tragically so.

9. Conclusion summarizes main points.

10. Fragment used for emphasis; shows a sophisticated writing style.

PRACTICE TEST 3: ENGLISH LITERATURE AND COMPOSITION

SECTION I: MULTIPLE-CHOICE QUESTIONS

Time—1 hour

Directions: This section contains selections from two passages of prose and two poems with questions on their content, style, form, and purpose. Read each selection closely and carefully. Then choose the best answer from the five choices.

Questions 1–17. Read the following selection carefully before you mark your answers.

Verses Upon the Burning of Our House July 18th, 1666

1   In silent night when rest I took,
    For sorrow near I did not look,
    I waken'd was with thund'ring noise
    And piteous shrieks of dreadful voice.

5   That fearful sound of fire and fire,
    Let no man know is my desire.
    I, starting up, the light did spy,
    And to my God my heart did cry
    To strengthen me in my distress

10 And not to leave me succorless.
    Then coming out beheld a space,
    The flame consume my dwelling place.
    And, when I could no longer look,
    I blest his Name that gave and took,

15 That laid my goods now in the dust:
    Yea so it was, and so 'twas just.
    It was his own: it was not mine;
    Far be it that I should repine.
    He might of all justly bereft,

20 But yet sufficient for us left.
    When by the ruins oft I past,
    My sorrowing eyes aside did cast,
    And here and there the places spy
    Where oft I sat, and long did lie.

25 Here stood that trunk, and there that chest;
    There lay that store I counted best:
    My pleasant things in ashes lie,
    And them behold no more shall I.
    Under thy roof no guest shall sit,

30 Nor at thy table eat a bit.
    No pleasant tale shall e'er be told,

Nor things recounted done of old.
No candle e'er shall shine in thee,
Nor bridegroom's voice ere heard shall be.

35 In silence ever shalt thou lie;
Adieu, adieu; all's vanity.
Then straight I gin my heart to chide,
And did thy wealth on earth abide?
Didst fix thy hope on mould'ring dust,

40 The arm of flesh didst make thy trust?
Raise up thy thoughts above the sky
That dunghill mists away may fly.
Thou hast an house on high erect,
Fram'd by that mighty Architect,

45 With glory richly furnished,
Stands permanent tho' this be fled.
It's purchased, and paid for too
By him who hath enough to do.
A prize so vast as is unknown,

50 Yet, by his gift, is made thine own.
There's wealth enough, I need no more;
Farewell my pelf, farewell, my store.
The world no longer let me love,
My hope and treasure lies above.
—Anne Bradstreet

1. The "arm of flesh" in line 40 refers to

(A) hope, promise.
(B) death, decay.
(C) secular, mundane concerns.
(D) the destruction of the fire.
(E) spiritual renewal.

2. "Pelf" in line 52 most nearly means

(A) a home.
(B) furniture.
(C) money or riches.
(D) a small shop.
(E) furs.

3. The connotation of the word "pelf" is

(A) the poet's earthly nature that must be overcome if she is to find salvation.
(B) the poet's greedy attitude toward her possessions.
(C) the poet's cavalier attitude toward her possessions.
(D) the poet's secret love of death and desire for release from her travails.
(E) the poet's deep love of God and His kingdom.

4. In the eighth stanza, the "house on high erect" is a symbol for

(A) heaven.
(B) her newly constructed house on the hill.
(C) her store.

(D) the richly furnished home provided by her architect friend.

(E) the finest house in her community.

5. When the poet finds herself unable to look at the fire any longer, she

(A) curses God and His unjust actions.

(B) blesses God but finds His action incomprehensible.

(C) consoles herself with plans for the new house on which a famous architect is already working.

(D) consoles herself with the thought of the new house her husband is building high on the hill.

(E) blesses God, for she believes His actions were just.

6. In which stanza does the speaker's attitude toward her home change?

(A) Sixth

(B) First

(C) Third

(D) Seventh

(E) Ninth

7. Which line best summarizes her change in feeling?

(A) "And to my God my heart did cry" (line 8)

(B) "Then straight I gin my heart to chide" (line 37)

(C) "Thou hast a house on high erect" (line 43)

(D) "I blest his Name that gave and took" (line 14)

(E) "In silent night when rest I took" (line 1)

8. The poet speaks of two homes in this poem. Who is the nominal owner of each home?

(A) The bridegroom owned the first home; the wealthy architect, the second.

(B) The poet owns the first home; the bridegroom, the second.

(C) The poet owns both homes.

(D) The plantation overseer owns both homes.

(E) The poet is the nominal owner of the first home; God, the second.

9. In a philosophical sense—the way the poet really intends it—who is the true owner of both homes?

(A) The poet feels she owns all homes, but she does have a mortgage on the first.

(B) God owns both homes, for the poet believes that everything people have is a gift from God.

(C) The homes are both really unowned, as lines 44 and 47 reveal.

(D) Humanity owns both homes, for all possessions are commonly shared.

(E) The reader is never sure of ownership here, for it is not critical to the poet's message.

10. Which adjective best describes the language of the poem?

(A) Ironic

(B) Argumentative

(C) Colloquial

(D) Pedantic

(E) Highly figurative

11. Which of the following is the most accurate description of the way material possessions are treated in the poem?

    (A) Their value diminishes when compared to God's treasures.
    (B) Although initially highly valued, the author realizes by the end of the poem that she can easily replace her goods. Thus, their value diminishes.
    (C) Select items—her trunk and chest especially—mean more than anything else to the author.
    (D) They were never highly regarded.
    (E) She is just thankful that her family has been spared.

12. The verse pattern here is

    (A) free verse.
    (B) rhymed couplets.
    (C) sprung rhythm.
    (D) highly alliterative.
    (E) irregular.

13. The point of view in this poem is

    (A) objective.
    (B) limited omniscient.
    (C) omniscient.
    (D) first-person participant.
    (E) first-person observer.

14. Many people try to find logical explanations for unfortunate events. Does the poet, anywhere in the poem, attempt to place blame for the fire?

    (A) She attributes the cause to God but not the blame.
    (B) Initially she blames the bridegroom, but she realizes that it is really God's fault.
    (C) She blames the first builder for his use of substandard materials and shoddy workmanship.
    (D) She really doesn't care that much about the loss of her possessions, for she already has another house in a better neighborhood.
    (E) She blames God, for He cruelly took back His possessions, as line 17 shows.

15. The attitude of the speaker can best be described as

    (A) ironic.
    (B) sarcastic.
    (C) moody.
    (D) religious.
    (E) irreligious.

16. Judging from the situation and its description, most probably

    (A) this is a true story.
    (B) this never could have occurred.
    (C) the author is not very religious.
    (D) this happened to someone the author knew very well.
    (E) this is a totally false story.

17. "The world no longer let me love,/My hope and treasure lies above" makes a suitable ending for all of the following reasons EXCEPT

    (A) the ending shows the speaker's growing realization of God's majesty and proves the theme.
    (B) the first thing the speaker did when she saw the fire was pray to God.
    (C) the author is really not very devout.
    (D) the thought behind the words helps console the author on the loss of her possessions.
    (E) the destruction of her worldly goods was followed by prayer to God.

Questions 18–29. Read the following selection carefully before you mark your answers.

Traveling

It is for want of self-culture that the superstition of Traveling, whose idols are Italy, England, Egypt, retains its fascination for all educated Americans. They who made England, Italy, or Greece venerable in the imagination, did so by sticking fast where they were, like an axis of the earth. In manly hours we feel that duty is our place. The soul is no traveler; the wise man stays at home, and when his necessities, his duties, on any occasion call him from his house, or into foreign lands, he is at home still and shall make men sensible by the expression of his countenance that he goes, the missionary of wisdom and virtue, and visits cities and men like a sovereign and not like an interloper or a valet.

I have no churlish objection to the circumnavigation of the globe for the purposes of art, of study, and benevolence, so that the man is first domesticated, or does not go abroad with the hope of finding somewhat greater than he knows. He who travels to be amused, or to get somewhat which he does not carry, travels away from himself, and grows old even in youth among old things. In Thebes, in Palmyra, his will and mind have become old and dilapidated as they. He carries ruins to ruins.

Traveling is a fool's paradise. Our first journeys discover to us the indifference of places. At home I dream that at Naples, at Rome, I can be intoxicated with beauty and lose my sadness. I pack my trunk, embrace my friends, embark on the sea and at last wake up in Naples, and there beside me is the same sad self, unrelenting, identical, that I fled from. I seek the Vatican and the palaces. I affect to be intoxicated with sights and suggestions, but I am not intoxicated. My giant goes with me wherever I go.

18. What figure of speech does the writer use in this sentence: "They who made England, Italy, or Greece venerable in the imagination, did so by sticking fast where they were, like an axis of the earth"?

    (A) Paradox
    (B) Hyperbole
    (C) Simile
    (D) Personification
    (E) An allusion

19. This figure of speech serves to

    (A) introduce the essential conflict in the essay.
    (B) underscore the immaturity of Europeans when compared to the sophistication of Americans.
    (C) berate people who choose to visit Europe before they tour America.

(D)   unify the essay's imagery.

(E)   convey the impression that the world revolves around Europe rather than America.

20.   In the end of the first paragraph, the writer compares someone who travels for the wrong reasons to a

(A)   great ruler.

(B)   weak monarch.

(C)   statue.

(D)   servant.

(E)   brave and masculine traveler.

21.   The word "churlish" in the phrase "I have no churlish objection" (paragraph 2) most nearly means

(A)   cantankerous.

(B)   intelligent.

(C)   logical.

(D)   defensible.

(E)   twisted.

22.   The connotation of the word "domesticated" in the phrase "so that the man is first domesticated" is

(A)   trained.

(B)   educated and well informed.

(C)   subdued.

(D)   tame.

(E)   well mannered.

23.   The phrase "He carries ruins to ruins" in paragraph 2 refers to

(A)   stealing valuable artifacts from foreign countries and smuggling them to America.

(B)   elderly people traveling to dangerous old cities.

(C)   traveling too much, which will result in premature aging.

(D)   traveling for the wrong reasons, which will deplete your sense of purpose and intelligence.

(E)   ruining the trip for others by traveling for selfish reasons.

24.   The writer believes that travel

(A)   provides a unique educational opportunity for people of all ages, but it is especially so for the mature and seasoned individual.

(B)   is too expensive to be undertaken without great thought.

(C)   can bridge the gap between the "haves" and the "have-nots."

(D)   enables people to run away from themselves and their inner lives.

(E)   enriches our soul by giving us a wider view of people who are different from us.

25.   The writer's topics and themes include all of the following EXCEPT

(A)   knowledge and wisdom.

(B)   cultural appreciation.

(C)   self-awareness.

(D)   spiritual growth.

(E)   nature and the natural world.

26.   The writer of this essay would be LEAST likely to

(A)   take a yearlong tour of Europe for pleasure and diversion.

(B)   stay home during his annual vacation to write and study.

(C)   travel to a foreign land to help the victims of a terrible natural tragedy, such as an earthquake or flood.

(D)   engage in contemplation and introspection.

(E)   encourage a young person to study abroad.

27.   Who or what is the "giant" of the last line?

(A)   People who travel too much

(B)   The self that is unable to find beauty at home and cannot be affected by the simple experiences of daily life

(C)   Our conscience

(D)   The guilt we carry as citizens of the richest nation on earth

(E)   Depression

28.   This passage is developed primarily through

(A)   comparison and contrast.

(B)   chronological order.

(C)   deduction.

(D)   induction.

(E)   most to least important reasons.

29.   Which line best summarizes the writer's theme?

(A)   There's no substitute for seeing the world.

(B)   Travel is wasted on the young, because they are too callow to appreciate the wonders they see.

(C)   No matter where we travel, we can never escape from ourselves.

(D)   Travel is a delightful diversion for people of all ages.

(E)   Only the young should travel; it is too dangerous for the elderly.

Questions 30–40. Read the following selection carefully before you mark your answers.

1 Death, be not proud, though some have called thee
   Mighty and dreadful, for thou art not so;
   For those whom thou think'st thou dost overthrow
   Die not, poor Death, nor yet canst thou kill me.

5 From rest and sleep, which but thy pictures be,
   Much pleasure; then from thee much more must flow;
   And soonest our best men with thee do go,
   Rest of their bones and souls' delivery.
   Thou'rt slave to fate, chance, kings, and desperate men,

10 And dost with poison, war, and sickness dwell;
   And poppy or charms can make us sleep as well
   And better than thy stroke. Why swell'st thou then?
   One short sleep past, we wake eternally,
   And Death shall be no more: Death, thou shalt die.
           —John Donne

30. In line 5, the phrase "From rest and sleep, which but thy pictures be" is best interpreted as meaning

    (A) when we are sleeping, we often look as though we are dead.
    (B) there are many pictures of sleeping people.
    (C) not all sleep is truly restful.
    (D) when you get more sleep, you look better in photographs.
    (E) Death eagerly watches us while we rest and sleep.

31. According to the speaker, Death is at the mercy of all of the following elements EXCEPT

    (A) destiny.
    (B) random events.
    (C) monarchs.
    (D) murderers.
    (E) poison.

32. With whom or what is Death allied?

    (A) Drugs and talismen
    (B) Combat and illness
    (C) Pleasure
    (D) Our best men and women
    (E) The soul

33. What aspect of death does the speaker attack?

    (A) Death's violent and cruel colleagues
    (B) Death's arrogance
    (C) Death's supposed invulnerability
    (D) The fear that Death inspires in us all
    (E) Death's violent reputation

34. The speaker's attitude toward death is best described as

    (A) calm and accepting.
    (B) disobedient.
    (C) obsequious.
    (D) fearful.
    (E) antagonistic and bold.

35. Which figure of speech does the poet use to unify his poem?

    (A) Rhyme
    (B) Personification
    (C) Rhythm
    (D) Irony
    (E) Alliteration

36. Between lines 12 and 14, there is a shift from

    (A) specific examples to a generalization or conclusion.
    (B) hyperbole to understatement.
    (C) fantasy to realism.
    (D) optimism to pessimism.
    (E) elevated diction to colloquial speech.

37. What form is this poem?

    (A) Rhymed couplets
    (B) Limerick
    (C) Free verse
    (D) Ballad
    (E) Sonnet

38. How does the poem's form affect its meaning?

    (A) The first eight lines provide specific examples; the last six lines draw conclusions.
    (B) The first two lines state the poet's thesis; the rest of the poem provides specific examples.
    (C) The final two lines indicate the poem's "turn," summing up the speaker's point.
    (D) Alternating couplets compare and contrast main ideas.
    (E) The first six lines state the problem; the last eight lines state the solution.

39. The poem's tone is best characterized as

    (A) neutral.
    (B) soothing.
    (C) horrified.
    (D) defiant.
    (E) angry.

40. In line 14, "Death, thou shalt die" is an example of a(n)

    (A) simile.
    (B) oxymoron.
    (C) metaphor.
    (D) inversion.
    (E) allusion.

Questions 41–51. Read the following selection carefully before you mark your answers.

Men are like plants; the goodness and flavor of the fruit proceeds from the peculiar soil and exposition in which they grow. We are nothing but what we derive from the air we breathe, the climate we inhabit, the government we obey, the system of religion we profess, and the nature of our employment. Here you will find but few crimes; these have acquired as yet no root among us. I wish I were able to trace all my ideas; if my ignorance prevents me from describing them properly, I hope I shall be able to delineate a few of the outlines, which is all I propose.

Those who live near the sea feed more on fish than on flesh and often encounter that boisterous element. This renders them more bold and enterprising; this leads them to neglect the confined occupations of the land. They see and converse with a variety of people; their intercourse with mankind becomes extensive. The sea inspires them with a love of traffic, a desire of transporting produce from one place to another, and leads them to a variety of resources which supply the place of labor. Those who inhabit the middle settlement, by far the most numerous, must be very different; the simple cultivation of the earth purifies them, but the indulgences of the government, the soft remonstrances of religion, the rank of independent freeholders, must necessarily inspire them with sentiments, very little known in Europe among a people of the same class of freemen, religious indifference, are their characteristics.

Exclusive of those general characteristics, each province has its own, founded on the government, climate, mode of husbandry, customs, and peculiarity of circumstances. Europeans submit insensibly to these great powers and become, in the course of a few generations, not only Americans in general, but either Pennsylvanians, Virginians, or provincials under some other name. Whoever traverses the continent must easily observe those strong differences, which will grow more evident in time. The inhabitants of Canada, Massachusetts, the middle provinces, the southern ones, will be as different as their climates; their only points of unity will be those of religion and language.

41. The comparison of men to plants in the first sentence is an example of a(n)

    (A) apostrophe.
    (B) epigram.
    (C) simile.
    (D) symbol.
    (E) euphemism.

42. In the second sentence, the main effect of using parallel phrases that elaborate on one another is to

    (A) emphasize the amount of time and effort it takes for a person to mature.
    (B) make the writing vigorous and logical.
    (C) establish the author's solemn and scholarly tone.
    (D) convince people to move to America.
    (E) temper the author's enthusiasm with unquestionable scientific facts.

43. In the context of the passage, the phrase "love of traffic" most nearly means

    (A) a desire to move goods from place to place.
    (B) an urge to drive.
    (C) an impulsive nature.
    (D) a passion for cars.
    (E) a craving for new sensations.

44. According to the author, our character is shaped by all of the following forces EXCEPT

    (A) our environment.
    (B) our government.
    (C) our career.
    (D) our genetic background.
    (E) our religious beliefs.

45. The author describes people who live near the sea as

    (A) deeply religious.
    (B) indifferent to their neighbors and other people around them.
    (C) courageous and adventurous.
    (D) pure and simple.
    (E) independent but not physically strong.

46. This essay is organized by

    (A) most to least important.
    (B) least to most important.
    (C) chronological order.
    (D) advantages and disadvantages.
    (E) spatial order, East to West.

47. The author would be most likely to describe America as a

    (A) "melting pot."
    (B) "glorious mosaic."
    (C) "crazy quilt."
    (D) "salad bowl."
    (E) "patchwork of people."

48. From what point of view is this essay written?

    (A) Third-person limited
    (B) First person
    (C) Omniscient
    (D) Third-person omniscient
    (E) All-knowing

49. Based on context clues, when was this essay most likely written?

    (A) 1400s
    (B) 1500s
    (C) 1700s
    (D) 1900s
    (E) Present day

50. The writer predicts that

    (A) people in different parts of America will become *less* similar as time passes.
    (B) people in different parts of America will become *more* similar as time passes.
    (C) Americans will never get along with each other because they are too individual.
    (D) people from all over the world will come to America.
    (E) Americans will deplete their rich natural resources through over-farming, fishing, and mining.

51. Based on the details, you can conclude that this essay reveals the author's

    (A) gratitude that he is not an American.
    (B) belief that Americans are an easily influenced group of people.
    (C) distrust of foreigners, especially immigrants.
    (D) mild support for America and Americans.
    (E) affection for and deep faith in the promise of America and Americans.

SECTION II: ESSAY QUESTIONS

Time—2 hours

Question 1
Suggested Time: 40 minutes

Directions: Read the following sonnet "How Soon Hath Time" by John Milton. Then show how the two parts of the poem are united by the theme. You will have to find and explain the two parts of the poem, describe the theme, and show how the theme unites the poem.

How Soon Hath Time

1   How soon hath Time, the subtle thief of youth,
    Stolen on his wing my three-and-twentieth year!
    My hasting days fly on with full career,
    But my late spring no bud or blossom shew'th.

5   Perhaps my semblance might deceive the truth
    That I to manhood am arrived so near;
    And inward ripeness doth much less appear,
    That some more timely-happy spirits endu'th.
    Yet be it less or more, or soon or slow,

10 It shall be still in strictest measure even
    To that same lot, however mean or high,
    Toward which Time leads me, and the will of Heaven;
    All is, if I have grace to use it so,
    As ever in my great Taskmaster's eye.
            —John Milton

Question 2
Suggested Time: 40 minutes

Directions: Analyze the following excerpt from Abraham Lincoln's Second Inaugural Address to explain how Lincoln uses stylistic elements to convey his point. You may wish to consider elements such as word choice, sentence variety, figurative language, and tone in answering this question.

...On the occasion corresponding to this four years ago, all thoughts were anxiously directed to an impending civil war. All dreaded it—all sought to avert it. While the inaugural address was being delivered from this place, devoted altogether to saving the Union without war, insurgent agents were in the city seeking to destroy it without war—seeking to dissolve the Union, and divide effects, by negotiation. Both parties deprecated war; but one of them would make war rather than let the nation survive; and the other would accept war rather than let it perish. And the war came.

One eighth of the whole population were colored slaves, not distributed generally over the Union, but localized in the southern part of it. These slaves constituted a peculiar and powerful interest. All knew that this interest was, somehow, the cause of the war. To strengthen, perpetuate, and extend this interest was the object for which the insurgents would rend the Union, even by war; while the government claimed no right to do more than to restrict the territorial enlargement of it....

The Almighty has His own purposes. "Woe unto the world because of offenses! for it must needs be that offenses come; but woe to that man by whom the offense cometh." If we shall suppose that American slavery is one of those offenses which in the providence of God, must needs come, but which, having continued through His appointed time, He now wills to remove, and that He gives to both North and South this terrible war, as the woe due to those by whom the offense came, shall we discern therein any departure from those divine attributes which the believers in a living God always ascribe to Him? Fondly do we hope—fervently do we pray—that this mighty scourge of war may speedily pass away. Yet, if God wills that it continue until all the wealth piled by the bondman's two hundred and fifty years of unrequited toil shall be sunk, and until every drop of blood drawn with the lash shall be paid by another drawn with the sword, as was said three thousand years ago, so still must be said, "The judgments of the Lord are true and righteous altogether."

With malice toward none; with charity for all; with firmness in the right, as God gives us to see the right, let us strive on to finish the work we are in; to bind up the nation's wounds; to care for him who shall have borne the battle, and for his widow and his orphan—to do all which may achieve and cherish a just and lasting peace among ourselves, and with all nations.

—Abraham Lincoln

Question 3
Suggested Time: 40 minutes

Directions: Private vs. public conscience—the desire to do what an individual perceives as right vs. the responsibility of carrying out the dictates of society—figures as a central conflict in many important works of literature. Select one literary work in which a character is faced with the choice of doing what he or she believes to be right or what society demands. You may select from the following works or from another of comparable quality.

Madame Bovary	*Ethan Frome*
Vanity Fair	*Moby Dick*
Lord Jim	*Catch-22*
Fahrenheit 451	*The Scarlet Letter*
The Turn of the Screw	*David Copperfield*
Native Son	*Invisible Man*
Like Water for Chocolate	*The Great Gatsby*
The Sun Also Rises	*Nicholas Nickleby*
Cry, the Beloved Country	*Julius Caesar*
Othello	*Romeo and Juliet*
Jane Eyre	*Our Town*
Pride and Prejudice	*The Sound and the Fury*

QUICK-SCORE ANSWERS

1. C	18. C	36. A
2. C	19. E	37. E
3. A	20. D	38. C
4. A	21. A	39. D
5. E	22. B	40. B
6. D	23. D	41. C
7. B	24. D	42. B
8. E	25. E	43. A
9. B	26. A	44. D
10. E	27. B	45. C
11. A	30. A	46. E
12. B	31. E	47. A
13. D	32. B	48. B
14. A	33. C	49. C
15. D	34. E	50. A
16. A	35. B	51. E
17. C		

COMPUTING YOUR SCORE

You can use the following worksheet to compute an approximate score on the practice test. Since it is difficult to be objective about your own writing and since you are not a trained ETS scorer or English teacher, you may wish to ask a friend who has already taken the test (and earned a high score of 4 or 5) to score your three essays.

Recognize that your score can only be an approximation (at best), as you are scoring yourself against yourself. In the actual AP English Literature and Composition Exam, you will be scored against every other student who takes the test as well.

Section I: Multiple-Choice Questions

	_____	number of correct answers
−	_____	.25 × number of wrong answers
=	_____	raw score
	_____	raw score
×	_____	1.25
=	_____	scaled score (out of a possible 67.5)

Section II: Essays

	_____	essay 1 (0–9)
	_____	essay 2 (0–9)
	_____	essay 3 (0–9)
×	_____	3.055
=	_____	scaled score (out of a possible 82.5)

Scaled Score

	_____	multiple-choice scaled score
+	_____	essay scaled score
=	_____	final scaled score (out of a possible 150)

AP Score Conversion Chart

Scaled Score	Likely AP Score
150–100	5
99–86	4
85–67	3
66–0	1 or 2

ANSWERS AND EXPLANATIONS

SECTION I: MULTIPLE-CHOICE QUESTIONS

1. **The correct answer is (C).** The "arm of flesh" in line 40 refers to secular, mundane concerns. Rather than an "arm of flesh," anchored to the mundane world, she knows now she ought to have realized that her "hope and treasure [lie] above" (line 54). Do not be confused and select the words with the opposite meaning: choice (A), *hope, promise*, or choice (E), *spiritual renewal*.

2. **The correct answer is (C).** "Pelf" in line 52 most nearly means *accumulated goods*. Don't be confused by choice (D), *a small shop*. The author uses the word "store" in line 52 to indicate a group of objects that she owns, not sells.

3. **The correct answer is (A).** She values her possessions very highly, especially since she would be unable to replace most of them, for there was no insurance and she lacked the means to send back to England for all the items, even if they were all available. Nonetheless, she believes that she must reject her reliance on earthly things if she is to achieve God's grace in heaven. These items are meaningless, of course, when she compares them to what God has to offer in salvation. Obviously, Bradstreet was very religious.

4. **The correct answer is (A).** In the eighth stanza, the "house on high erect" is a symbol for heaven. This symbolism is shown in the following stanza: "Then straight I gin my heart to chide,/And did thy wealth on earth abide?/Didst fix thy hope on mould'ring dust,/The arm of flesh didst make thy trust?/Raise up thy thoughts above the sky/That dunghill mists away may fly."

5. **The correct answer is (E).** When the poet finds herself unable to look at the fire any longer, she blesses God, for she believes His actions were just. This is shown in the third stanza: "And, when I could no longer look,/I blest his Name that gave and took,/That laid my goods now in the dust:/Yea so it was, and so 'twas just./It was his own: it was not mine;/Far be it that I should repine." This is clearly the opposite of choice (A). Choice (B) is incomplete. Choice (C) is a misreading, as the house is symbolic of heaven. The same misreading is shown with choice (D).

6. **The correct answer is (D).** The speaker's attitude toward her home changes in the seventh stanza when she says, "Then straight I gin my heart to chide,/And did thy wealth on earth abide?/Didst fix thy hope on mould'ring dust,/The arm of flesh didst make thy trust?/Raise up thy thoughts above the sky/That dunghill mists away may fly."

7. **The correct answer is (B).** Line 37—"Then straight I gin my heart to chide"—best summarizes her change in feeling.

8. **The correct answer is (E).** The poet speaks of two homes in this poem: her home on earth and her home in heaven. Who is the nominal owner of each home? The poet is the nominal owner of the first home; God, the second. "Nominal" is the key word here.

9. **The correct answer is (B).** In a philosophical sense—the way the poet really intends it—the true owner of both homes is God. He owns both homes, because the poet believes that everything people have is a gift from God. This is shown most clearly in the third stanza.

10. **The correct answer is (E).** The language uses many figures of speech. Choice (A) is incorrect because the term "ironic" means that the words express a meaning that is often the direct opposite of what is intended; Bradstreet makes her meaning quite clear. Choice (B) is wrong because there is no argumentative tone here; rather, she assumes

that her reader will agree with her conclusion. Choice (C) is wrong because *colloquial language* is characteristic of ordinary conversation rather than formal speech or writing. Bradstreet uses a great many inversions ("For sorrow near I did not look"—line 2—rather than "I did not look near for sorrow' "), and thus her language is not characteristic of the way people usually speak. Choice (D) is wrong because the term "pedantic" refers to an excessive or inappropriate show of learning, which is not the case here. However, it was typical of much of the writing of the seventeenth century, when this poem was written.

11. **The correct answer is (A).** The poet believes that the value of material possessions diminishes when compared to God's treasures. This theme is introduced in lines 19–20: "He might of all justly bereft,/But yet sufficient for us left."

12. **The correct answer is (B).** The verse pattern here is rhymed couplets. In the first stanza, for example, "took" and "look," "noise" and "voice," and "fire" and "desire" all rhyme. Thus, the rhymes are in pairs, also called *couplets*. Choice (A) has unrhymed lines without regular rhythm. Choice (C) is characterized by the use of strongly accented syllables pushed up against unaccented syllables. It was brought into favor by Gerard Manley Hopkins in the late nineteenth and early twentieth centuries. Choice (D) is not a verse pattern. Rather, *alliteration* refers to repeated sounds throughout a poem. Rhymed couplets are not irregular verse, so choice (E) is wrong.

13. **The correct answer is (D).** The point of view in this poem is *first-person participant*. The author is a participant in the action, as mentioned above. Far from objective, choice (A), she is very much involved in what happened. *Omniscient,* choices (B) and (C), means having complete or infinite knowledge, and this could be true only in God's case, in her way of thinking. She finds out what is happening as events unfold.

14. **The correct answer is (A).** Many people try to find logical explanations for unfortunate events. The poet attributes the cause to God, but not the blame. Lines 14–18 tell us that God "gave and took" and that His actions were "just." The other house she mentions is not a physical house at all, as in choice (D), and she assigns no blame to God.

15. **The correct answer is (D).** The speaker's attitude can best be described as *religious*. This is shown in lines 8–9 ("And to my God my heart did cry/To strengthen me in my distress"), lines 13–14 ("And, when I could, no longer look,/I blest his Name that gave and took"), and lines 53–54 ("The world no longer let me love,/My hope and treasure lies above.") Nowhere is she *sarcastic,* choice (B), or *ironic,* choice (A), about her subject.

16. **The correct answer is (A).** Judging from the situation and its description, most probably this is a true story. At the age of 18, Anne Bradstreet, the author of "Upon the Burning of Our House," came to America with her husband, settling in the Massachusetts Bay Colony. She had received a better education than most women of her day, and in spite of the demands made upon her as the mother of eight children, she found time to write poetry. Her brother-in-law took some of her verse back with him to England and had it published, establishing her as the first published poet of the New World. This particular poem is based on a true incident, as the language conveys.

17. **The correct answer is (C).** "The world no longer let me love,/My hope and treasure lies above" makes a suitable ending for all of the following reasons EXCEPT the fact that the author is really not very devout. As proven earlier, the poet is very religious.

18. **The correct answer is (C).** In the sentence "They who made England, Italy, or Greece venerable in the imagination, did so by sticking fast where they were, like an axis of the earth," the writer uses a simile. The writer compares travelers enthusiastic about Europe ("they") to the axis of the earth, using the word "like." Choice (A) is wrong

because a *paradox* is a seeming contradiction. In addition, a paradox is not a figure of speech. Choice (B) is wrong because *hyperbole* is exaggeration for literary effect. Choice (D) is wrong because *personification* is giving human traits to nonhuman objects, as in "the wind howled." Choice (E) is wrong because an *allusion* is a reference to a well-known place, event, person, work of art, or other work of literature. Allusions enrich a story or poem by suggesting powerful and exciting comparisons.

19. **The correct answer is (E).** The *simile* in the previous example serves to convey the impression that the world revolves around Europe rather than America. This is conveyed through the phrase "like an axis of the earth." The simile does not introduce the essential conflict in the essay, choice (A), because the essay does not have a conflict. A *conflict* in literature is a struggle or fight. There are two kinds of conflict. In an *external conflict*, characters struggle against a force outside themselves. In an *internal conflict*, characters battle a force within themselves. The author, Ralph Waldo Emerson, is expressing his opinion on travel and trying to convince us that his point of view is correct or at least deserves serious consideration. Choice (B) is wrong because neither the simile nor the essay underscores the immaturity of Europeans when compared to the sophistication of Americans. Indeed, the topic of immaturity never comes up. Choice (C) is wrong because Emerson does not berate people who choose to visit Europe before they tour America; rather, he believes that we should look into our souls for enlightenment rather than seeking diversion through travel. Choice (D) is wrong because this simile does not serve to unify the essay's imagery.

20. **The correct answer is (D).** In the end of the first paragraph, the writer compares someone who travels for the wrong reasons to a servant. You can figure this out by knowing that a *valet* is a *servant*: "... and visits cities and men like a sovereign and not like an interloper or a valet." Choice (A) is a result of misreading: "and visits cities and men *like a sovereign* and not like an interloper or a valet."

21. **The correct answer is (A).** The word "churlish" most nearly means *cantankerous*. "I have no churlish objection to the circumnavigation of the globe for the purposes of art..." Emerson says, suggesting that he is not being cranky in his objection.

22. **The correct answer is (B).** The connotation of the word "domesticated" in the phrase "so that the man is first domesticated" is *educated and well informed*. This is a difficult question because "domesticated" has several different meanings. Choices (A) and (D) are the most common meaning but not the one that fits the context. Choice (C) does not make sense in context. Choice (E) is wrong because Emerson does not discuss how Americans act when they travel abroad, only that such travel rarely serves its purpose of enlightenment.

23. **The correct answer is (D).** The phrase "He carries ruins to ruins" in paragraph 2 refers to traveling for the wrong reasons, which will deplete your sense of purpose and intelligence. A close reading of the passage reveals Emerson's belief that someone who "travels to be amused, or to get somewhat which he does not carry, travels away from himself" will find his soul grows weary through the useless search. The misguided traveler becomes a ruin visiting the ancient cities and monuments.

24. **The correct answer is (D).** The writer believes that travel enables people to run away from themselves and their inner lives. You can infer this from the passage in the second paragraph cited above as well as from sentences such as this one: "Traveling is a fool's paradise." Choice (A) is wrong because Emerson believes just the opposite of this statement: travel does NOT provide a unique educational opportunity for people of all ages—but especially the mature and seasoned individual. The same is true for choice (E), which is again the opposite of Emerson's thesis: travel does NOT enrich our souls by giving us a wider view of people who differ from us. Emerson never deals with the issue of cost, so choice (B) cannot be correct. The same is true for choice (C).

25. **The correct answer is (E).** The writer's topics and themes include all of the following EXCEPT nature and the natural world. Emerson treats knowledge and wisdom, choice (A), at great length, as shown in this quote: "...by the expression of his countenance that he goes, the missionary of wisdom and virtue, and visits cities and men like a sovereign and not like an interloper or a valet." He also discusses cultural appreciation, choice (B), revealed in this passage: "I have no churlish objection to the circumnavigation of the globe for the purposes of art, of study, and benevolence..." The entire passage focuses on self-awareness, choice (C), and spiritual growth, choice (D), as shown in the passages cited earlier in this explanation.

26. **The correct answer is (A).** The writer of this essay would be LEAST likely to take a yearlong tour of Europe for pleasure and diversion because that is precisely what he condemns. This is evident in the following passage: "He who travels to be amused, or to get somewhat which he does not carry, travels away from himself, and grows old even in youth among old things. " He is in favor of looking inward to find knowledge, so choice (B) is wrong. He would be in favor of traveling to a foreign land to help the victims of a terrible natural tragedy such as an earthquake or flood, so choice (C) is wrong. This is shown in the sentence "I have no churlish objection to the circumnavigation of the globe for the purposes of art, of study, and benevolence." The word "contemplation" shows that choice (D) cannot be correct. The same is true for choice (E), thanks to the prepositional phrase "of study."

27. **The correct answer is (B).** The "giant" of the last line is the self that is unable to find beauty at home and cannot be affected by the simple experiences of daily life. We carry this with us always because it defines who we are. Since Emerson does not travel too much (or at all, if he can avoid it), choice (A) cannot be correct. Choice (C) is close, but choice (B) is more precise. Since he does not discuss the unequal distribution of assets, choice (D) cannot be correct. Choice (E) is too big a leap, for we have no proof at all that he is depressed. On the contrary, he seems quite content with his life of study and introspection at home.

30. **The correct answer is (A).** In line 5, the phrase "From rest and sleep, which but thy pictures be" is best interpreted as meaning that when we are sleeping, we often look as though we are dead. The poet is mocking Death's pretensions to greatness by arguing that sleep looks just like death. Do not be misled into choosing choice (B) by the word "pictures". The same is true of choice (D). Choice (E) assumes that Death stalks us, which the poet does not discuss here. Choice (C) is not the point at all.

31. **The correct answer is (E).** According to the speaker, Death is at the mercy of all of the following elements EXCEPT poison. You can find all the other choices in line 9: "Thou'rt slave to fate, chance, kings, and desperate men." Choices (A) and (B) match with "chance," choice (C) matches with "kings," and choice (D) matches with "desperate men." Poison is mentioned in line 10: "And dost with poison, war, and sickness dwell." This means that Death lives with poison, not that it is at poison's mercy.

32. **The correct answer is (B).** Death is allied with combat and illness. You can infer this from line 10: "And dost with poison, war, and sickness dwell." *Combat* is the same as "war"; *illness* is the same as "sickness."

33. **The correct answer is (C).** The speaker attacks Death's supposed invulnerability. This is stated in the very beginning: "Death, be not proud, though some have called thee/Mighty and dreadful, for thou art not so" (lines 1–2).

34. **The correct answer is (E).** The speaker's attitude toward death is best described as *antagonistic and bold*. Again, you can infer the speaker's attitude from the defiance in the first two lines: "Death, be not proud, though some have called thee/Mighty and dreadful, for thou art not so."

35. **The correct answer is (B).** The poet uses *personification* to unify his poem. Recall that *personification* is giving human traits to nonhuman things. For example: "The book begged to be read." In this poem, Death is personified as a living, human being. You can eliminate choices (A), (C), and (D) because they are not figures of speech. Choice (E) is the repetition of initial consonant sounds in several words in a sentence or line of poetry. Writers use alliteration to create musical effects, link related ideas, stress certain words, or mimic specific sounds. The repeated *d* sounds in line 4 show alliteration ("Die not, poor Death..."), but alliteration is not the primary way that the author unifies the poem.

36. **The correct answer is (A).** Between lines 12 and 14, there is a shift from specific examples to a generalization or conclusion. There are many specific examples in lines 10–11 "And dost with poison, war, and sickness dwell;/And poppy or charms can make us sleep as well. The poet draws this together in the conclusion: "One short sleep past, we wake eternally,/And Death shall be no more: Death, thou shalt die." Choice (B) is wrong because there isn't any hyperbole or exaggeration in the poem. Choice (C) is wrong because the entire poem can be said to concern fantasy, by attributing human qualities to Death. Choice (D) is wrong because the entire poem has an optimistic tone in its defiance of death. Choice (E) is wrong because the entire speech is written in elevated diction; there isn't any everyday speech here.

37. **The correct answer is (E).** The poem is a *sonnet,* a fourteen-line poem with a set rhythm and rhyme scheme. Choice (A) is wrong because every set of two lines does not rhyme, as we see in lines 1–2: "Death, be not proud, though some have called *thee*/Mighty and dreadful, for thou art not *so*." Choice (B) is wrong because a *limerick* is a type of humorous poetry. Limericks have five lines, a strong rhyme, and a set rhythm. The first, second, and fifth lines rhyme, and the third and fourth rhyme. The rhyming words are sometimes misspelled to create humor. Choice (C) is wrong because *free verse* is poetry that does not have regular beat, rhyme, or line length. Walt Whitman's poetry is an example of free verse. Choice (D) is wrong because a *ballad* is a story told in song form. Since ballads were passed down by word of mouth from person to person, the words are simple and have a strong beat. Ballads often tell stories about adventure and love.

38. **The correct answer is (C).** The poem's form affects its meaning because the final two lines indicate the poem's "turn," summing up the speaker's point. Reread these lines: "One short sleep past, we wake eternally,/And Death shall be no more: Death, thou shalt die." This is the poet's message.

39. **The correct answer is (D).** The poem's tone is best characterized as *defiant.* The poet refuses to be cowed by Death's power. Instead, the poet mocks Death's pretensions to mastery of humanity: "Death, be not proud, though some have called thee/Mighty and dreadful, for thou art not so" (lines 1–2).

40. **The correct answer is (B).** In line 14, "Death, thou shalt die" is an example of an *oxymoron,* a seeming contradiction. Since death is already dead, it cannot die. Choice (A) is wrong because a *simile* is a figure of speech that compares two unlike things. Similes use the words "like" or "as" to make the comparison. "A dream put off dries up like a raisin in the sun" is an example of a simile. Choice (C) is wrong because a *metaphor* is a comparison that does not use the words "like" or "as" to make the comparison. Choice (D) is wrong because an *inversion* is switching the words or phrases in a sentence for literary effect. Choice (E) is wrong because an *allusion* is a reference to a well-known place, event, person, work of art, or other work of literature. Allusions enrich a story or poem by suggesting powerful and exciting comparisons.

41. **The correct answer is (C).** The comparison of men to plants in the first sentence is an example of a *simile,* a figure of speech that compares two unlike things. Similes use

the words "like" or "as" to make the comparison, as is the case here: "Men are *like* plants." Choice (A) is wrong because an *apostrophe* is a direct address. Choice (B) is wrong because an *epigram* is a witty statement. Choice (D) is wrong because a *symbol* is a person, place, or object that represents an abstract idea. For example, a dove may symbolize peace or a rose may symbolize love. Choice (E) is wrong because a *euphemism* is the substitution of a pleasant expression for a harsh or offensive one, such as "kick the bucket" or "pushing up daises" for "dead."

42. **The correct answer is (B).** In the second sentence, the main effect of using parallel phrases that elaborate on one another is to make the writing vigorous and logical. Parallelism does not emphasize the amount of time and effort it takes for a person to mature, so choice (A) is wrong. Authors use diction (word choice) and sentence length to establish a solemn and scholarly tone, so choice (C) is wrong. Matching phrases and clauses will not help convince people to move to America, so choice (D) is wrong. Choice (E) makes no sense in context, since there aren't any scientific facts in the essay.

43. **The correct answer is (A).** In the context of the passage, the phrase "love of traffic" most nearly means a desire to move goods from place to place. You can infer this from the juxtaposition of the phrases "a love of traffic" with "a desire of transporting produce from one place to another" in this sentence: "The sea inspires them with a love of traffic, a desire of transporting produce from one place to another, and leads them to a variety of resources which supply the place of labor."

44. **The correct answer is (D).** According to the author, our character is shaped by all of the following forces BUT our genetic background. That our *environment*, choice (A), shapes us is shown in this sentence: "Men are like plants; the goodness and flavor of the fruit proceeds from the peculiar soil and exposition in which they grow." The influence of *government,* choice (B); *careers,* choice (C); and *religious beliefs,* choice (E) are shown in this sentence: "We are nothing but what we derive from the air we breathe, the climate we inhabit, the government we obey, the system of religion we profess, and the nature of our employment."

45. **The correct answer is (C).** The author describes people who live near the sea as courageous and adventurous. This is shown in the following sentences: "Those who live near the sea feed more on fish than on flesh and often encounter that boisterous element. This renders them more bold and enterprising; this leads them to neglect the confined occupations of the land...." *Bold* is the same as "courageous"; *enterprising* is the same as "adventurous."

46. **The correct answer is (E).** This essay is organized by spatial order, east to west. The writer starts by describing people near the sea and moves across the continent to the "middle settlement."

47. **The correct answer is (A).** The author would be most likely to describe America as a "melting pot" since he sees Europeans losing their previous characteristics to become "Americans." You can infer this from the following passage: "Europeans submit insensibly to these great powers and become, in the course of a few generations, not only Americans in general, but either Pennsylvanians, Virginians, or provincials under some other name." All the other choices show Americans retaining their heritage and clinging to their differences.

48. **The correct answer is (B).** This essay is written from the first-person point of view. *Point of view* is the position from which a story is told. In the *first-person point of view,* the narrator is one of the characters in the story. As a result, the narrator explains the events through his or her own eyes, using the pronouns *I* and *me.* In the *third-person limited point of view,* the narrator tells the story through the eyes of only one character, using the pronouns *he, she,* and *they.* In the *omniscient point of view,* the

narrator is not a character in the story. Instead, the narrator looks through the eyes of all the characters. As a result, the narrator is all-knowing.

49. **The correct answer is (C).** Based on context clues, this essay was most likely written in the 1700s when America was first being settled. You can infer this from clues such as the author's use of the word "provinces" for "states" (since states had not yet been established): "Exclusive of those general characteristics, each province has its own, founded on the government..."

50. **The correct answer is (A).** The writer predicts that people in different parts of America will become less similar as time passes. This is stated in the following passage: "Europeans submit insensibly to these great powers and become, in the course of a few generations, not only Americans in general, but either Pennsylvanians, Virginians, or provincials under some other name."

51. **The correct answer is (E).** Based on the details, you can conclude that this essay reveals the author's affection for and deep faith in the promise of America and Americans. The author celebrates America's vibrant people and great energy.

SECTION II: ESSAY QUESTIONS

Question 1

To earn a high score on this question,

- follow the directions precisely. There are three essential parts of your response: isolating the two parts of the poem, describing the theme, and showing how the theme unites the poem.

- demonstrate a complete understanding of the poem.

- clearly link form (Italian sonnet) to function (express the theme).

- provide specific examples from the poem to make your point.

- be concise but complete.

The following model response would earn a top score because it fulfills the requirements of this question and the standards of good writing:

1. Topic sentence is a clear response to prompt.

2. Explains first part of poem.

3. Explains second part of poem.

4. Specific examples.

5. Specific examples.

6. Explains the theme.

7. Essential background on sonnet form.

8. Relates form to function—the theme.

9. Relates form to function—the theme.

10. Conclusion sums up main points.

1 Writers often use the form of their literary work to help them create meaning. This is the case with John Milton's sonnet "How Soon Hath Time," in which the two parts of the poem are united by the theme.

2 The first part of the sonnet, lines 1–8, discusses the outward changes the speaker has undergone. Such changes are reflected in the statement "Perhaps my semblance might deceive the truth/That I to manhood am arrived so near" (lines 5–6), which
3 shows, in the word "semblance," the outward changes time has
4 wrought. The second part of the poem concerns inward changes,
5 as found in the phrase "inward ripeness" (line 7). The theme, stated in the final six lines, is that the changes the speaker has
6 experienced are a result of the will of heaven.

Sonnets can take two forms, Italian (Petrarchan) and English (Elizabethan). "How Soon Hath Time" is an Italian sonnet. The
7 Italian sonnet has an eight line octave, rhyming *abbaabba*, which presents the poet's subject. This is followed by a six line sestet, rhyming *cdecde*, which indicates the importance of the facts set forth in the octave and resolves the problem established there. Milton used the Italian sonnet form rather than the Elizabethan (abab/cdcd/efef/gg rhyme) because the Elizabethan form resolves the conflict in the final couplet (gg) and usually has a witty turn of phrase. The Italian form allows Milton eight lines to make his
8 point—the changes God wills in man—without any wit at the end. Since the subject is so serious, Milton did not want a humorous ending.

9 Milton also selected the sonnet form because it allows for a brief and clear presentation of theme. He did not need a narrative (a long story) or an ode (a long poem in elevated language) to make his point about the changes he has undergone and their reason.

10 The intertwining of form and function in literature allows writers to reinforce meaning, often with great subtlety. Using the Italian sonnet enabled Milton to provide examples in the first eight lines and use them to draw a conclusion in the final six lines.

Question 2

To earn a high score on this question,

- read the essay through several times. Each time, focus on a different stylistic element. Begin by looking at overall meaning and tone. Is the essay fiery, calm, or antagonistic, for example? Then turn your attention to word choice. Which words especially help the writer convey meaning?

- be sure to provide specific examples to prove your point.

- interweave the elements, as you have been taught in class and in this book. Cluster them around a common point. This results in a more articulate and cohesive response.

- you are not expected to provide startling or original insight (after all, you have only 40 minutes to frame your response), but making an intelligent point can go a long way toward impressing your reader. That's because nearly all the essays submitted tend to have a numbing sameness. An essay with an original thought, sophisticated insight, or clever point will impress your reader and result in a better grade (all things being equal).

The following model response would earn a top score because it fulfills the requirements of this question and the standards of good writing:

1 Lincoln's speech is extraordinarily effective in what it seeks to accomplish. It is especially effective for the glimpse that it gives us of the speaker, who reveals himself here to be a wise and compassionate man. In addition, the speech is also almost free from recrimination, the assignment of blame.

    Slavery is attacked on moral grounds, but the ethics of men
2 "wringing their bread from the sweat of other men's faces" is set forth with little heat, while the "two hundred and fifty years of unrequited toil" and the "blood drawn with the lash"—which are the most emotional lines in the speech—are presented in almost
3 biblical language and thus are missing a vengeful quality. Quotes from the Bible are used to indicate a share in the responsibility.
4 The quotation from Matthew 7:1 foreshadows the lack of vindictiveness in the final paragraph: "With malice toward none; with charity for all."

    The diction is simple for the most part, but there are times when
5 the choice of words is especially precise and apt. This is evident in the second sentence of the third paragraph, for example: "These slaves constituted a peculiar and powerful interest." There is nothing that could be substituted for "interest" and "peculiar" without seriously changing the exact meaning that the author desired. Lincoln is also subtly alluding to the slave trade's nickname, "that peculiar institution." It is also a sign of good writing that so much of American history is contained in the words "strengthen, perpetuate, and extend this interest," which follows in the next sentence. Lincoln is also adept at varying his
6 sentences to achieve specific effects. For example, he uses *inversion*, the switching of the normal, expected order of words within the sentence, to attract attention to specific sentences.

1. Point stated clearly.

2. Specific examples support main point.

3. Specific examples support main point.

4. Sophisticated insight.

5. Analysis of diction addresses the main point.

6. Great insight and examples.

7. Sentence variety analyzed.

8. Sophisticated analysis of diction; original insight, too.

9. Figurative language analyzed.

10. Summarizes with tone, right on target.

7   Thus, "Fondly do we hope" and the opening sentences of the last paragraph attract our attention by their difference. We would expect the phrase to read "We fondly hope." While Lincoln's sentences tend to be long and complex in style, he is careful to mix in some short statements for balance. This can be seen in the second and third paragraphs, for instance.

8   At some points his prose borders on the poetic, as "Fondly do we hope—/ fervently do we pray—/that this mighty scourge of war/may speedily pass away." There are also numerous instances of specific poetic techniques such as assonance and alliteration, metaphor, and personification. "Bind up the nation's wounds" in

9   the final paragraph is an example of personification.

10   In the end, it is not the poetic devices that achieve the success here, but the writer's compassionate and restrained tone. The calm and rational tone helps to convey the message of utter sincerity, especially in the final paragraph. The language of this address evokes the ugly realities of the war as well as the hope of people everywhere for a just and lasting peace. As a result of these stylistic elements, Abraham Lincoln's Second Inaugural Address is a lasting example of clear, persuasive prose.

Question 3

To earn a high score on this question,

- select a novel, biography, autobiography, or play in which the character experiences a clear moral conflict.

- explain the conflict.

- analyze its effect.

- provide specific examples.

The following model response would earn a top score because it fulfills the requirements of this question and the standards of good writing:

1   Huckleberry Finn, the protagonist in Mark Twain's *The Adventures of Huckleberry Finn*, is torn between what he knows is right and what society has taught him is right. The topic is slavery, and the conflict is a brutal one.

1. Huck has a clear moral conflict.

2   Huck's mother is dead and his father Pap is a drunken wastrel. Huck has been adopted and "sivilized" by Miss Watson. In keeping with the dictates of pre-Civil War America, she teaches Huck that slavery is both natural and morally right. Miss Watson owns a slave, Jim. Miss Watson has always promised not to sell Jim down the Mississippi River to New Orleans, which would separate him from his family. She changes her mind, however, when a slave trader offers her $800 for Jim. When Jim hears that he is about to be sold away from his family, he runs away. He is determined to earn the money to buy his freedom. Meanwhile, Huck has run away from his abusive father. When Huck and Jim accidentally meet as they hide on Jackson's Island, Huck decides to team up with Jim and sail down the Mississippi River. Of course, a white man traveling with a slave as equals was outside the bounds of acceptable behavior. But since Huck is already outside the bounds of society as the son of the town drunk, he is relatively comfortable with this arrangement—until the a conman who calls himself the "King" sells Jim out. Jim is taken prisoner at the Phelps' farm.

2. Essential background.

3   The novel reaches its climax as Huck is faced with the crucial moral dilemma of his life: does he return Jim to his rightful owner, Miss Watson, or continue to harbor a fugitive? At first, Huck decides to turn Jim in, as he has been taught by a corrupt society that slavery is acceptable. He is very concerned that it will get around that he helped a slave escape. Then he will be further dishonored in society. To save himself the shame, Huck writes a letter to Miss Watson, revealing Jim's whereabouts.

3. Moral conflict.

4   However, the longer Huck thinks about his actions, the more he realizes the conflict between what he has been taught about slavery and what he knows is morally right about owning another human being. As his private conscience wars with his public conscience, Huck rejects the responsibility of carrying out the

4. Conflict developed with examples.

5. Results of conflict.

5   dictates of society and decides to do what he perceives as morally right. Huck decides to risk eternal damnation rather than return his friend to slavery. "All right, then, I'll go to hell," Huck says,

6   and tears up the letter.

6. Quote is excellent specific detail.

7. Clever way to segue
into conclusion.

8. Major points tied
together.

7   Huck takes "the road less traveled by," as poet Robert Frost said,
when he chooses to protect Jim rather than turn him in. Even
though he has been taught that slavery is desirable, he knows that
it is never acceptable to enslave another person. Huck was able to
8   live with himself because he did what he knew was right.

PRACTICE TEST 4: ENGLISH LITERATURE AND COMPOSITION

SECTION I: MULTIPLE-CHOICE QUESTIONS

Time—1 hour

Directions: This section contains selections from two passages of prose and two poems with questions on their content, style, form, and purpose. Read each selection closely and carefully. Then choose the best answer from the five choices.

Questions 1–20 refer to the following poem.

Thanatopsis

1   To him who in the love of Nature holds
   Communion with her visible forms, she speaks
   A various language; for his gayer hours
   She has a voice of gladness, and a smile

5   And eloquence of beauty, and she glides
   Into his darker musings with a mild
   And healing sympathy that steals away
   Their sharpness ere he is aware. When thoughts
   Of the last bitter hour come like a blight

10 Over thy spirit, and sad images
   Of the stern agony, and shroud, and pall,
   And breathless darkness, and the narrow house
   Make thee to shudder and grow sick at heart—
   Go forth, under the open sky, and list

15 To Nature's teachings, while from all around—
   Earth and her waters, and the depths of air—
   Comes a still voice—
   Yet a few days, and thee
   The all-beholding sun shall see no more
   In all his course; nor yet in the cold ground,

20 Where thy pale form was laid with many tears,
   Nor in the embrace of ocean shall exist
   Thy image. Earth, that nourished thee, shall claim
   Thy growth, to be resolved to earth again,
   And, lost each human trace, surrendering up

25 Thine individual being, shalt thou go
   To mix forever with the elements,
   To be a brother to the insensible rock
   And to the sluggish clod which the rude swain
   Turns with his share and treads upon. The oak

30   Shall send his roots abroad and pierce thy mold.
       Yet not to thine eternal resting place
       Shalt thou retire alone; nor couldst thou wish
       Couch more magnificent. Thou shalt lie down
       With patriarchs of the infant world—with kings,

35   The powerful of the earth—the wise, the good.
       Fair forms, and hoary seers of ages past,
       All in one mighty sepulcher. The hills
       Rock-ribbed and ancient as the sun; the vales
       Stretching in pensive quietness between;

40   The venerable woods; rivers that move
       In majesty; and the complaining brooks
       That make the meadows green; and, poured round all
       Old Ocean's gray and melancholy waste—
       Are but the solemn decorations all

45   Of the great tomb of man. The golden sun,
       The planets, all the infinite host of heaven,
       Are shining on the sad abodes of death
       Through the still lapse of ages. All that tread
       The globe are but a handful to the tribes

50   That slumber in its bosom. Take the wings
       Of morning, pierce the Barcan wilderness,
       Or lose thyself in the continuous woods
       Where rolls the Oregon, and hears no sound
       Save his own dashings—yet the dead are there;

55   And millions in those solitudes, since first
       The flight of years began, have laid them down
       In their last sleep—the dead reign there alone.
       So shalt thou rest, and what if thou withdraw
       In silence from the living, and no friend

60   Take note of thy departure? All that breathe
       Will share thy destiny. The gay will laugh
       When thou art gone, the solemn brood of care
       Plod on, and each one as before will chase
       His favorite phantom; yet all these shall leave

65   Their mirth and their employments, and shall
         come
       And make their bed with thee. As the long train
       Of ages glides away, the sons of men,
       The youth in life's green spring, and he who goes
       In the full strength of years, matron and maid,

70   The speechless babe, and the gray-headed man—
       Shall one by one be gathered to thy side,
       By those who in their turn shall follow them.
       So live, that when thy summons comes to join
       The innumerable caravan which moves

75   To that mysterious realm, where each shall take
      His chamber in the silent halls of death,
      Thou go not, like the quarry slave at night,
      Scourged to his dungeon, but, sustained and
        soothed
      By an unfaltering trust, approach thy grave

80   Like one who wraps the drapery of his couch
      About him, and lies down to pleasant dreams.

1. In lines 1–17, what does the poet say humanity should do when torn by thoughts of death?

    (A)   Seek diversion
    (B)   Think instead of "darker musings" and the "eloquence of beauty"
    (C)   Listen to Nature
    (D)   Ignore Nature's promptings, for they offer false hopes
    (E)   Continue our daily routine and push such thoughts firmly aside

2. What will Nature be able to offer humanity, according to the poet?

    (A)   The sluggish clod
    (B)   The insensible rock
    (C)   Healing sympathy
    (D)   The magnificent oak
    (E)   The company of fascinating people

3. In lines 17–57, what comfort does the poet believe Nature offers people when they are facing death?

    (A)   The beauty of the open sky and still waters
    (B)   A "magnificent couch" decorated with glories
    (C)   The warm embrace of the ocean
    (D)   Old friends and fond memories
    (E)   None at all; Nature is cold and unyielding.

4. Who has NOT shared Nature's "magnificent couch"?

    (A)   Great leaders
    (B)   Upstanding citizens
    (C)   Wise men and women
    (D)   Prophets
    (E)   Murderers

5. In lines 57–72, why is dying without being mourned not important?

    (A)   Since you are already dead, you have little use for what the living say.
    (B)   It is actually very important, for it determines your fate.
    (C)   Mourning customs are hypocritical at best, for few of us are really concerned about anyone else's mortality.
    (D)   Mourning is unnecessary, for all who are unaware of the person's passing will be joining him or her soon enough.
    (E)   Mourning offers little comfort to the survivors.

6. In lines 73–81, what is important to the poet and the poem's meaning?

   (A) That people will live in continuing trust with Nature
   (B) That people set their affairs in order before their death
   (C) That people make their peace with their neighbors
   (D) That people summon their friends and relatives to their side before dying
   (E) That people fight death to the last, not surrendering their will to Nature's

7. Why must people base their faith in Nature?

   (A) There is nothing else to comfort them.
   (B) So that when we face death, we can be secure in the knowledge that Nature will sustain us and make us a part of the natural order.
   (C) Nature will reward us with riches beyond our wildest dreams.
   (D) There is no Supreme Being for people to seek.
   (E) There is no reason.

8. What does the "mighty sepulcher" in line 37 most nearly mean?

   (A) The tomb
   (B) Clay
   (C) Nature
   (D) Earth
   (E) The individual grave

9. To what does the above term refer?

   (A) The final resting place of the wicked
   (B) The mighty grave of all
   (C) The mighty grave of the worthy
   (D) The afterlife
   (E) The process by which humans are forgotten

10. What is the "destiny" spoken of in lines 60–61?

    (A) Rebirth
    (B) Death
    (C) Joining with the Supreme Being
    (D) Mourning
    (E) Accepting Nature

11. What poetic technique does the author use in the final two lines?

    (A) Simile
    (B) Personification
    (C) Alliteration
    (D) Apostrophe
    (E) Inversion

12. To what is death compared in these final two lines?

    (A) Mourning
    (B) Nature
    (C) Rebirth
    (D) Sleep
    (E) The ocean

13. When the author published this poem in a new edition, he added lines 1–17, up to "Yet a few days." What purpose did these new lines serve?

    (A) They explained the theme more fully.
    (B) They established the tone more firmly.
    (C) They framed the poem by clearly defining the subject matter.
    (D) They made the poem conform to an established literary form.
    (E) They offered a bit of hope.

14. At the same time as the above additions were made, the poet also added the final 16 lines, beginning with "As the long train." Why did he do this?

    (A) These lines allow the poet more room for additional figures of speech.
    (B) These lines offer hope and consolation.
    (C) These lines establish the poem as a ballad.
    (D) These lines ask people to fear death as a worthy opponent.
    (E) These lines complete the rhyme pattern.

15. The poem presents a movement from

    (A) life to death.
    (B) death to rebirth.
    (C) doubt to hope to doubt.
    (D) ecstasy to joy to sorrow.
    (E) faith to rebirth.

16. All of the following are true about the language of the poem EXCEPT that

    (A) the poet uses poetic contraction such as "list" for "listen."
    (B) sentences and phrases are inverted for poetic effect.
    (C) the words are selected to call for two different levels of interpretation.
    (D) the words are not unusual or difficult to define.
    (E) the poet makes frequent references to Nature.

17. The language of the poem can best be described as

    (A) labored.
    (B) economical.
    (C) extravagant.
    (D) awkward.
    (E) ill suited to the subject matter.

18. The speaker of the poem is

    (A) Nature.
    (B) the dead.
    (C) the "powerful of the earth."
    (D) the poet.
    (E) different in different stanzas.

19. The following line is an example of what poetic technique? "Yet a few days, and thee/The all-beholding sun shall see no more/In all his course."

    (A) Oxymoron
    (B) Conceit
    (C) Inversion
    (D) Personification
    (E) Synecdoche

20. The tone in this poem is intended to be
    (A) comforting.
    (B) frightening.
    (C) neutral.
    (D) passive.
    (E) excited.

Questions 21–31 refer to the following essay.

Man Thinking

It is one of those fables which out of an unknown antiquity convey an unlooked-for wisdom, that the gods, in the beginning, divided Man into men, that he might be more helpful to himself; just as the hand was divided into fingers, the better to answer its end.

The old fable covers a doctrine ever new and sublime; that there is One Man,—present to all particular men only partially, or through one faculty; and that you must take the whole society to find the whole man. Man is not a farmer, or a professor, or an engineer, but he is all. Man is priest, and scholar, and statesman, and producer, and soldier. In the divided or social state these functions are parceled out to individuals, each of whom aims to do his stint of the joint work, whilst each other performs his. But, unfortunately, this original unit, this fountain of power, has been so distributed to multitudes, has been so minutely subdivided and peddled out, that it is spilled into drops, and cannot be gathered. The state of society is one in which the members have suffered amputation from the trunk, and strut about so many walking monsters,—a good finger, a neck, a stomach, an elbow, but never a man.

Man is thus metamorphosed into a thing, into many things. The planter, who is Man sent out into the field to gather food, is seldom cheered by any idea of the true dignity of his ministry. He sees his bushel and his cart, and nothing beyond, and sinks into the farmer, instead of Man on the farm. The tradesman scarcely ever gives an ideal worth to his work, but is ridden by the routine of his craft, and the soul is subject to dollars. The priest becomes a form; the attorney a statute-book; the mechanic a machine; the sailor a rope of the ship.

In this distribution of functions the scholar is the delegated intellect. In the right state he is Man Thinking. In the degenerate state, when the victim of society, he tends to become a mere thinker, or still worse, the parrot of other men's thinking.

21. The phrase "just as the hand was divided into fingers" functions here as a(n)
    I. simile.
    II. example.
    III. personification.

    (A) I only
    (B) II only
    (C) III only
    (D) I and II
    (E) I and III

22. The phrase "the better to answer its end" at the end of the first paragraph can best be interpreted to mean to

    (A) signal the specific type of division.
    (B) show defeat.
    (C) better serve its purpose.
    (D) destroy the strength of the whole.
    (E) signal the conclusion of the fable.

23. The "old fable" in paragraph two refers to

    (A) a legend about the naming of parts.
    (B) a myth about the beginning of the world.
    (C) an allegory about regeneration.
    (D) the belief that individuals possess only certain talents.
    (E) a parable concerning change and metamorphosis.

24. As used in context, the word "faculty" most nearly means

    (A) a department of learning.
    (B) aptitude.
    (C) power.
    (D) authority.
    (E) staff.

25. The phrase "But, unfortunately" in the second paragraph does which of the following things?

    (A) It signals a transition to a new idea.
    (B) It shifts the focus from generalities to individual cases.
    (C) It emphasizes the abstract in place of the concrete.
    (D) It signals a continuation of a previous line of reasoning.
    (E) It shows the distribution of power among individual members of society.

26. Which of the following statements best expresses the writer's attitude toward society?

    (A) Society is necessary to ensure that all labor is accomplished.
    (B) Government is best that governs least.
    (C) Society has destroyed humanity's wholeness.
    (D) Society alone can distribute tasks equably among its members.
    (E) Lack of social controls has resulted in a sharp rise in industrial accidents.

27. The writer uses the word "ministry" in relation to the planter to suggest

    (A) the inherent holiness of farming.
    (B) the farmer would rather be a minister.
    (C) the farmer worships the soil and its abundance.
    (D) farming's dependence on the whims of nature.
    (E) it is important that we have jobs that we like and in which we can excel.

28. The author's thesis in the third paragraph is developed through

    (A) repetition of key words.
    (B) comparison and contrast.
    (C) a series of examples.
    (D) alliteration.
    (E) aphorisms.

29. The writer concludes the third paragraph with a series of metaphors to suggest

    (A) the situation is hopeless.
    (B) our identity is subsumed in our work.
    (C) work gives life meaning.
    (D) we constantly compare ourselves to others.
    (E) work robs life of meaning.

30. The tone of this essay is best described as

    (A) despairing.
    (B) fiery.
    (C) soothing.
    (D) angry.
    (E) neutral.

31. The language of this essay is best described as

    (A) colloquial.
    (B) scholarly and elevated.
    (C) florid.
    (D) biased.
    (E) vague and colorless.

Questions 32–41 refer to the following poem.

His Excellency General Washington

1   Celestial choir! enthron'd in realms of light,
    Columbia's scenes of glorious toils I write.
    While freedom's cause her anxious breast alarms,
    She flashes dreadful in refulgent arms.

5   See mother earth her offspring's fate bemoan,
    And nations gaze at scenes before unknown!
    See the bright beams of heaven's revolving light
    Involved in sorrows and the veil of night!
    The goddess comes, she moves divinely fair,

10 Olive and laurel binds her golden hair:
    Wherever shines this native of the skies,
    Unnumber'd charms and recent graces rise.
    Muse! bow propitious while my pen relates
    How pour her armies through a thousand gates;

15 As when Eolus heaven's fair face deforms,
    Enwrapped in tempest and a night of storms;
    Astonish'd ocean feels the wild uproar,
    The refulgent surges beat the sounding shore,
    Or thick as leaves in Autumn's golden reign,

20 Such, and so many, moves the warrior's train.
    In bright array they seek the work of war,
    Where high unfurl'd the ensign waves in air.
    Shall I to Washington their praise recite?
    Enough thou know'st them in the fields of fight.

25 Thee, first in place and honors,—we demand
    The grace and glory of thy martial band.
    Fam'd, for thy valor, for thy virtues more,
    Here every tongue thy guardian aid implore!
    One century scarce performed its destin'd round,

30 When Gallic powers Columbia's fury found;
    And so may you, whoever dares disgrace
    The land of freedom's heaven-defended race!
    Fix'd are the eyes of nations on the scales,
    For in their hopes Columbia's arm prevails.

35 Anon Britannia droops the pensive head,
    While round increase the rising hills of dead.
    Ah! cruel blindness to Columbia's state!
    Lament thy thirst of boundless power too late.
    Proceed, great chief, with virtue on thy side,

40 Thy every action let the goddess guide.
    A crown, a mansion, and a throne that shine,
    With gold unfading, Washington, be thine.

32. What purpose do the two opening lines serve?

    (A)   They introduce the poem and state its subject.
    (B)   They establish the poem's tone and theme.
    (C)   They explain Washington's role as a leader.
    (D)   They explain the suitability of Washington as a subject for the poem.
    (E)   They establish the poet's unconventional style.

33. What is Columbia?

    (A)   A metaphor for the future
    (B)   A metaphor for the past
    (C)   A metaphor for the Gallic powers
    (D)   A metaphor for Washington
    (E)   The personification of America

34. What figure of speech is used in line 2?

    (A)   Metaphor
    (B)   Simile
    (C)   Irony
    (D)   Assonance
    (E)   Personification

35. In context, what do the olive branch and laurel symbolize (line 10)?

    (A)   The olive is a symbol of abundance; the laurel, a symbol of fertility.
    (B)   The olive is a symbol of victory; the laurel, a symbol of peace.
    (C)   The olive is a symbol of peace; the laurel, a symbol of victory.
    (D)   The olive is a symbol of food; the laurel, a symbol of harvests.
    (E)   The olive is a symbol of tradition; the laurel, a symbol of innovation.

36. How does the poet regard Washington?

    (A) He is the unquestioned leader of Columbia's army, strong and virtuous.
    (B) He is a strong leader, but he is by no means omnipotent.
    (C) He is brave and forceful, but he is subject to enormous human doubt.
    (D) He is a fine leader, but he is no match for the Gallic powers.
    (E) He is soon to be replaced by Columbia, a true leader.

37. What does the god Eolus personify?

    (A) Tempests and other wild storms
    (B) The fierce British warriors
    (C) Autumn
    (D) The unbeatable American forces
    (E) Aspects of the natural world

38. The rhyme scheme of this poem is

    (A) aa bb cc dd.
    (B) abc abc def def.
    (C) abba cddc effg.
    (D) aaab bbbc ddde.
    (E) There is no rhyme scheme; this poem is written in free verse.

39. "Celestial choir" (line 1) is an example of

    (A) personification.
    (B) symbolism.
    (C) alliteration.
    (D) metaphor.
    (E) irony.

40. What do the last two lines suggest about the influence of British social and political systems on American thinking?

    (A) The British political system has corrupted American values of democracy and individuality.
    (B) The British social system is fatally flawed, but Americans are intelligent enough to recognize this and strike out on their own.
    (C) Since the British political system has shown that elected governments are doomed to failure, we should appoint Washington to be our king.
    (D) The British social structure correctly identifies natural rulers, men such as the heroic and glorious George Washington.
    (E) The British monarchy has been so influential that the poet suggests that Washington be crowned king when he is victorious.

41. The tone of the poem is best described as

    (A) condemning.
    (B) laudatory.
    (C) sarcastic.
    (D) ironic.
    (E) resigned.

Questions 42–52 refer to the following essay.

On Eating

[1763] At supper this night he talked of good eating with uncommon satisfaction.

"Some people (said he) have a foolish way of not minding, or pretending not to mind, what they eat. For my part, I mind my belly very studiously, and very carefully; for I look upon it that he who does not mind his belly will hardly mind anything else."

He was, for the moment, not only studious but vehement. Yet I have heard him, upon other occasions, talk with great contempt of people who were anxious to gratify their palates; and the 206th number of his *Rambler* is a masterly essay against gluosity. His practice, indeed, I must acknowledge, may be considered as casting the balance of his different opinions upon this subject, for I never knew a man who relished good eating more than he did. When at table, he was totally absorbed in the business of the moment; his looks seemed riveted to his plate; nor would he, unless when in very high company, say one word, or even pay the least attention to what was said by others, till he had satisfied his appetite, which was so fierce, and indulged with such intenseness, that while in the act of eating, the veins of his forehead swelled, and generally strong perspiration was visible.

To those whose sensations were delicate, this could not but be disgusting; and it was doubtless not very suitable to the character of a philosopher, who should be distinguished by self-command. But it must be owned that Johnson, though he could be rigidly abstemious, was not a temperate man either in eating or drinking. He could refrain, but he could not use moderately. He told me that he had fasted two days without inconvenience, and that he had never been hungry but once. They who beheld with wonder how much he ate upon all occasions when his dinner was to his taste could not easily conceive what he must have meant by hunger, and not only was he remarkable for the extraordinary quantity which he ate, but he was, or affected to be, a man of very nice discernment in the science of cookery. He used to descant critically on the dishes which had been at table where he had dined or supped, and to recollect minutely what he had liked...

When invited to dine, even with an intimate friend, he was not pleased if something better than a plain dinner was not prepared for him. I have heard him say on such an occasion, "This was a good dinner enough, to be sure; but it was not a dinner to *ask* a man to." On the other hand, he was wont to express, with great glee, his satisfaction when he had been entertained quite to his mind.

42. In the first paragraph, what rhetorical strategy does the writer use with the word "mind"?

    (A) Word play
    (B) Metaphor
    (C) Allegory
    (D) Understatement
    (E) Hyperbole

43. What does the word "mind" mean as it is used in the last sentence of the first paragraph?

    (A) To obey
    (B) To object to
    (C) To recall
    (D) To be intelligent
    (E) To take care of

44. The phrase "I must acknowledge" in the second paragraph does which of the following?

    (A) Makes Johnson seem disingenuous, even hypocritical
    (B) Shifts the focus from the author to his subject
    (C) Emphasizes Boswell's own love of good food
    (D) Portrays Johnson in a more flattering light
    (E) Replaces general statements with specific examples

45. The long sentences in paragraph 2 serve to

    (A) emphasize the theoretical rather than the practical aspects of the discussion.
    (B) demonstrate that the writer knows his subject well.
    (C) mirror the length of Johnson's eating binges.
    (D) reveal how Johnson scandalizes the other people at the table with him.
    (E) suggest the food shortages of the time.

46. How can someone be *abstemious* but not *temperate*?

    (A) They can deny themselves pleasure because of an adherence to principle but secretly indulge in that which they abjure.
    (B) They can deny themselves pleasure as long as they're not exposed to it, but once they have a little, they cannot stop.
    (C) They can deny only certain pleasures, depending on their whims.
    (D) They can do one thing in public and the opposite in private.
    (E) They can indulge in moderate rather than excessive pleasure.

47. At the end of the third paragraph, "nice" is used to mean

    (A) superior.
    (B) agreeable.
    (C) pleasant.
    (D) exacting.
    (E) good.

48. The passage suggests contrasts between

    (A) Johnson and other philosophers.
    (B) youth and old age.
    (C) Boswell (the author) and Johnson (the subject).
    (D) appearance and reality.
    (E) virtue and vice.

49. The writer, Boswell, emerges as somewhat

    (A) gluttonous.
    (B) hypocritical.
    (C) cool.
    (D) jealous.
    (E) prissy.

50. This essay is constructed primarily on

    (A) chronological order.
    (B) comparison and contrast.
    (C) order of importance.

(D)   spatial order.
(E)   cause and effect.

51. James Boswell most likely discussed Johnson's eating habits for all of the following reasons EXCEPT

(A)   to strike back at Johnson for his slights and petty cruelties.
(B)   to make his account of Johnson more balanced.
(C)   to present a more complete portrait of his subject, "warts and all."
(D)   to be more accurate in his reporting.
(E)   to make his account more interesting and thus more commercially viable.

52. What picture emerges of Johnson from this passage?

(A)   He is arrogant and ungrateful.
(B)   He is hypocritical, saying one thing and doing quite another.
(C)   He is gross and vulgar, a dreadful houseguest.
(D)   He is larger-than-life, a nonconformist with great appetites in everything.
(E)   He is studious, careful, and picky.

Question 1
Suggested Time: 40 minutes

Directions: The following passage is an excerpt from Virginia Woolf's 1929 essay "A Room of One's Own." Read the excerpt carefully. Then write an essay in which you describe Woolf's thesis. What does a woman need to be a writer? Then agree or disagree with her argument.

...For my belief is that if we live another century or so—I am talking of the common life which is the real life and not of little separate lives which we live as individuals—and have five hundred a year each of us and rooms of our own; if we have the habit of freedom and the courage to write exactly what we think; if we escape a little from the common sitting room and see human beings not always in their relation to each other but in reality to reality; and the sky, too, and the trees or whatever it may be in themselves; if we face the fact, for it is a fact, that there is no arm to cling to, but that we go alone and that our relation is to the world of reality and not to the world of men and women, then the opportunity will come and the dead poet who was Shakespeare's sister will put on the body which she has so often laid down. Drawing her life from the lives of the unknown who were her forerunners, as her brother did before her, she will be born. As for her coming without that preparation, without that effort on our part, without that determination that when she is born again she shall find it possible to live and write her poetry, that we cannot expect, for that would be impossible. But I maintain that she would come if we worked for her, and that so to work, even in poverty and obscurity, is worth while.

Question 2
Suggested Time: 40 minutes

Directions: Read the following poem by Robert Frost. Then write an essay in which you discuss how the poem's imagery, symbolism, and form express its theme.

Design

1   I found a dimpled spider, fat and white,
    On a white heal-all, holding up a moth
    Like a white piece of rigid satin cloth—
    Assorted characters of death and blight

5   Mixed ready to begin with morning right,
    Like the ingredients of a witches' broth—
    A snow-drop spider, a flower like a froth,
    And dead wings carried like a paper kite.
    What had that flower to do with being white,

10 The wayside blue and innocent heal-all?
    What brought the kindred spider to that height,
    Then steered the white moth thither in the night?
    What but design of darkness to appall?—
    If design govern in a thing so small.

Question 3
Suggested Time: 40 minutes

Directions: Suffering can be a challenge to grow or an occasion to surrender to defeat. Choose a novel or play of recognized literary merit in which a character had to cope with a crucial, painful experience. Describe the character's experience and tell how it became a challenge to grow or an occasion to surrender. Show the effect the character's response had on his or her life. You may choose a work from the list below or another novel or play of literary merit.

Othello	*Macbeth*
King Lear	*Hamlet*
All My Sons	*The Crucible*
A Doll's House	*Jane Eyre*
The Sound and the Fury	*David Copperfield*
Jude the Obscure	*Wuthering Heights*
As I Lay Dying	*Lord Jim*
Sons and Lovers	*Catch-22*
Saint Joan	*Waiting for Godot*
The Iceman Cometh	*Gulliver's Travels*
Moby Dick	*The Turn of the Screw*
1984	*The Oresteia*

QUICK-SCORE ANSWERS

1. C	19. C	36. A
2. C	20. A	37. D
3. B	21. D	38. A
4. E	22. C	39. C
5. D	23. D	40. E
6. A	24. B	41. B
7. B	25. A	42. A
8. D	26. C	43. E
9. B	27. A	44. A
10. B	28. C	45. C
11. A	29. B	46. B
12. D	30. E	47. D
13. E	31. B	48. A
14. B	32. B	49. E
15. A	33. E	50. B
16. C	34. E	51. A
17. A	35. C	52. D
18. D		

COMPUTING YOUR SCORE

You can use the following worksheet to compute an approximate score on the practice test. Since it is difficult to be objective about your own writing and since you are not a trained ETS scorer or English teacher, you may wish to ask a friend who has already taken the test (and earned a score of 4 or 5) to score your three essays.

Recognize that your score can only be an approximation (at best), as you are scoring yourself against yourself. In the actual AP English Literature and Composition Exam, you will be scored against every other student who takes the test as well.

Section I: Multiple-Choice Questions

	_____	number of correct answers
−	_____	.25 × number of wrong answers
=	_____	raw score

	_____	raw score
×	_____	1.25
=	_____	scaled score (out of a possible 67.5)

Section II: Essays

_____	essay 1 (0–9)
_____	essay 2 (0–9)
_____	essay 3 (0–9)
× _____	3.055
= _____	scaled score (out of a possible 82.5)

Scaled Score

_____	multiple-choice scaled score
+ _____	essay scaled score
= _____	final scaled score (out of a possible 150)

AP Score Conversion Chart

Scaled Score	Likely AP Score
150–100	5
99–86	4
85–67	3
66–0	1 or 2

ANSWERS AND EXPLANATIONS

SECTION I: MULTIPLE-CHOICE QUESTIONS

A note on "Thanatopsis":

The major influence on William Cullen Bryant's "Thanatopsis" is a movement called Romanticism, which flourished during the nineteenth century. Some of the ideas of the movement reflected in this poem include a belief in the changeable, variable state of the physical world (often called "mutability") and the feeling that all is prey to decline and decay. The Romantics also felt that even though everything changes and declines, God remains absolute and reveals Himself through that changeable creation—Nature. Bryant also used many of the writing techniques of the Romantic school. There is a great reliance on artificially inflated diction and syntax. The Romantics felt that old-fashioned, out-of-date word order and choice could be used to establish a serious and philosophical tone. Thus we find words like "thou," "thy," and "shalt," as well as contractions such as "list" for "listen." Even in the nineteenth century, which seems so long ago, no one was speaking in this manner. Inversion was also a Romantic technique. Also referred to as *anastrophe*, it is the movement of a word or phrase from its normal and expected position in the sentence for poetic effect or emphasis. It can also be used to maintain poetic rhythm and rhyme. As shown in the poem, Bryant made extensive use of this technique.

1. **The correct answer is (C).** The poet feels that people should listen to Nature when thoughts of death obsess them. Lines 2–3 tell us that "she [Nature] speaks/A various language," and line 7 explains Nature's "healing sympathy." Lines 8–15 specifically instruct people to shake off their thoughts of the "last bitter hour" by going forth to Nature under the open sky and listening to what the Earth and waters and air can tell.

2. **The correct answer is (C).** According to the poet, Nature will be able to offer humanity healing sympathy. You can find the direct reference in line 7: "Into his darker musings with a mild/And healing sympathy that steals away."

3. **The correct answer is (B).** In lines 17–57, the poet believes Nature offers people a "couch more magnificent" as comfort when they are facing death (line 33). The author is saying that nothing could be more majestic than to share eternity with the most powerful people the earth has known—kings, the wise, and the good.

4. **The correct answer is (E).** Only murderers, choice (E), have not shared Nature's "magnificent couch"—the grave. Lines 34–37 list all those who are buried in the earth: "With patriarchs of the infant world—with kings,/The powerful of the earth—the wise, the good./Fair forms, and hoary seers of ages past,/All in one mighty sepulcher." *Great leaders,* choice (A), is shown in the words "The powerful of the earth." *Upstanding citizens,* choice (B), and *wise men and women,* choice (C), are shown in the words "the wise, the good." *Prophets,* choice (D), is shown in the phrase "hoary seers."

5. **The correct answer is (D).** The line "All that breathe/Will share thy destiny" (lines 60–61) explains that mourning is not necessary, for in time all will pass on to Nature's bed.

6. **The correct answer is (A).** In lines 73–81, it is important to the poet and the poem's meaning that humanity live in trust with Nature. Lines 77–81—"Thou go not, like the quarry slave at night,/Scourged to his dungeon, but, sustained and soothed/By an unfaltering trust, approach thy grave and lies down to pleasant dreams"—reveal this.

7. **The correct answer is (B).** People must base their faith in Nature so that when we face death, we can be secure in the knowledge that Nature will sustain us and make us a part of the natural order. The entire poem is concerned with humanity's acceptance of the natural order, that people live and die according to Nature's rule, and thus all

will work in a great cosmic harmony. None of the other choices fits with the poem's meaning.

8. **The correct answer is (D).** A "sepulcher" is a tomb, and "mighty" means *grand*. Here, the earth is the grandest tomb of all, for it is the largest and holds all the great, wise, and mighty from all time.

9. **The correct answer is (B).** The "sepulcher" refers to the mighty grave of all. Choice (A) cannot be correct because the poet has already included "The powerful of the earth—the wise, the good./Fair forms, and hoary seers of ages past." They are all to be entombed "All in one mighty sepulcher." Choice (C) cannot be correct because the sepulcher is in the ground. It is made by nature, not human hands. Choice (D) is wrong because the poet does not refer to an afterlife here in relationship to the tomb. The same is true of choice (E).

10. **The correct answer is (B).** The "destiny" in lines 60–61 is death, what all people, no matter how great or small, hold in common. None of the other choices is always true, for we have no assurance that *all will have to mourn,* choice (D), or *accept Nature,* choice (E).

11. **The correct answer is (A).** In the final two lines, the poet uses a *simile*. This figure of speech is a comparison using "like" or "as." The simile is "Like one who wraps the drapery of his couch/About him," which compares sleep with a warm and comfortable blanket to the grave's shroud. Both death and sleep, the poet claims, should be approached calmly and with trust. Choice (B) is giving human qualities to inanimate objects, and choice (C) is the repetition of the initial letter, as in "Peter Piper picked a peck of pickled peppers." Choice (D) is addressing someone who is not present, as if the author said, "Dear Nature." Choice (E) occurs when portions of the sentence are switched around for literary effect. That is not the case in this instance.

12. **The correct answer is (D).** In the final two lines, death is compared to sleep. The reader is instructed to approach death as if it were but sleep on a warm couch: "Like one who wraps the drapery of his couch/About him, and lies down to pleasant dreams." This is especially clear in the poet's use of the word "dreams."

13. **The correct answer is (E).** When the author published this poem in a new edition, he added lines 1–17, up to "Yet a few days." These lines serve to offer more hope, speaking as they do of "gayer hours" (line 3), "voice of gladness" (line 4), and "healing sympathy" (line 7). The poet had come under fire for what many saw as a bleak picture of death in this poem, although he intended to offer great comfort.

14. **The correct answer is (B).** At the same time as the above additions were made, he also added the final 16 lines, beginning with "As the long train." He did this to offer a bit of hope and unify the beginning and the end of the poem. Rarely will an author add anything simply to allow room for more figures of speech, as choice (A) suggests. Rather, the poetic devices add to the meaning, not substitute for it. The poem is not a *ballad,* choice (C), and nowhere is *death to be feared or battled,* as choice (D) states. (They ask man to fear death as a worthy opponent.) The final lines have a warm and soothing tone and calming imagery.

15. **The correct answer is (A).** The poem presents a movement from life to death. The poet speaks of life in the beginning and concludes with a discussion of the way in which a person should approach death—calmly and with trust in Nature.

16. **The correct answer is (C).** All of the following are true about the language of the poem EXCEPT choice (C),"The words are selected to call for two different levels of interpretation." There is only one level of interpretation here: the poet's belief that Nature will welcome us, comfort us, and that our death will unite us firmly with the

universe and the natural order of life. Be careful with questions that have the word EXCEPT in them, for they can be tricky to read.

17. **The correct answer is (A).** The language of the poem can best be described as *labored.* The inversions and poetic contractions, such as "list" for "listen," make the poem difficult to read. This is the same as "labored." The poet uses a great many words, so the language cannot be described as *economical,* choice (B). Indeed, we could make a case that the poem would have been more effective if the poet *had* been more economical in his use of language. The language is not *best* described as *extravagant,* choice (C), or *awkward,* choice (D), although a case could be made for both. Choice (E) is weak. Remember to select the answer that *best* completes the question. Even though there will be answers that appear to be correct, you should look for the *best* response.

18. **The correct answer is (D).** The speaker of the poem is the poet. The speaker makes no pretensions to be *Nature,* choice (A), or the *powerful of the earth,* choice (C). The voice remains the same throughout the poem, so choice (E) is not correct.

19. **The correct answer is (C).** "Yet a few days, and the all-beholding sun shall see no more in all his course" is an example of an *inversion,* as the words are switched out of their expected order. The sentence would usually read, "Yet a few days, and the all-beholding sun shall not see any more in all his course." Choice (A), an *oxymoron,* is a seeming contradiction, such as "cruel kindness." Choice (B), *a conceit,* is an elaborate metaphor or extended comparison, and choice (D), *personification,* is giving human qualities to inanimate objects. A *synecdoche,* choice (E), is the use of a part for a whole or a whole for a part, such as "five sails" for five ships.

20. **The correct answer is (A).** The tone here is intended to be *comforting.* This is the opposite of choice (B), *frightening.* In the same way, *neutral,* choice (C); *passive,* choice (D); and *excited,* choice (E), cannot be correct.

21. **The correct answer is (D).** The phrase "just as the hand was divided into fingers" functions as a *simile* and an *example.* Recall that a *simile* is a comparison that uses "like" or "as." In addition to being a simile, however, the phrase functions as an example to illustrate the point that "Man [was divided] into men." Choice III, *personification,* is giving human qualities to inanimate objects. Since a hand and fingers are already human parts, the phrase cannot be personification.

22. **The correct answer is (C).** The phrase "the better to answer its end" at the end of the first paragraph can best be interpreted to mean to better serve its purpose. The word "end" is used here to mean "purpose" or "means." None of the other answer choices conveys this meaning.

23. **The correct answer is (D).** The "old fable" in paragraph two refers to the belief that individuals possess only certain talents. You can infer this from the first sentence, especially the last clause: "The old fable covers a doctrine ever new and sublime; that there is One Man,—present to all particular men only partially, or through one faculty; and that you must take the whole society to find the whole man." If you must consider everyone together to find the "whole man," each individual must have only certain abilities. Choices (A), (B), (C), and (E) sound sufficiently "myth-like" to mislead casual readers, but none of these choices expresses the correct meaning.

24. **The correct answer is (B).** As used in context, the word "faculty" most nearly means *aptitude.* Look back at the sentence: "The old fable covers a doctrine ever new and sublime; that there is One Man,—present to all particular men only partially, or through one faculty..." Substitute the word "aptitude" for "faculty" to verify meaning in context. While "faculty" does mean a *department of learning,* choice (A), and *staff,*

choice (E), those meanings are not required by the context. As you read, be careful to correctly define multiple-meaning words.

25. **The correct answer is (A).** The phrase "But, unfortunately" in the second paragraph signals a transition to a new idea. The conjunction "but" is always used to show contrast, as is the case here. None of the other choices conveys this meaning.

26. **The correct answer is (C).** The author suggests that society has destroyed humanity's wholeness. This can be seen most clearly in the following excerpt: "The state of society is one in which the members have suffered amputation from the trunk, and strut about so many walking monsters,—a good finger, a neck, a stomach, an elbow, but never a man." None of the other choices shows the correct interpretation.

27. **The correct answer is (A).** The writer uses the word "ministry" in relation to the planter to suggest the inherent holiness of farming. The writer suggests that all occupations have their own divinity, but few of us are able to appreciate the dignity and holiness of our work.

28. **The correct answer is (C).** The author's thesis in the third paragraph is developed through a series of examples. These include the planter, tradesman, priest, attorney, mechanic, and sailor. While the author does repeat key words (especially "man" and "thinking"), this is not the way he develops his ideas. *Comparison and contrast,* choice (B), is also a technique that he uses, but it is not the key method of development in this paragraph. Choice (D), *alliteration,* is the repetition of initial consonants. It is not the means of paragraph development in this instance. Choice (E), *aphorisms,* are pithy statements. Again, they are not the chief means of paragraph development here.

29. **The correct answer is (B).** The writer concludes the third paragraph with a series of metaphors to suggest our identity is subsumed in our work. You can infer this from the following statement: "The priest becomes a form; the attorney a statute-book; the mechanic a machine; the sailor a rope of the ship."

30. **The correct answer is (E).** The tone of this essay is best described as *neutral.* This is another instance of selecting the *best* choice. *Despairing,* choice (A); *fiery,* choice (B); *soothing,* choice (C); and *angry,* choice (D), do not accurately reflect the tone.

31. **The correct answer is (B).** The language of this essay is best described as *scholarly and elevated.* Note the long, complex sentences and the sophisticated use of punctuation (especially semicolons and dashes to show emphasis). This is the opposite of choice (A), *colloquial.* The language is too straightforward to be accurately described as *florid,* choice (C). *Florid* means "excessively ornate," which is not the case here. The same is true of choice (D), *biased.* Since the author provides specific examples, the language cannot be described as *vague and colorless,* choice (E).

32. **The correct answer is (B).** The two opening lines establish the tone and theme. The two lines read, "Celestial choir! enthron'd in realms of light,/Columbia's scenes of glorious toils I write." The tone is celebratory; the theme, America's victory over the British. Choice (A) is close, but choice (B) is more accurate in capturing the praiseful tone. Choices (C) and (D) are too narrow to be correct. Choice (E) is clearly incorrect because the poem's style is very conventional, comprised of rhymed couplets and traditional rhythms.

33. **The correct answer is (E).** Columbia stands for America, as the poem tells of America's quest for freedom under General Washington. This comparison shows her beauty and strength.

34. **The correct answer is (E).** In line 2, the poet uses personification to describe the battle. *Personification* is giving human characteristics to inanimate objects. When the poet writes "Columbia's scenes of glorious toils I write," she is making Columbia seem to be human and be able to "toil." Both *metaphor,* choice (A), and *simile,* choice

(B), are figures of speech that make comparisons. There is no comparison being made here. *Irony,* choice (C), is a reversal of the reader's expectations. We would expect Columbia to be "glorious," so the reference can't be ironic. Finally, *assonance,* choice (D), is the repetition of consonants within a line of poetry or prose. This is not the case here.

35. **The correct answer is (C).** The olive is a symbol of peace; the laurel, a symbol of victory. Readers can infer this from the lines "Muse! bow propitious while my pen relates/How pour her armies through a thousand gates" (lines 13–14). According to the poet, America will be victorious in her battle for victory and "first in peace and honors" (line 25) because of her leader George Washington and her virtuous cause.

36. **The correct answer is (A).** The poet believes in Washington without reservation. She sees him as the unquestioned leader of Columbia's army, strong and virtuous. The praise increases as the poem continues, and the final four lines sum up the poet's admiration.

37. **The correct answer is (D).** *Personification* is giving human characteristics to inanimate objects. Here, the god Eolus is used to personify the unbeatable American forces.

38. **The correct answer is (A).** The rhyme scheme of this poem is *aa bb cc dd.* Therefore, the poem is written in rhymed couplets (pairs): light/write (aa), alarms/arms (bb), bemoan/unknown (cc), etc.

39. **The correct answer is (C).** "Celestial choir" (line 1) is an example of *alliteration,* the repetition of two or more initial sounds within a line of poetry or prose. The two c's in "celestial choir" show alliteration. All the other answers have been previously explained; see the glossary for a further explanation of terms.

40. **The correct answer is (E).** The last two lines suggest that the British monarchy has been so influential that the poet thinks that Washington should be crowned king when he is victorious. This is a curious twist in a poem so devoted to the American cause.

41. **The correct answer is (B).** The tone of the poem is best described *laudatory.* The poet enthusiastically celebrates America and its brilliant leader, George Washington. This is the opposite of choice (A), *condemning,* and choice (C), *sarcastic.* It's also clear that the poet is being straightforward rather than *ironic,* so choice (D) cannot be correct. Finally, if she is laudatory and enthusiastic, she cannot be *resigned,* choice (E).

42. **The correct answer is (A).** In the first paragraph, the writer uses word play with the word "mind." Notice that he uses the word "mind" five times in one sentence: "Some people (said he) have a foolish way of not *minding,* or pretending not to *mind,* what they eat. For my part, I *mind* my belly very studiously, and very carefully; for I look upon it that he who does not *mind* his belly will hardly *mind* anything else." There's neither *metaphor,* choice (B), a comparison, nor any *allegory,* choice (C), which occurs when one idea or object is represented in the shape of another. There is no *understatement,* choice (D), a statement that states less than it indirectly suggests, or *hyperbole,* choice (E), an exaggeration.

43. **The correct answer is (E).** As used in the last sentence of the first paragraph, the word "mind" means *to take care of.* Reread the passage: "For my part, I *mind* my belly very studiously, and very carefully; for I look upon it that he who does not *mind* his belly will hardly *mind* anything else." He is not *obeying* his belly, choice (A), or *objecting to it,* choice (B). Choices (C) and (D) do not make sense in context.

44. **The correct answer is (A).** The phrase "I must acknowledge" in the second paragraph makes Johnson seem disingenuous, even hypocritical. Johnson has written against gluttony, yet he loves to overeat. This is shown in the following passage: "Yet I have heard him, upon other occasions, talk with great contempt of people who were anxious

to gratify their palates; and the 206th number of his *Rambler* is a masterly essay against gluosity. His practice, indeed, I must acknowledge, may be considered as casting the balance of his different opinions upon this subject, for I never knew a man who relished good eating more than he did." This is the direct opposite of choice (D). The phrase has nothing to do with Boswell, so you can eliminate choices (B) and (C). Choice (E) does not fit the context because the entire essay is built on specific examples rather than generalities.

45. **The correct answer is (C).** The long sentences in the second paragraph serve to mirror the length of Johnson's eating binges. This is a clever marrying of form and function. Choice (A) has nothing to do with context. The same is true of choice (B). The length of the sentence cannot reveal how Johnson scandalizes the other people at the table with him, so choice (D) is not valid. Choice (E) makes no sense.

46. **The correct answer is (B).** Someone can be *abstemious* but not *temperate* if they can deny themselves pleasure as long as they're not exposed to it, but once they have a little, they cannot stop. This describes Johnson: he can fast for two days, yet once he sees food, he cannot stop eating. The following sentence states the issue clearly: "He could refrain, but he could not use moderately."

47. **The correct answer is (D).** At the end of the third paragraph, "nice" is used to mean *exacting*: "but he was, or affected to be, a man of very nice discernment in the science of cookery." The context clue is the word "discernment."

48. **The correct answer is (A).** The passage suggests contrasts between Johnson and other philosophers. The contrast is suggested outright in this sentence: "To those whose sensations were delicate, this could not but be disgusting; and it was doubtless not very suitable to the character of a philosopher, who should be distinguished by self-command." There is no mention of youth and old age, so you eliminate choice (B). We do not know anything about Boswell's appetites, so choice (C) cannot be correct. Since appearance and reality match here (Johnson says that he likes to eat and he eats with gusto), you can eliminate choice (D). While Boswell does seem to look down his nose at Johnson's magnificent appetite, it's too big a leap to go for choice (E).

49. **The correct answer is (E).** The writer, Boswell, emerges as somewhat *prissy*. He seems shocked at Johnson's capacity for food and his total devotion to it while eating. This can be seen in the following passage: "... or even pay the least attention to what was said by others, till he had satisfied his appetite, which was so fierce, and indulged with such intenseness, that while in the act of eating, the veins of his forehead swelled, and generally strong perspiration was visible." Since Boswell has a strong reaction to Johnson's eating habits, *cool,* choice (C), cannot be right. Johnson—not Boswell—emerges as gluttonous, so choice (A) can't be correct. We don't know anything about Boswell's eating habits, so *hypocritical,* choice (B), cannot be right. Finally, there's no reason for Boswell to be *jealous* of Johnson's prodigious appetites, so choice (D) is wrong.

50. **The correct answer is (B).** This essay is constructed primarily on *comparison and contrast.* Boswell compares and contrasts Johnson's different attitudes about food, eating, and being a dinner guest. The other choices do not make sense. The essay is not constructed in *chronological order,* choice (A): Boswell does not trace Johnson's eating habits over a period of time. Neither does he use *order of importance,* choice (C), or show which aspects of Johnson's character are more important than any other. The passage is not arranged by *spatial order,* choice (D), or *cause and effect,* choice (E).

51. **The correct answer is (A).** James Boswell most likely discussed Johnson's eating habits for all of the following reasons EXCEPT to strike back at Johnson for his slights and petty cruelties. We do not have any textual support that Johnson was anything but

kind to his biographer. Indeed, only the most foolish subjects would alienate their biographers!

52. **The correct answer is (D).** Johnson emerges as larger-than-life, a nonconformist with great appetites in everything. As this passage shows, he likes to eat mass quantities of food. Most people probably wouldn't say anything to their host if they didn't like the food, but Johnson apparently didn't hesitate to say that the meal had not been good enough for a guest. You might argue that Johnson is *hypocritical,* saying one thing and doing quite another, choice (B), because he argues against overeating and then overeats on my occasions, but choice (D) offers a more complete picture of Johnson as presented in this passage.

SECTION II: ESSAY QUESTIONS

Question 1

To earn a high score on this question,

- first describe Woolf's main idea.

- explain what Woolf believes a woman needs to be a writer.

- take a stand regarding her thesis.

- use specific examples drawn from the essay and your reading.

The following model response would earn a top score because it fulfills the requirements of this question and the standards of good writing:

1. Catchy opening on the topic.

2. Describes Woolf's main idea.

3. Takes a stand on the thesis.

4. First main point.

5. Supporting detail.

6. Counter argument.

7. Supporting detail.

8. Detail very specific.

9. Third main point.

1 Are writers made or born? In an excerpt from her 1929 essay "A Room of One's Own," Virginia Woolf argues that female writers
2 need four things to be successful: a room, an independent income, experience, and determination. While Woolf's argument
3 has merit, it is not without flaws.

4 No doubt having "a room of one's own" and enough money to avoid having to toil daily makes it easier for anyone to be a writer—both men and women. Certainly having a separate writing room confers a legitimacy to a person's effort to become a writer. It announces to the world: "My creative efforts are serious stuff. My writing is more than a hobby like tennis, golf, or painting-by-the numbers." A separate space also affords a writer privacy and the assurance that papers will stay put and not become toys for the dog or thrown out accidentally. In the same
5 way, having a steady income from a trust fund or generous patron gives writers (or any artist) the time to devote to the craft.

6 However, much of our great literature has been produced in times of great deprivation by people under seemingly insurmountable stress. Waves of great literature have been produced during each World War. For example, Harriet Beecher Stowe wrote *Uncle Tom's Cabin* on the eve of the Civil War. She had neither a room
7 nor an income; rather, she had many children, tubs of laundry, and piles of bills. During World War I, Rupert Brooke, Wilfred Owen, and Siegfried Sassoon wrote streams of poetry about their experiences—and they certainly had no office space! James Jones' *From Here to Eternity* was a result of his life-and-death
8 experiences in World War II; George Orwell created the classics *1984* and *Animal Farm* while close to starvation. It does not appear that comfort is a catalyst to creativity, judging by the number of people who have the means yet do not produce the words.

9 No doubt a writer needs determination. You can't win it if you're not in it, as the popular slogan goes. However, an "escape a little from the common sitting room" doesn't seem to be required for all good writers, judging by the brilliant poems of recluse Emily Dickinson and classic essays of homebody Henry David

10 Thoreau. Writers clearly need courage to be successful, the "habit of freedom and the courage to write exactly what we think."

11. What writers really need, however, is that rare quality called *talent*. Just about anyone can become a *competent* writer, but few can become *great* writers. Americans in particular cling to the so-called "American Dream" that with hard work and a little bit of luck, anyone can be successful. It also takes talent, creativity, and a touch of genius to become a great writer. A room, some

12 money, and the desire alone are just not sufficient.

10. Excellent detail.

11. Student's opinion on Woolf's thesis.

12. Clear conclusion.

Question 2

To earn a high score on this question,

- include examples of imagery.

- explain the symbolism.

- identify the poem's form (sonnet) and link it to the theme (determination).

- pull together all the elements (imagery, symbolism, form, and theme).

The following model response would earn a top score because it fulfills the requirements of this question and the standards of good writing:

1. Intelligent and catchy opening.

2. Thesis directly addresses the question.

3. Focus on imagery.

4. Addresses symbolism.

5. Specific examples drawn from poem.

6. Theme addressed.

7. Form and theme linked.

8. Focused and precise examples.

9. Intriguing conclusion.

1 In Herman Melville's novel *Moby Dick*, Captain Ahab is appalled by the "whiteness" of Moby Dick, the great whale. Robert Frost is working with the same symbolism in his sonnet "Design." The images of death and destruction centered on 2 "whiteness" combine to convey his theme: humans appear to be powerless to control their lives. Instead, we are pieces trapped in a grand design. However, Frost shows that we have far more control than we think, especially when it comes to the creation of art.

3 The images in the first three lines all concern disease and dying: the "spider, fat and white" (line 1); the "white heal-all" (line 2); and a moth, "Like a white piece of rigid satin cloth" (lines 2-3). All these images are linked by the remark in line 4: "Assorted characters of death and blight." Notice especially that they are all 4 white. The color white is used in this poem to symbolize death. 5 These images of death and decay—all white—continue: "A snow-drop spider"(line 7); "a flower like a froth" (line 7); and "And dead wings carried like a paper kite" (line 8).

The images listed above are pulled together in the final two lines 6 as the speaker expresses surprise that there is some power governing even the formation and design of items as small and seemingly insignificant as the ones he lists. If there is a hand behind even these petty items, he suggests, what rules something as significant as our life?

The poem's rigid form reinforces our apparent lack of control. 7 "Design" is a sonnet, perhaps the least flexible lyric form. The rhyme scheme is abba abba acaacc. This is a variation on the Italian sonnet, whose form is abba abba cdecde. This pattern is followed through the octave (abbaabba), but breaks form in the sestet, to acaacc, with a final rhyming couplet, the cc. It seems 8 likely that the sonnet form is followed in the first eight lines because Frost is talking about design and so follows a rigid form. In the conclusion, though, he breaks out of the plan to create a new pattern. This is reflected in the theme of design ruling even the smallest item in nature, but not in his creation, the poem. In 9 our art, Frost suggests, we have the power to create our own design. Then we are masters of our lives.

Question 3

To earn a high score on this question,

- isolate a character who really suffers.

- the suffering must be major, as in "crucial and painful."

- tell about the character's experience, using details from the work.

- demonstrate whether the character rose to the challenge or faltered.

The following model response would earn a top score because it fulfills the requirements of this question and the standards of good writing:

1   What do you do when the foundation of your life falls away because you discover that the most important person in your life is a fraud? This is the situation Elizabeth Proctor faces in Arthur Miller's play *The Crucible* when she discovers that her husband John has cheated on her with their servant girl, Abigail Williams.

2   Elizabeth certainly has cause to crumble, but instead she rises to the challenge. She revives the ashes of her marriage to stand beside her husband in his time of greatest need. In so doing, she becomes a heroic figure in her own right.

3   About seven months before the play opens, Elizabeth suspects that John has had an affair with Abigail. She confronts him with her suspicions, and he confesses. Abigail is promptly fired, but afterward, there is a clear rift in the Williams' marriage. Both John and Elizabeth are uncomfortable around each other: he feels guilty; she, hurt yet superior. Elizabeth is so cold toward John 4   that he even cries out, "Elizabeth, your justice would freeze beer."

But when Abigail accuses John of witchcraft, Elizabeth lies to protect him. She thinks that in lying she is saving him, but ironically, her lie condemns him to death. Elizabeth learns through her ordeal with false accusations and imprisonment that 5   she is partially to blame for her husband's transgressions because she could not let go of her anger. At the end of the novel, she does not deny him his death, even though she very much wants him living. She has come to understand that he needs this sacrifice to cleanse his soul and validate his life.

6   As John stands on the scaffold, Elizabeth refuses to plead with him to lie and so save his life. Hale, the minister who realizes that he was deluded about the witchcraft hysteria, begs Elizabeth to change her mind. "He have his goodness now!" she cries. "God forbid I take it from him!"

7   Suffering can be a challenge to grow or an occasion to surrender to defeat. In Elizabeth Proctor's case, anguish becomes the spark that ignites great change and personal growth. Elizabeth learns to set aside her anger, take responsibility for her own role in the disintegration of her marriage, and so rebuild her life as an 8   individual and a wife. Tested in the "crucible" of fire, Elizabeth emerges far stronger than before.

1. Elizabeth really suffers.

2. She has a "crucial and painful" experience.

3. Traces the experience.

4. Describes her character before the change.

5. Shows how she changes.

6. Quotes are great specific details.

7. Summary right on target.

8. Clever use of title in ending.

Glossary of Literary Terms

A

Accent   Emphasis or stress on certain words or parts of words.

Accentual Verse   A system of verse in which accents are used to determine the length of lines of poetry. The number of syllables per line is unimportant. Accentual verse is found mainly in the works of the earliest poets, dating from the eighth century.

Accentual-Syllabic Verse   A type of verse in which the counting of accents and syllables occurs within the same line. It is the type of poetry most people instantly recognize as "poetic," for it has a definite beat and often rhymes.

Aesthetic Movement   In the early nineteenth century, a devotion to beauty developed in France. The movement rejected the notion that the value of literature was related to morality—a sense of right and wrong—or some sort of usefulness. Instead, it put forth the idea that art was independent of any moral or didactic (instructive) end. The Aesthetics' slogan was "art for art's sake" ("*l'art pour l'art*"), and many of the writers involved actively attacked the idea that art should serve any "purpose" in the traditional sense. In the late 1900s in England, the movement was represented by Oscar Wilde and Walter Pater. The term "*fin de siècle*" ("end of the century"), which earlier stood for progress, came to imply decadence—great refinement of style but a marked tendency toward the abnormal or freakish in content. When used as a proper noun, *Decadence* refers to the Aesthetic Movement.

Allegory   *Allegory* occurs when one idea or object is represented in the shape of another. In medieval morality plays, abstract ideas such as virtues and vices appear as people to help readers understand the moral (lesson) more easily. In Emily Dickinson's poem "Because I Could Not Stop for Death," death appears as the allegorical figure of a coachman, kindly stopping to pick her up on the road to eternity.

Alliteration   The repetition of initial consonant sounds in several words in a sentence or line of poetry. Writers use alliteration to create musical effects, link related ideas, stress certain words, or mimic specific sounds. Here is an example:

About the lilting house and happy as the grass was green

Note the repetition of *h* in "house" and "happy" and the *gr* in "grass" and "green." Alliteration is also called *initial rhyme*. In Macbeth's line, "after life's fitful fever," alliteration is found in the repeated *f*'s of "fitful fever" and hidden alliteration is found in the repetition of *f* in "after," "life," and "fitful."

Allusion   A reference to a well-known place, event, person, work of art, or other work of literature. Allusions enrich a story or poem by suggesting powerful and exciting comparisons.

Ambiguity   *Ambiguity* allows multiple meanings to coexist in a word or a metaphor. It does not mean that the word or term is unclear; rather, it means that the perceptive reader can see more than one possible interpretation at the same time. Puns, for example, offer ambiguity, as these lines from Wyatt's "They Flee From Me" show: "But since that I so kindely am served/I fain would know what she hath deserved." The word "kindely" means both "served by a group" and "courteously."

Anecdote   A brief story that gets the reader's interest and sheds light on the writer's main idea and theme. To accomplish the writer's aims, anecdotes often describe funny, interesting, and unusual events or people.

Antagonist   The force or person in conflict with the main character in a work of literature. An antagonist can be another character, a force of nature, society, or something within the character.

Apostrophe   A thing is addressed directly, as though it were a person listening to the conversation. For example we have Wordsworth's "Milton! thou should'st be living at this hour," although Milton had been dead for a long time. Apostrophe and personification go hand-in-hand in Donne's "Busy old fool, unruly Sun" and Wyatt's "My lute, awake."

Article   A short work of nonfiction. You can find articles in magazines, newspapers, and books.

Assonance   A type of rhyme in which the vowels in the words are the same but the consonants are not. (for example, the words "seat" and "weak")

Atmosphere   See *Mood*.

Author's Purpose   The author's goal in writing a selection. Common purposes include to entertain, instruct, persuade, or describe. A selection may have more than one author's purpose, but one purpose is often the most important.

Autobiography   A person's story of his or her own life. An autobiography is nonfiction and describes key events from the person's life.

B

Ballad   A story told in song form. Since ballads were passed down by word of mouth from person to person, the words are simple and have a strong beat. Ballads often tell stories about adventure and love. When professional poets write stanzas of this type, such as Auden's "I Walked Out One Evening," they are called *literary ballads*. Probably the most famous ballads are Coleridge's "Rime of the Ancient Mariner" and Keats's "La Belle Dame sans Merci." The ballad stanza rhymes *abcb*. Ballads often contain *refrains,* musical repetitions of words or phrases. Some critics believe that ballads were originally two-line rhyming songs, thus explaining why there are only two rhymes in a four line stanza. Because early ballads were nonliterary, half-rhymes and slant rhymes are often used. Ballads sometimes employ incremental repetition, the repetition of a previous line or lines, but with a slight variation to advance the narrative, as in these lines from "The Cruel Brother":

> O what will you leave to your father dear?
> The silver-shode steed that brought me here.
> And what will you leave to your mother clear?
> My velvet pall and my silken gear.

Biography   A true story about a person's life written by another person. Biographies are often written about well-known, important people, although any person can be the subject.

Blank Verse   Unrhymed iambic pentameter. Blank verse was introduced into English poetry in the middle of the sixteenth century. By the end of the century, it had become the standard medium of English drama. Here is an example by William Shakespeare: "Time hath, my Lord, a wallet at his back,/Wherein he puts alms for oblivion."

Breve   ˘ mark over a syllable to indicate that it is not accented.

Broadside Ballad   A poem of any sort printed on a large sheet—thus the "broadside"—and sold by street singers in the sixteenth century. Not until the eighteenth century was the word "ballad" limited to traditional narrative song.

Burlesque   Any imitation of people or literary type that, by distortion, aims to amuse. Burlesque tends to ridicule faults, not serious vices. Thus it is not to be confused with satire, for burlesque makes fun of a minor fault with the aim of arousing amusement rather than contempt or indignation. Also, it need not make us devalue the original. For example, T. S. Eliot's "The Hollow Men" is parodied in Myra Buttle's "Sweeniad." An excerpt from the original poem reads as follows:

> Between the conception
> And the creation
> Between the emotion
> And the response
> Falls the shadow

while the burlesque is as follows:

> Between the mustification
> And the deception
> Between the multiplication
> And the division
> Falls the Tower of London.

C

Character   A person or an animal in a story. *Main characters* have important roles in the literary work; *minor characters* have smaller parts.

Characterization   The different ways an author tells readers about characters. Writers can tell about characters directly or let readers reach their own decisions about a character indirectly by showing the comments, thoughts, and actions of the other characters.

Chronological Order   The arrangement of the events of a story in time order from first to last.

Climax   The highest point in the action. During the climax, the conflict is resolved and the end of the story becomes clear. The climax is also called the *turning point*.

Comedy   A humorous play that has a happy ending.

Conceit   A long, complex metaphor. In John Donne's "A Valediction Forbidding Mourning," the souls of two lovers become the same as the two legs of a draftsman's compass:

> If they be two, they are two so
> As stiff twin compasses are two;
> Thy soul, the fixed foot, makes no show
> To move, but doth, if th'other do.
> And through it in the center sit,
> Yet when the other far doth roam,
> It leans and harkens after it,
> And grows erect, as that comes home.

Conclusion   The end of an article, play, poem, or book. The term can also refer to an opinion.

Concrete Poems   Poems in which the shape, not the words, is what matters. George Herbert's "Easter Wings" is an example. Also called *emblematic poetry*.

Conflict   A struggle or fight. Conflict makes a story interesting because readers want to find out the outcome. There are two kinds of conflict. In an *external conflict*, characters struggle against a force outside themselves. In an *internal conflict*, characters battle a force within themselves. Stories often contain both external and internal conflicts.

Connotation and Denotation   *Connotation* is the generally accepted meaning(s) of a word, in contrast to the *denotation,* which is the dictionary meaning. Connotation adds additional richness to a word's meaning. In the line, "She was the sickle; I, poor I, the rake," the word "rake" has a clear denotation—a gardening tool designed to pick up clippings from a lawn or a garden that a sickle might have cut down. In the context of the entire poem, though, the word "rake" has the connotative meaning of a debauched man. The two meanings work together to give the poem greater depth and further the author's theme.

Context   The part of a selection that contains a particular word or group of words. Effective readers use the context to help them define the meaning of a word.

Contrast   Contrast shows the difference between two objects. Contrast is the opposite of *comparison*, which shows similarities. In the following example by William Shakespeare, we see his mistress contrasted to various accepted symbols of adoration:

> My mistress' eyes are nothing like the sun;
> Coral is far more red than her lips' red;
> If snow be white, why then her breasts are dun;
> If hairs be wires, black wires grow on her head.

Consonance   A type of half-rhyme in which the consonants agree but the vowels do not, as in the words "luck" and "lick."

Couplet   Two related lines of poetry. A couplet often rhymes.

D

Dead Metaphor   A metaphor that has lost its figurative value through overuse. "Foot of a hill" or "eye of a needle" are examples.

Detail   A small piece of information. In a paragraph, the main idea tells what the paragraph is about, and the details give information to support or explain the main idea.

Denouement   The resolution of a story. At the denouement, all the loose ends of the plot are tied up to leave the reader feeling satisfied.

Description   A word picture of what something or someone is like. Description is made up of sensory details that help readers form pictures in their minds.

Dialect   The way people speak in a certain region or area. In a dialect, certain words are spelled and pronounced differently. Writers use dialects to describe their characters and setting more fully. Mark Twain's *The Adventures of Huckleberry Finn* used dialect extensively.

Dialogue   The conversation in fiction or drama, the exact words a character says. In a story or novel, quotation marks are used to point out the dialogue. In a drama, quotation marks are usually not included.

Diary   A writer's record of his or her experiences, ideas, and feelings.

Didactic Literature   Literature that intends to instruct or teach rather than merely to delight and entertain. The term need not be pejorative, though many use it in this manner. A good case can be made that almost all of the world's finest poetry is didactic in some way. Satire makes fun of certain modes of behavior; Milton wrote his epic poem *Paradise Lost* to "justify the ways of God to men." The problem, then, is one of degree, as true didactic literature deals mainly with instruction. This does not make it any less "poetic." The following lines by John

Gay, explaining how to clean worms, are an illustration of didactic literature:

> Cleanse them from filth, to give a tempting gloss,
> Cherish the sully'd reptile race with moss;
> Amid the verdant bed they twine, they toil,
> And from their bodies wipe the native soil.

Diphthong   Two syllables that are counted and pronounced as one, used in poetry to make the words fit the metrical requirements.

Doggerel   Verse made comic because irregular metrics are made regular by stressing normally unstressed syllables. In Butler's lines:

> More peevish, cross, and splenetic
> Than dog distract or monkey sick.

If the subject matter is mock heroic and the lines are iambic tetrameter couplets (as in the example quoted above), the poem is also referred to as *hudibrastic*, after Samuel Butler's "Hudibras."

Drama   A piece of literature written to be performed in front of an audience. The actors tell the story through their actions. Dramas can be read as well as acted.

Dramatic Monologue   The speaker in a dramatic monologue is usually a fictional character or a historical figure caught at a critical moment. His or her words are established by the situation and are usually directed at a silent audience. The speaker usually reveals aspects of his personality of which he or she is unaware. To some extent, every poem is a dramatic monologue, as an individual speaker is saying something to someone, even if only to himself, but in a true dramatic monologue, the above conventions are observed. A famous example of a dramatic monologue is Robert Browning's "My Last Duchess," in which a duke who has eliminated his last duchess reveals his cruelty to an emissary, who wants to arrange for the marriage to the latest duchess. T. S. Eliot's "The Love Song of J. Alfred Prufrock," in which the speaker's timid self addresses his aggressively amorous self, is another famous example.

Dramatic Poetry   A play written in poem form.

E

Elegy   A poem that deals solemnly with death. Gray's "Elegy Written in a Country Churchyard" is an example. If an elegy is a short funeral lament, it may be called a *dirge*, which in ancient times was a funeral song. Walt Whitman's elegy on Abraham Lincoln, "When Lilacs Last in the Dooryard Bloomed," and Milton's "Lycidas" are famous examples.

Elision   The elimination of a vowel, consonant, or syllable in pronunciation. It usually occurs in verse at the end of a word when the next word begins with a vowel and is used to shorten or lengthen a line to make it fit metrical requirements.

Emblematic Poems   A poem that takes the shape of the subject of the poem. An emblematic poem on a swan, for example, would be in the shape of a swan. George Herbert's "Easter Wings" is an example of an emblematic poem. Also called *concrete poetry*.

Epic   A long and serious narrative poem (a poem that tells a story) about a hero and his heroic companions often set in a past that is pictured as greater than the present. The hero often possesses superhuman and/or divine traits. In Homer's *Iliad*, for example, the hero, Achilles, is the son of a goddess; in Milton's *Paradise Lost*, the characters are God the Father, Christ, angels, and Adam and Eve. The action is usually rather simple—Achilles' anger in the *Iliad* and the fall of man in *Paradise Lost*—but it is increased by figurative language and allusions that often give it cosmic importance. The style is elevated to reflect the greatness of the events, and certain traditional procedures are employed. For example, the poet usually calls to the muses for help, asks them what initiated the action (*the epic question*), and often begins his tale in the middle of the action (*in medias res*). At this point, the hero is at his lowest fortunes and later recounts the earlier part of the tale. Gods often participate in the tale, helping the heroes.

There are two types of epics: the *primary epic* (sometimes called a *folk epic*), which is a stately narrative about the noble class recited to the noble class; and the *literary epic,* a stately narrative about great events designed to be read. Primary epics include Homer's *Iliad* and *Odyssey* and the anonymous Old English *Beowulf.* Literary epics include Vergil's *Aeneid* and Milton's *Paradise Lost.* The poet of the primary epic speaks as the voice of the community, whereas the poet of the literary epic may show more individuality.

Modern epics include Hart Crane's "The Bridge," William Carlos Williams's "Paterson," and Ezra Pound's "Cantos." The first two are examples of American epics; the last is a case for Western civilization. Epics vary in structure. *Beowulf,* for example, uses alliteration and accentual stress rather than rhyme or stanza length to structure the poem.

Epigram   Originally meaning an "inscription," the epigram became for the Greeks a short poem, usually solemn. The Romans used the term to mean a short witty poem, with the sting at the end. The term has come to mean any cleverly expressed thought in verse or prose. An example by John Wilmot:

> We have a pretty witty King,
> Whose word no man relies on,
> Who never said a foolish thing,
> Nor ever did a wise one.

Epitaph   A burial inscription, usually serious but sometimes humorous. John Gay's own serves as an example: "Life is a jest and all things show it:/I thought so once, but now I know it."

Epithalamion   (also spelled epithalamium) A lyric poem in honor of a bride, bridegroom, or both. It is usually ceremonial and happy and is not simply in praise of marriage, but of a particular marriage. Spenser's "Epithalamion" is the greatest epithalamion in English. It begins with an invocation, calls on young people to attend the bride, praises the bride, and welcomes the night. Spenser added deep Christian feeling and realistic description of landscape.

Essay   A brief prose writing on a particular subject or idea.

Eulogy   Frequently confused with *elegy,* a *eulogy* is a poem praising the memory of a living or dead person.

Exaggeration   Overstating an idea to achieve a specific literary effect.

Excerpt   A part of a literary work that is printed on its own, separate from the whole.

Existentialism   The writings of this literary movement stress the loneliness, insecurity, and irrevocability of human experience. It also focuses on people's anxious attempts to face these situations and their ultimately useless attempts to escape them. Our free choice asserts our actions as valid: in Jean-Paul Sartre's own words, "man makes himself." Existentialist criticism approached literature by asking how well a literary work depicts these complexities of the human situation.

Exposition   A kind of writing that explains, shows, or tells about a subject. The word "exposition" can also be used to mean the opening parts of a play or story. During the exposition, the characters, action, and setting are introduced.

Expressionism   This literary movement presents life as the author (or his character) passionately feels it to be, not as it appears on the surface. Thus the Expressionist's work often consciously distorts the external appearance of an object in order to picture the object as the writer or artist feels it really is. Scenery in an Expressionist drama, for example, would not be photographically accurate but would be distorted so that, for instance, the wall of a courtroom may tilt at a weird angle to reveal the accused person's state of mind. The movement was especially dominant in German painting during the decade following World War I.

Extended Metaphor   An extended metaphor results when a metaphor becomes long, elaborate, and complex.

Eye-rhyme   Words that are spelled the same and look alike but have a different sound. This is shown in the following lines from Sir Walter Raleigh's poem "The Nymph's Reply to the Shepherd":

> "These pretty pleasures might me move
> To live with thee and be thy love"

The words "move" and "love" have eye rhyme. These rhymes are also called *historical rhymes,* as their pronunciation has changed over the years. The word "tea," for example, once rhymed with "day," but today these two words are, at best, half-rhymes.

F

Fable   A short, easy-to-read story that teaches a lesson about people. Fables often feature animals that talk and act like people.

Fantasy   A kind of writing that describes events that could not take place in real life. Fantasy has unrealistic characters, settings, and events.

Farce   A humorous play that is based on a silly plot, ridiculous situations, and comic dialogue. The characters are usually one-dimensional stereotypical figures. They often find themselves in situations that start out normally but soon turn absurd. Often, humor is created through an identity switch and the other characters' reaction to it.

Feminine Ending   A line that ends on an accented syllable.

Fiction   Writing that tells about made-up events and characters. Novels and short stories are examples of fiction. Fiction that contains imaginary situations and characters that are very similar to real life is called *realistic fiction.*

Figurative Language   Words and expressions not meant to be taken literally. Figurative language uses words in fresh, new ways to appeal to the imagination. Figures of speech include *similes, metaphors, extended metaphors, hyperbole,* and *personification.* What is impossible or difficult to convey to a reader through the literal use of language may be highly possible through the use of figures of speech. When taken literally, "my love is a rose" is ridiculous, for few people love a plant with a prickly, thorny stem. But "rose" suggests many other possible interpretations—delicate beauty, soft, rare, costly, etc.—and so it can be implied in a figurative sense to mean "love" or "loved one."

Figure of Speech   See *Figurative Language.*

Flashback   A scene that breaks into the story to show an earlier part of the action. Flashbacks help fill in missing information, explain the characters' actions, and advance the plot.

Folk Tale   A story that has been handed down from generation to generation. Fables, fairy tales, legends, tall tales, and myths are different types of folktales. Many folktales contain unusual characters and a moral (a lesson).

Foot   A group of stressed and unstressed syllables combining to form a unit of verse. A foot is composed of either two or three syllables, such that the nature of the foot is determined by the placement of the accent. Every English sentence, no matter whether classified poetry or prose, is made up of these units. Their placement determines the rhythm of a line. One particular foot determines the poem's rhythm. There are four basic types of metrical feet in

English verse:

iamb ˘ʹ
trochee ʹ˘
anapest ˘˘ʹ
dactyl ʹ˘˘

And two uncommon ones:

spondee ʹʹ
phyrrhic ˘˘

The most common foot in English is the *iamb*, perhaps because the use of articles—the, a, an—establishes that an unstressed syllable will occur before a stressed one. Children's verse, such as nursery rhymes, often has trochees dominating. This is also because children don't use as many articles as adults do in speech. The most common line in English poetry is the iambic pentameter line, in part because a line greater than ten syllables in length requires an intake of breath, which translates as requiring another line.

Poetic lines are usually not composed of only one type of metrical foot, for this would sound dull. Variations are constructed to give the line more exciting movement.

Foreshadowing   Clues that hint at what will happen later on in the story. Writers use foreshadowing to create suspense and link related details.

Frame Story   A shorter story within a larger one. Often, the longer story introduces and closes the frame story.

Free Verse   Poetry composed of rhythmical lines varying in length, following no fixed metrical pattern, usually unrhymed. Often, the pattern is based on repetition and parallel grammatical structure. Although free verse may appear unrestrained, it does follow the rules outlined above. An example from Walt Whitman's "Song of Myself":

I celebrate myself, and sing myself,
And what I assume you shall assume,
For every atom belonging to me as good belongs to you.

G

Genre   A major literary category. The three genres are prose, drama, and poetry.

H

Haiku   A type of Japanese verse form composed of seventeen syllables in three lines. The first and third lines have five syllables each; the second line has seven syllables. Most haiku describe images from nature. Haiku were greatly admired models for the Imagist school, an early twentieth-century movement that attempted to shed excess words to create poems of clear, concise details.

Half-rhyme (also called *slant rhyme, approximate rhyme, near rhyme,* or *off-rhyme*)   A type of rhyme in which only the final consonant sounds of the words are identical. The stressed vowel sounds as well as the initial consonant sounds (if any) differ. Examples include *soul: oil, firth: forth,* and *trolley: bully.* The following lines from William Whitehead's "Je Ne Sais Quoi" exemplify half-rhyme:

Tis not her face that love creates,
For there no grace revel;
'Tis not her shape, for there the Fates
Had rather been uncivil.

"Revel" and "uncivil in lines 2 and 4 above illustrate half-rhyme because the vowel sound changes, but the "vl" sound has remained the same.

Hero/Heroine   Literary characters that we admire for their noble traits, such as bravery, selflessness, or cleverness. In the past, the term "hero" was used to refer to a male character; the term "heroine" for a female character. Today, "hero" is used for both male or female characters.

Hubris   A Greek word for a character's excessive pride, confidence, or arrogance. In tragedies, the hero's hubris usually causes his or her downfall. The word can also be spelled "hybris."

Humor   Parts of a story that are funny. Humor can be created through sarcasm, word play, irony, and exaggeration.

Hyperbole   (also called *Overstatement*)   Exaggeration used for a literary effect such as emphasis, drama, or humor. Shakespeare's Sonnet 97 contains this example:

> How like a winter hath my absence been
> From thee, the pleasure of the fleeting year!
> What freezings have I felt, what dark days seen!
> What old December's bareness everywhere!

We realize that Shakespeare did not literally freeze with real cold when he was apart from his loved one. We also realize that the days did not turn dark or June turn to December; however, Shakespeare is saying this to illustrate the depth of his despair at the separation from his beloved.

The same process is at work in Lovelace's "When I lie tangled in her hair/And fetter'd to her eye." Obviously, he is neither captured in her hair nor chained to her eye; what he is suggesting, however, is that he is a prisoner to her beauty and finds himself unable to escape its spell.

I

Ictus   ' mark over a syllable to indicate that it is accented.

Idiom   An expression whose meaning cannot be taken literally. "It's raining buckets" and "He hit the ceiling" are examples of idioms.

Idyll   A short picturesque piece, usually about shepherds. It presents an episode from the heroic past but stresses the pictorial rather than the heroic. The most famous English example is Tennyson's "Idylls of the King," with its detailed descriptions of several aspects of the Arthurian legends.

Image   A word that appeals to one or more of our five senses: sight, hearing, taste, touch, or smell. Imagery can be found in all sorts of writing, but it is most common in poetry.

Imagery   See *Image*.

Imagists/Imagism   At their peak between 1912 and 1914, these poets sought to use common language, to regard all the world as possible subject matter, and to present in vivid and sharp detail a concentrated visual image. "There should be no ideas but things," said poet William Carlos Williams. Imagists usually wrote in free verse. The most frequently cited example of their aims is summed up in the following brief poem by Ezra Pound, the leader of the Imagist movement:

> The apparition of these faces in the crowd;
> Petals on a wet, black bough.

The title of this brief poem, "In a Station of the Metro," informs the reader that the poem is about a metro, a European subway, but the poem presents its statement without directly telling the reader what conclusions to draw. The images in the poem suggest that the colorful faces of people in the subway are like flower petals against dark branches. The poet selects his images and arranges them, but the reader must sense the relationships to experience the picture the poem presents.

Poems of all kinds contain imagery, carefully described objects of the world, but the Imagist movement went further than describing what was seen to create a theory of verse around the idea of the picture.

Implicit or Submerged Metaphor If both terms of the metaphor ("My winged heart" instead of "My heart is a bird") are not present, we have a *submerged metaphor.*

Internal Rhyme A type of rhyme that occurs *within* the line instead of at the end. Oscar Wilde's "Each narrow cell within which we dwell" is an example of internal rhyme because the words "cell" and "dwell" rhyme.

Inciting Moment The beginning of the conflict.

Invocation An address to a god or muse whose aid is sought. Invocation is commonly found at the beginning of an epic. (for example, Milton's "Sing, Heavenly Muse" at the opening of his *Paradise Lost)*

Irony *Irony* occurs when something happens that is different from what was expected. In *verbal irony*, there is a contrast between what is stated and what is suggested. In *dramatic irony,* there is a contrast between what a character believes and what the audience knows is true. In *irony of situation*, an event reverses what the readers or characters expected.

Auden's "Unknown Citizen," for example, is ironic in that it condemns the State by using the State's own terms of praise: "Was he free? Was he happy? The question is absurd;/Had anything been wrong, we should certainly have heard."

L

Legend A story handed down through time that explains how or why something in nature originated. Legends are sometimes based in historical facts, but they often contain exaggerated details and characters.

Light Verse Playful poetry that often combines lightheartedness or whimsy with mild satire as in Suckling's "Why So Pale and Wan, Fond Lover?" that concludes, "If of herself she will not love,/Nothing can make her;/The devil take her." The definition of light verse changed in the late nineteenth century, however, to include less polished pieces such as nursery songs with funny rhymes and distorted pronunciations.

Limerick A form of light verse, a *limerick* is a jingling poem composed of three long and two short lines, the long lines (first, second, and fifth) rhyming with each other and the short lines (third and fourth) rhyming with each other. The rhyming words in the first line can sometimes be misspelled to produce a humorous effect. The following limerick from an early sixteenth-century songbook is an example:

> Once a Frenchman who'd promptly said "oui"
> To some ladies who'd asked him if houi
> Cared to drink, threw a fit
> Upon finding that it
> Was a tipple no stronger than toui

Literature A type of art expressed in writing. Literature includes poetry, fiction, nonfiction, and drama.

Litote A special form of understatement. It affirms something by negating its opposite. For example, "He's no fool" means that he is very shrewd.

Lyric   Brief, musical poems that present a speaker's feelings. In the past, people sang lyrics as they played string-like instruments called "lyres." Lyrics have regular rhyme schemes and are brief, as in the fourteen-line sonnet. Burns' famous drinking song "Auld Lang Syne," Robert Frost's short poems, and George Herbert's religious meditations are lyrics. If the emotion is hate or contempt, and its expression is witty, the poem is usually called a *satire,* or if very brief, an *epigram.* A *complaint* is a lyric expressing dissatisfaction, usually to an unresponsive lover. Chaucer's humorous "Complaint to His Purse," for example, begins, "To you, my purse, and to noon other wight,/Complayne I, for ye be my lady dere!" For a brief period in the 1800s, nature as well as love became a major subject for lyrics, and poets such as William Wordsworth wrote more lyrics on clouds and daffodils than on love.

M

Macaronic Verse   Verse containing words resembling a foreign language or a mixture of languages. For example,

> Mademoiselle got the croix de guerre,
> For washing soldiers' underwear,
> Hinky-dinky, parley-vous.

Main Character   The most important figure in a novel, short story, poem, or play.

Masculine Ending   A line that ends on an unaccented syllable.

Masculine and Feminine Rhymes   Types of rhymes that are the equivalents of masculine and feminine line endings. Rhymes that end on a stress, such as "van" and "span," are masculine, while those ending on an unstressed syllable, such as "falling" and "calling," are called feminine. Thus, "stark/mark" and "support/retort" would be masculine, while "revival/arrival" and "flatter/batter" are feminine. Feminine rhyme is also referred to as *double rhyme.*

Memoir   A first-person prose selection about an event.

Metamorphosis   A *metamorphosis* occurs when a person changes form or shape. For example, in ancient myths, different characters often change into stars, animals, and trees.

Metaphor   A figure of speech that compares two unlike things. The more familiar thing helps describe the less familiar one. Metaphors do not use the words "like" or "as" to make the comparison. "My heart is a singing bird" is an example of a metaphor. In the following metaphor by John Donne, the poet's doctors become the map-makers of the heavens, while the poet's body becomes the map in which the ultimate destiny of his soul can be divined:

> Whilst my physicians by their love are grown
> Cosmographers, and I their map, who lie
> Flat on this bed.

Metaphysical Poets   The most important Metaphysical poets include John Donne (1572–1631) and his seventeenth-century followers, Andrew Marvell, George Herbert, Abraham Cowley, Richard Crashaw, and Henry Vaughan. These poets reacted against the traditions and rules of Elizabethan love poetry to create a more witty and ironic poetry. Modern critics have also concluded that the verse was more passionately intense and psychologically probing than the Elizabethan poems. Instead of penning smooth lines comparing a woman's beauty to something traditional like a rose, these poets wrote colloquial and often metrically irregular lines, filled with difficult and more searching comparisons. These comparisons are called *conceits,* which came to refer to a striking parallel of two highly unlike objects, such as the sun partly hidden by a cloud to a lover's head reclining on a pillow. Certain Petrarchan conceits were often used in English poetry during this time. They included a lover as a ship tossed by a storm, shaken by his tears, or frozen by the coldness of his love.

Meter   The beat or rhythm in a poem. It is created by a pattern of stressed and unstressed syllables. The most common meter in English poetry is called *iambic pentameter*. It is a pattern of five *feet* (groups of syllables), each having one unstressed syllable and one stressed one. Here are the most common meters in English poetry:

Length	Name of Meter
one	monometer
two	dimeter
three	trimeter
four	tetrameter
five	pentameter
six	hexameter
seven	heptameter

Metonymy   The substitution of one item for another item that it suggests or to which it is closely related. For example, if a letter is said to be in Milton's own *hand*, it means that the letter is in Milton's own *handwriting*. Sidney wrote in his sonnet "With How Sad Steps, O Moon," "What, may be that even in heav'nly place/That busy archer his sharp arrows tries?" "That busy archer" is a reference to Cupid, the god of love frequently depicted as a cherubic little boy with a quiver full of arrows. Thus an archer, by relating to the god of love, describes love without specifically using the word "love."

Minor Character   A less important figure in a literary work. A minor character serves as a contrast to the main character or to advance the plot.

Mixed Metaphor   A combination of two metaphors, often with absurd results. For example, "Let's iron out the bottlenecks" would be silly, for it is obvious that it is an impossibility.

Mock Epic or Mock Heroic   Also known as *high burlesque,* a mock epic pokes fun at low activities by treating them in the elevated style of the epic. The humor results from the difference between the low subject and the lofty treatment it is accorded. Alexander Pope's epic poem "The Rape of the Lock" is a famous mock epic. It deals with the cutting of a lock of hair. In the theatre, a burlesque may be a play that humorously criticizes another play by imitating aspects of it in a grotesque manner, as in John Gay's "Beggar's Opera," which make fun of serious operas.

Mood   The strong feeling we get from a literary work. The mood is created by characterization, description, images, and dialogue. Some possible moods include terror, horror, tension, calmness, and suspense. Also called *atmosphere.*

Moral   A lesson about right and wrong. Sometimes, the moral can be stated directly. Other times, readers have to infer the moral from the plot, characters, and setting.

Myth   A story from ancient days that explains certain aspects of life and nature. The Greek and Roman myths, as with many other myths, are about gods and goddesses.

N

Narration   Writing that tells a story. Narrations that tell about real events include biographies and autobiographies. Narrations that deal with fictional events include short stories, myths, narrative poems, and novels.

Narrative   See *Narration.*

Narrative Poem   A poem that tells a story in poetic form. As with a narrative story, a narrative poem has a plot, characters, and theme.

Narrator   The person who tells a story. The narrator may also be a character in the work.

Naturalism   This movement attempted to portray a scientifically accurate, detached picture of life, including everything and selecting nothing for particular emphasis. This is often called the "slice of life" technique when focused on a narrow bit of scientific realism. Many of the Naturalists were very much influenced by evolutionary thought and regarded people as devoid of free will and soul, creatures whose fate was determined by environment and heredity. The movement was represented in the works of Emile Zola, Theodore Dreiser, Frank Norris, Stephen Crane, and others to a lesser extent. The emphasis on scientific determinism, heredity, and environment—Social Darwinism—differentiates Naturalism from Realism.

Nonfiction   A type of writing about real people and events. Essays, biographies, autobiographies, and articles are all examples of nonfiction.

Novel   A long work of fiction. The elements of a novel—plot, characterization, setting, and theme—are developed in detail. Novels usually have one main plot and several less important subplots.

O

Octets   Eight-line stanzas.

Ode   A very long lyric poem characterized by elevated feelings. The Pindaric ode, named for the Greek poet Pindar (c. 522–443 B.C.E.), has two structurally identical stanzas, the *strophe* and *antistrophe* (Greek for "turn" and "counterturn"). These are followed by a stanza with a different structure, the *epode* (Greek for "stand"). The line length and rhyming patterns are determined by the individual poet. The odes were characterized by great passion. Notable English Pindaric odes are Gray's "The Progress of Poesy" and Wordsworth's "Ode: Intimations of Immortality." Horatian odes, named after the Latin poet Horace (65–8 B.C.E.), are composed of matched regular stanzas of four lines that usually celebrate love, patriotism, or simple Roman morality. Notable English Horatian odes include Marvell's "Horatian Ode Upon Cromwell's Return to Ireland" and Collins' "Ode to Evening." Keats' "Ode to a Grecian Urn" is probably the best-known Horatian Ode. Although the ode is a serious poem expressing the speaker's passion, it may be passion about almost anything. Especially during the 1800s, the ode tended to become less public and more personal and introspective. Shelley's "Ode to the West Wind" and Keats' "Ode to a Nightingale" are examples of this introspection. The irregular ode, such as Wordworth's "Intimations on Immortality," has stanzas of various shapes, irregular rhyme schemes, and elaborate rhythms.

Onomatopoeia   The sound of a word echoes or suggests the meaning of the word. "Hiss" and "buzz" are examples. There is a tendency for readers to see onomatopoeia in far too many instances, in words such as "thunder" and "horror." Many words that are thought to echo the sound they suggest merely contain some sound that seems to have a resemblance to the thing it suggests. Tennyson's lines from "Come Down, O Maid" are often cited to explain true onomatopoeia:

> "The moan of doves in immemorial elms
> And murmuring of innumerable bees."

Oral Tradition   Passing songs, poems, and stories down through the ages by word of mouth. Since these selections are spoken rather than written, their words get changed. As a result, there are many different versions of each work, and the original writers and tellers are no longer known.

Oxymoron   The combination of contradictory or incongruous terms. "Living death," "mute cry," and Milton's description of hell as "no light, but rather darkness visible" are all examples of this process. The two words that are brought together to form a description of this nature ought to cancel each other out by the nature of their contradictions; instead, they increase the sense of each word. Thus "sweet pain" aptly describes certain experiences of love.

P

Parable   A short story that contains a moral or lesson. Parables are very similar to fables.

Pastoral   Any writing concerning itself with shepherds may be called *pastoral*. Often set in Arcadia, a mountainous area in Greece known for its simple shepherds who live an uncomplicated and contented life, a pastoral can also be called a *bucolic, idyll,* or an *eclogue*. Rural life is usually shown as superior to tainted city life.

Pathetic Fallacy   This is a specific kind of personification in which inanimate objects are given human emotions. John Ruskin originated the term in *Modern Painters* (1856). Ruskin uses the example of "the cruel crawling foam" of the ocean to discuss the pathetic fallacy: the ocean is not cruel, happy to inflict pain on others, as a person may be, although it may well seem cruel to those who have suffered because of it. Ruskin obviously disapproved of such misstatement and allowed it only in verse where the poet was so moved by passion that he could not be expected to speak with greater accuracy. But in all truly great poetry, Ruskin held, the speaker is able to contain his excess emotion to express himself accurately. The term is used today, however, without this negative implication.

Personification   Giving human traits to nonhuman things. For example: "The book begged to be read."

Persuasion   A type of writing or speech that tries to move an audience to thought or action. Newspaper editorials, advertisements, and letters to the editor are all examples of persuasive writing.

Play   See *Drama*.

Playwright   A person who writes a play.

Plot   The arrangement of events in a work of literature. Plots have a beginning, middle, and end. The writer arranges the events of the plot to keep the reader's interest and convey the theme. In many stories and novels, the events of the plot can be divided as follows:

- *Exposition*: Introduces the characters, setting, and conflict.

- *Rising Action*: Builds the conflict and develops the characters.

- *Climax*: Shows the highest point of the action.

- *Denouement:* Resolves the story and ties up all the loose ends.

Poetry   A type of literature in which words are selected for their beauty, sound, and power to express feelings. Traditionally, poems had a specific rhythm and rhyme, but such modern poetry as *free verse* does not have regular beat, rhyme, or line length. Most poems are written in lines, which are arranged together in groups called *stanzas*.

Point of View   The position from which a story is told. Here are the three different points of view you will encounter most often in literature.

First-person point of view: The narrator is one of the characters in the story. The narrator explains the events through his or her own eyes, using the pronouns *I* and *me*.

Third-person omniscient point of view: The narrator is not a character in the story. Instead, the narrator looks through the eyes of all the characters. As a result, the narrator is all-knowing. The narrator uses the pronouns *he, she,* and *they*.

Third-person limited point of view: The narrator tells the story through the eyes of only one character, using the pronouns *he, she,* and *they.*

Prose   All written work that is not poetry, drama, or song. Examples of prose include articles, autobiographies, biographies, novels, essays, and editorials.

Protagonist   The most important character in a work of literature. The protagonist is at the center of the conflict and the focus of our attention.

Purpose   See *Author's Purpose.*

Q

Quatrains   Four-line stanzas

R

Realism   In contrast to Naturalism, Realism is the detailed presentation of appearances of everyday life. William Dean Howells, a notable Realist, said that the movement "sought to front the every-day world and catch the charm of its work-worn, care-worn, brave, kindly faces." This movement is closely linked to the Local Color school, which concentrated on picturesque details—scenery, customs, and language—characteristic of a certain region. Though often sentimental, Local Color could go beyond externals and delve into character and thus is an important part of realism. In its humble, everyday subject matter, Realism has its roots in Romanticism, but Realism generally shuns the Romantic interest in the exotic and mysterious. After the Civil War, American Realism showed a note of disillusionment not present in Howells, painting little people who had their share of petty vices. This can be found in the work of Mark Twain, Stephen Crane, and Hamlin Garland. Realism is not the same as Naturalism, which usually paints a picture of life determined by the twin forces of heredity and environment.

Refrain   A line or a group of lines that are repeated at the end of a poem or song. Refrains serve to reinforce the main point and create musical effects.

Repetition   Using the same sound, word, phrase, line, or grammatical structure over and over. Authors use repetition to link related ideas and emphasize key points.

Resolution   The *resolution* of a plot occurs near the end when all the remaining strands of the story are woven together.

Rhyme   The repeated use of identical or nearly identical sounds. *End rhyme* occurs when words at the end of lines of poetry have the same sound. Lines that end with the words *bat, cat, sat,* or *rat* would have end rhyme. *Internal rhyme* occurs when words within a sentence share the same sound. Poets use rhyme to create a musical sound, meaning, and structure.

Rhyme Scheme   A regular pattern of words that end with the same sound.

Rhythm   A pattern of stressed and unstressed syllables that create a beat, as in music. The *meter* of a poem is its rhythm. When you read a poem, use the punctuation and capitalization in each line to help you decide where to pause and what words to stress to make the rhythm clear.

Romance   The Romance describes strange lands and wonderful adventures. It allows the writer greater latitude to "mingle the Marvelous as a slight, delicate, and evanescent favor," in Nathaniel Hawthorne's words (in his preface to *The House of the Seven Gables*). A novel, in contrast to a Romance, assumes the writer will aim at a very minute fidelity to facts, but here the writer may, as Hawthorne again remarks, "swerve aside from the truth of the human heart." The Romance may include the traditional hero with the white hat on the white horse, the evil villain with the long black mustache, the lovely young woman in need of rescue, and the hairbreadth rescue.

S

Sarcasm   Crude and heavy-handed verbal irony.

Scan/Scanning   To *scan* a poem is to figure out its meter (its pattern of stressed and unstressed syllables).

Scene   A part of a play. Each scene in a play takes place during a set time and in one place.

Science Fiction   Fantasy writing that tells about make-believe events that include science or technology. Often, science fiction is set in the future, on distant planets, or among alien races.

Sensory Language   Words that appeal to the five senses: sight, hearing, taste, touch, or smell.

Setting   The time and place where the events take place. The setting may be stated outright, or you may have to infer it from details in the story. To infer the setting, look for words that tell *when* and *where*. Also look for clues in the characters' speech, clothing, or means of transportation.

Sextets   Six-line stanzas.

Short Story   A narrative prose fiction shorter than a novel that focuses on a single character and a single event. Most short stories can be read in one sitting and convey a single overall impression.

Simile   A figure of speech that compares two unlike things. Similes use the words "like" or "as" to make the comparison. "A dream put off dries up like a raisin in the sun" is an example of a simile. Here are some additional examples:

> My heart is like a singing bird. (C. Rossetti)
> I am weaker than a woman's tear. (Shakespeare)
> Seems he a dove? His feathers are but borrowed. (Shakespeare)

Slash   A slash (/) is used as a divider to separate feet in a line. It is also used to separate lines of poetry written as straight text.

Socratic Irony   This form of irony is named for Socrates, who usually pretended to be ignorant when he was in fact cautious or tentative. People who state "I do not understand; please explain this to me" are Socratic ironists, and their words are ironic, for they *do* understand.

Soliloquy   A speech one character speaks while alone on the stage. In the soliloquy, the character often voices his or her deepest thoughts or concerns. Hamlet's "To be or not to be" speech is a famous example.

Sonnet   A fourteen-line lyric poem, written in iambic pentameter (five accents per line). There are two main sonnet forms. Originally, both forms came into the language as love verse, but sonnets have been used for many different themes and subjects.

The first was originated by the Italian poets in the thirteenth century and reached its final form a century later in the work of Petrarch; thus, it came to be called the *Petrarchan* or *Italian sonnet*. The first eight lines, called the *octave*, rhyme *abbaabba* and present the subject of the poem; the final six lines, called the *sestet,* rhyme *cdecde* and resolve the problem or situation set forth in the first eight lines.

The English poets of the sixteenth century altered the rhyme scheme of the Italian sonnet, creating an *abab/cdcd/efef/gg* pattern, which has come to be called the *Shakespearean* or *English sonnet*.

Speaker   The personality the writer assumes when telling a story. For example, the writer can tell the story as a young girl, old man, or figure from history. It is important not to confuse the speaker with the author. Also called *personae*.

Sprung Rhythm   A reintroduction of accentual verse in the works of Gerard Manley Hopkins (1844–1889) in which strongly accented syllables are pushed up against unaccented ones to produce greater tension and emphasis within the verse.

Stage Directions   Instructions to the actors, producer, and director telling how to perform the play. Stage directions are included in the text of the play, written in parentheses or *italics*. Stage directions can describe how actors should speak, what they should wear, and what scenery should be used, for example.

Stanza   A group of lines in a poem. Lines of poems are grouped into stanzas, just as sentences of prose are grouped into paragraphs. Each stanza presents one complete idea.

Stanzas may be classified as follows:

Couplets	Two-line stanzas
Quatrains	Four-line stanzas
Sextets	Six-line stanzas
Octets	Eight-line stanzas

Style   An author's distinctive way of writing. Style is made up of elements such as word choice, sentence length and structure, figures of speech, and tone. An author may change his or her style for different kinds of writing and to suit different audiences. In poetry, for example, authors might use more imagery than they would use in prose.

Surprise Ending   A conclusion that is different from what the reader expected. In most stories, the ending follows logically from the arrangement of events in the plot. In a surprise ending, however, final events take an unexpected twist. A surprise ending always makes sense in retrospect, however.

Surrealism   The Surrealist aims to go beyond what is usually considered "real" to the "super real," which would include the world of dreams and the unconscious. Surrealists especially shun middle-class ideals and artistic traditions, believing that all these deform the creations of the artist's unconscious. With its emphasis on spontaneity, feeling, and sincerity, Surrealism is linked to Romanticism. The movement was especially strong in France in the 1920s and 1930s.

Suspense   The feeling or tension or anticipation an author creates in a work. Authors create suspense by unexpected plot twists. This keeps readers interested in the story and makes them want to read on to find out what will happen.

Syllabic Verse   A system of verse in which syllables are used to determine the length of a line of poetry. This type of verse flourished mainly in the period between 1066–1400, although modern poets have experimented with it.

Symbol   A person, place, or object that represents an abstract idea. For example, a dove may symbolize peace, or a rose may symbolize love.

Symbolism   Symbolism occurs when an image stands for something other than what was expected. The ocean, for example, may be said to symbolize "eternity," and the phrase "river to the sea" could stand for "life flowing into afterlife." In most instances, the symbol does not directly reveal what it stands for; rather, the meaning must be discovered through a close reading of the literary work and an understanding of conventional literary and cultural symbols. For example, we realize that the "stars and stripes" stands for the American flag. We know this because we are told it is so, for the flag itself in no way looks like the United States. Without cultural agreement, many of the symbols we commonly accept would be meaningless.

Symbolist Movement   The Symbolist movement arose in France in the second half of the nineteenth century and included writers Mallarmé and Valéry. W. B. Yeats, the Irish writer, was influenced by the movement. Some Symbolists believed in an invisible world beyond that of concrete events—Yeats, for example, experimented with automatic writing—but other Symbolists found that the concrete world stimulated their writings. Symbolists believed that an object was neither a real thing nor the holder of divine essence; it simply called forth emotions, which were communicated by words whose sounds would be able, they thought, to call forth the same emotion in the reader. Extreme followers of the Symbolist movement believed that poetry was sound with associations rather than words with meanings.

Synecdoche   The substitution of a part of something for the whole, or the whole is used in place of one of the parts. "Ten sails" would thus stand for ten ships. In the stanza below by American poet Emily Dickinson, "morning" and "noon," parts of the day, are used to refer to the whole day. In the same manner, "Rafter of Satin" refers to a coffin, by describing its inner lining rather than the entire object:

> Safe in their Alabaster Chambers—
> Untouched by Morning—
> And untouched by Noon—
> Lie the meek members of the Resurrection—
> Rafter of Satin—and Roof of Stone!

Synesthesia   This figure of speech takes one of the five senses and creates a picture or image of sensation as perceived by another. For example, "the golden cry of the trumpet" combines "golden," a visual perception of color, with "cry," hearing. In the same manner, Emily Dickinson speaks of a fly's "blue, uncertain stumbling buzz."

T

Tall Tale   A folk tale that exaggerates the main events or the characters' abilities. Tall tales came from the oral tradition, as pioneers sitting around the campfires at night tried to top each other's outrageous stories. Twain's short story "The Celebrated Jumping Frog of Calaveras County" is a tall tale.

Theme   The main idea of a literary work, it's a general statement about life. The theme can be stated outright in the work, or readers will have to infer it from details about plot, characters, and setting.

Tone   The writer's attitude toward his or her subject matter. For example, the tone can be angry, bitter, sad, or frightening.

Transferred Epithet   A word or phrase shifted from the noun it would usually describe to one that has no logical connection with it, as in Gray's "drowsy tinklings," where "drowsy" literally describes the sheep who wear the bells but here is figuratively applied to the bells. In current usage, the distinction between metonymy, synecdoche, and transferred epithet is so slight that the word *metonymy* is often used to cover them all.

Travesty   Also known as *low burlesque,* travesty takes a high theme and treats it in trivial terms, as in the Greek "Battle of the Frogs and Mice," which travesties Homer.

True, Exact, or Perfect Rhyme   When the first consonants change but following consonants or vowels stay the same. These involve identity of sound, not spelling. "Fix" and "sticks," like "buffer" and "rougher," though spelled differently, are perfect rhymes. Anne Bradstreet's "Before the Birth of One of Her Children" (1678) illustrates true rhyme:

> All things within this fading world hath end,
> Adversity doth still our joys attend;
> No ties so strong, no friends so dear and sweet,

But with death's parting blow is sure to meet.

In the lines quoted, "end," which we shall call *a*, rhymes with "attend," also called *a*, while "sweet," called *b*, rhymes with "meet." The rhyme scheme, then, is *aabb*, etc.

Turning Point   See *Climax.*

U

Understatement   The opposite of *exaggeration*, an understatement states less than it indirectly suggests, as in Jonathan Swift's "Last week I saw a woman flayed, and you will hardly believe how much it altered her person for the worst." In the same way, Auden's ironic poem "The Unknown Citizen" has a great many examples of understatement that combine to show how numbers cannot evaluate the ultimate happiness of a person's life.

V

Verse   A stanza in a poem.

Villanelle   A poetic form that not only rhymes but also repeats lines in a predetermined manner, both as a refrain and as an important part of the poem itself. Five stanzas of three lines each are followed by a quatrain. The first and third lines of the first stanza are repeated in a prescribed alternating order as the last lines of the remaining tercets, becoming the last two lines of the final quatrain. Dylan Thomas's "Do Not Go Gentle Into That Good Night" is a modern villanelle.

Voice   The author's unique attitude toward the material.

7

Guide to Grammar and Usage

CRIB SHEET

ROAD MAP

- *Crib Sheet*
- *Grammar 101*

Use the following section for a quick review of grammar and usage.

Adjectives are words that modify (describe or limit) nouns and pronouns.

Adjective clauses describe nouns and pronouns.

Adverb clause is a dependent clause that describes a verb, adjective, or other adverb.

Adverbial phrase is a prepositional phrase that modifies a verb, an adjective, or an adverb.

Agreement means that sentence parts match. Subjects must agree with verbs, and pronouns must agree with antecedents.

Appositive is a noun or a pronoun that renames another noun or pronoun.

Appositive phrases are nouns or pronouns with modifiers.

Bias-free language uses words and phrases that don't discriminate on the basis of gender, physical condition, age, race, or anything else.

Case is the form of a noun or pronoun that shows how it is used in a sentence. Case is the grammatical role a noun or pronoun plays in a sentence. English has three cases: *nominative, objective,* and *possessive.*

Clause is a group of words with its own subject and verb.

Collective nouns name a group of people or things. Collective nouns include the words *class, committee, flock, herd, team, audience, assembly, team, club,* and so on.

Complex sentences have one independent clause and at least one dependent clause.

Compound-complex sentences have at least two independent clauses and at least one dependent clause.

Conjugate a verb to list the singular and plural forms of the verb in a specific tense.

Conjunctions connect words or groups of words.

Conjunctive adverbs are used to connect other words. Conjunctive adverbs are also called *transitions* because they link ideas.

Connotation is a word's emotional overtones.

Dangling modifiers are words or phrases that describe something that has been left out of the sentence.

Denotation is a word's dictionary meaning.

Dependent (subordinate) clause is part of a sentence; it cannot stand alone.

Doublespeak is artificial, evasive language.

Diction is a writer's choice of words.

Compound sentences have two or more independent clauses.

Grammar is a branch of linguistics that deals with the form and structure of words.

Indefinite pronouns refer to people, places, objects, or things without pointing to a specific one.

Independent clause is a complete sentence; it can stand alone.

Indirect objects tell *to* or *for* whom something is done.

Infinitive is a verb form that comes after the word "to" and functions as a noun, adjective, or adverb.

Interjections show strong emotion. Often, interjections will be set off with an exclamation mark.

Linking verbs indicate a state of being (*am, is, are*, etc.), relate to the senses (*look, smell, taste*, etc.), or indicate a condition (*appear, seem, become*, etc.).

Mechanics include punctuation, numbers, quotation marks, capitalization, abbreviations, and italics.

Misplaced modifiers are a phrase, clause, or word placed too far from the word or words it modifies.

Mixed metaphors are a combination of images that do not work well together. They occur when writers string together clichés.

Mood shows the attitude expressed toward the action. It refers to the ability of verbs to convey a writer's attitude toward a subject.

Nouns name a person, place, or thing.

Noun clause is a dependent clause that functions as a noun.

Number refers to the two forms of a word: *singular* (one) or *plural* (more than one).

Parallel structure means putting ideas of the same rank in the same grammatical structure.

Participle is a form of a verb that functions as an adjective. There are two kinds of participles: *present participles* and *past participles*.

Phrase is a group of words, without a subject or a verb, that functions in a sentence as a single part of speech.

Predicate adjectives are adjectives separated from the noun or pronoun by a linking verb. Predicate adjectives describe the subject of the sentence.

Predicate nominatives are a noun or pronoun that follow a linking verb. A predicate nominative renames or identifies the subject.

Prepositions are words that link a noun or a pronoun to another word in the sentence.

Prepositional phrases are groups of words that begin with a preposition and end with a noun or a pronoun.

Pronouns are words used in place of a noun or another pronoun. An *antecedent* is the noun the pronoun stands for.

Redundancy is unnecessary repetition of words and ideas.

Relative clause is an adjective clause that begins with one of the relative pronouns.

Run-on sentences are two incorrectly joined independent clauses. A *comma splice* is a run-on with a comma where the two sentences run together.

Sentence is a group of words that express a complete thought.

Sentence coordination links ideas of equal importance.

Sentence fragments are a group of words that do not express a complete thought.

Sexist language assigns qualities to people on the basis of their gender. It reflects prejudiced attitudes and stereotypical thinking about the sex roles and traits of both men and women.

Simple sentence is a sentence with one independent clause.

Slang is coined words and phrases or new meanings for established terms.

Split infinitives occur when an adverb or adverbial phrase is placed between *to* and the verb.

Style is a writer's distinctive way of writing.

Subordination is connecting two unequal but related ideas with a subordinating conjunction to form a complex sentence.

Tense shows the time of a verb.

Tone is the writer's attitude toward his or her subject and audience.

Usage is the customary way we use language in speech and writing. The correct level of usage is the one that is appropriate for the occasion.

Verbal is a verb form used as another part of speech.

Verbs are words that name an action or describe a state of being.

Voice is the form of the verb that shows whether the subject performed the action or received the action.

GRAMMAR 101

Use this section to review grammar and usage in depth.

Adjectives and Adverbs
Adjectives

Adjectives describe nouns and pronouns. Adjectives answer the questions *What kind? How much? Which one?* or *How many?*

There are four kinds of adjectives: *articles, common adjectives, compound adjectives,* and *proper adjectives.*

Articles: A, an, and *the* are "articles."

The is called the "definite article" because it refers to a specific thing.

Examples: <u>The</u> poem   <u>The</u> novel   <u>The</u> student

A and *an* are "indefinite articles" because they refer to general things.

Examples: <u>A</u> poem   <u>A</u> novel   <u>An</u> author

Use *an* in place of *a* when it precedes a vowel sound, not just a vowel.

Examples: <u>an</u> honor <u>a</u> UFO

Common adjectives: They describe nouns or pronouns.

Examples: <u>big</u> book   <u>excellent</u> poem   <u>superb</u> style

Compound adjectives: These adjectives are comprised of more than one word.

Examples: <u>nearsighted</u> reader   <u>first-time</u> test taker
<u>hard-working</u> student

Proper adjectives: These adjectives are formed from proper nouns.

Examples: <u>Mexican</u> poet   <u>French</u> bread

Here are two hints for using adjectives well:

- Use an adjective to describe a noun or a pronoun.
- Choose precise adjectives rather than piling them on. One perfect adjective is far more powerful than a string of inaccurate ones.

Predicate adjectives are adjectives separated from the noun or pronoun by a linking verb. Predicate adjectives describe the subject of the sentence.

Example: The weather was *cold* all week.

Adverbs

Adverbs describe verbs, adjectives, or other adverbs. Adverbs answer the following questions: *When? Where? How?* or *To What Extent?*

Most adverbs are formed by adding -*ly* to an adjective.

Examples: wrote <u>quickly</u> edited <u>slowly</u> worked <u>carefully</u>

Here is a list of the most common adverbs that don't end in -*ly*:

Adverbs that Don't End in -ly

afterward	almost	already	also	back
even	far	fast	hard	here
how	late	long	low	more
never	next	now	often	rather
so soon	still	then	there	today
too	tomorrow	when	where	yesterday

Here are hints for using adverbs well:

- Use an adverb to describe a verb, an adjective, or another adverb.
- As with adjectives, choose the precise adverb to get just the meaning you want. You can use an online or print thesaurus to help you find the exact adjectives and adverbs you want.

Comparing with Adjectives and Adverbs

Adjectives and adverbs are often used to compare by showing that one thing is larger, smaller, bigger, or more important than something else. English makes this easy by giving us a special way to compare two things (the *comparative degree*) and a special way to compare more than two things (the *superlative degree*). Here's how to do it.

Use the *comparative degree* (-*er* or *more* form) to compare two things.

Examples: John is <u>taller</u> than Chris. Jess is <u>younger</u> than Nicole.

Use the *superlative form* (-*est* or *most* form) to compare more than two things.

Examples: This is the <u>finest</u> novel I have ever read!

Don't you think writing is the <u>nicest</u> way to spend a day?

Never use -*er* and *more* or -*est* and *most* together.

Examples: I have a <u>more slower</u> computer. I have a <u>slower</u> computer.

I have the <u>most biggest</u> monitor. I have the <u>biggest</u> monitor.

Good and *bad* do not follow these guidelines. They have irregular forms, as follows:

Part of Speech	Positive	Comparative	Superlative
adjective	good	better	best
adverb	well	better	best
adjective	bad	worse	worst
adverb	badly	worse	worst

Agreement

Agreement means matching parts of a sentence. When sentence parts match, your writing sounds smooth. If they don't match, it sounds jarring or awkward.

Agreement of Pronoun and Antecedent

Pronouns and antecedents (the words to which they refer) must *agree* or match. Here's the basic guideline: a personal pronoun must agree with its antecedent in number, person, and gender.

Number is amount: singular or plural.

Person refers to first person, second person, or third person (the person

speaking, the person spoken to, or the person spoken about).

Gender refers to masculine, feminine, or neuter references. *He* and *him* are masculine in gender, *she* and *her* are feminine, and *it* and *its* are neuter.

Examples:

Number: Marla and Carol wrote their essays.

Person: Leigh wrote in her journal every night.

Gender: Jim studies grammar, a subject he needs to do well on the AP Language exam.

In the past, the pronouns *he* and *his* were used to refer to both men and women. We would write or say: "A writer should try his hand at different kinds of poetry," or "Anyone can learn to write well if he applies himself."

Today, using the pronouns *he* and *his* to refer to both men and women is considered sexist language. As a result, avoid this usage. Try these ideas:

• Rewrite the sentence into the third-person *they* or *them*.

Example: Writers should try their hands at different kinds of poetry.

• Rewrite the sentence into the second person *you*.

Example: You should try your hand at different kinds of poetry.

• Eliminate the pronoun altogether.

Example: Try writing different kinds of poetry.

Agreement of Subject and Verb

To make your writing sound polished, be sure that subjects and verbs are in the same form. Here are some guidelines.

A singular subject takes a singular verb.

Example: <u>He edits</u> (not <u>edit</u>) everything he writes.

A plural subject takes a plural verb.

Example: <u>Luis and Marc edit</u> (not <u>edits</u>) everything they write.

Prepositional phrases that come between the subject and the verb don't affect agreement.

Example: Too many *mistakes* in a poem can *block* meaning.

(The plural subject *mistakes* requires the plural verb *block*. Ignore the prepositional phrase "in a poem.")

Subjects that are singular in meaning but plural in form take a singular verb. These subjects include words such as *measles, news,* and *economics*.

Example: The <u>news was</u> encouraging.

Singular subjects connected by *either/or, neither/nor,* and *not only/but also* take a singular verb.

Example: Either the student <u>or</u> the teacher <u>was</u> going to proofead the essay.

If the subject is made up of two or more nouns or pronouns connected by *or, nor, not only,* or *but also*, the verb agrees with the noun closest to the pronoun.

Examples: Neither Chris nor the <u>scorers are </u>done working.

Neither the scorers nor <u>Chris is </u>done working.

NOTE

A pronoun replaces a noun. To make sure that your writing is clear, always use the noun first before using the pronoun.

Example: <u>Justin</u> read his practice AP essay to his friends. <u>He</u> read with great emotion.

Biased Language

Avoid *biased language*, words and phrases that assign qualities to people on the basis of their gender, race, religion, or health. Here are some guidelines:

* Avoid using *he* to refer to both men and women.
* Avoid using *man* to refer to both men and women.
* Avoid language that denigrates people.

Capitalization

Capitalization is one of the writer's most useful tools, because it helps convey meaning. For example, when readers see a capital letter, they know they've reached the beginning of a sentence, a quotation, or a person's name. This helps your audience read your writing the way you intended it to be read! Below are the rules for using capital letters correctly.

Capitalize the first word of a sentence, the greeting of a letter, the complimentary close of a letter, and each item in an outline.

Capitalize geographical places and sections of the country; the names of historical events, eras, and documents; and abbreviations that appear after a person's name.

Capitalize the names of languages, races, and nationalities.

Capitalize proper nouns, proper adjectives, and brand names.

Capitalize the names of organizations, institutions, courses, and famous buildings.

Capitalize days, months, and holidays.

Capitalize abbreviations for time.

Conjunctions

Conjunctions are words or pairs of words that link ideas. Use them to help create meaning and logic in writing. As you draft, select the conjunctions that give you the precise shade of meaning you want. To make your job easier, you may wish to choose conjunctions from this list as you write:

Conjunctions

after	although	and	as
as if	because	before	both...and
but	either...or	even though	for
if	neither...nor	or	not only...but also
nor	since	so	so that
than	though	unless	until
when	where	wherever	while

Contractions

Contractions are two words combined into one. When you contract words, add an apostrophe in the space where the letter or letters have been taken out.

Examples:

I + am	=	I'm	she + is	=	she's
you + are	=	you're	we + are	=	we're
he + is	=	he's	it + is	=	it's

Contractions are often confused with *possessive pronouns*. You may wish to use this chart to keep the two clear:

Contraction	Possessive Pronoun
it's (it is)	its
you're (you are)	your
they're (they are)	their
who's (who is)	whose

Double Negatives

Use only one negative word to express a negative idea. Using two negative words cancels them both out.

Example: I do<u>n't</u> have <u>no</u> ideas.   I do<u>n't</u> have any ideas.

The most common negative words are *n't (don't, etc.), no, nobody, not, no one, nothing, nowhere, never,* and *neither.*

Interjections

Interjections are words that show strong emotion. Often, interjections will be set off with an exclamation mark. For example: *Watch out!*, *Oh!*, *Wow!*

Nonstandard English

Nonstandard English consists of words and phrases that are not considered standard written English.

Examples:	*Nonstandard:*	irregardless	being that	hisself
	Standard:	regardless	since	himself

Nonstandard English can work effectively in dialogue, as Mark Twain showed in *The Adventures of Huckleberry Finn,* however.

Nouns

A *noun* is a word that names a person, place, or thing. There are different kinds of nouns, as follows:

Common nouns name a type of person, place, or thing.

Examples: play   poem   movie

Proper nouns name a specific person, place, or thing

Examples: *Hamlet*   "Trees"   *Citizen Kane*

Plural Nouns

Plural nouns name more than one person, place, or thing. Here are the guidelines for forming plural nouns.

Add *s* to form the plural of most nouns.

Examples: book/books   play/plays   noun/nouns

Add *es* if the noun ends in *s, sh, ch,* or *x.*

Examples: inch/inches   box/boxes

If the noun ends in *y* preceded by a *consonant,* change the *y* to *i* and add *es.*

Examples: city/cities   baby/babies

If the noun ends in *y* preceded by a *vowel,* add *s.*

Examples: essay/essays   journey/journeys

If the noun ends in *o* preceded by a *consonant,* some nouns take *es,* some take *s,* and some take either *s* or *es.*

Examples: hero/heroes   piano/pianos   motto/mottos, mottoes

Some nouns ending in *f* take *s;* others change the *f* or *fe* to *v* and add *es.*

Examples: belief/beliefs   life/lives

Some nouns change their spelling when they become plural.

Examples: child/children   foot/feet

Some nouns have the same form whether they are singular or plural.

Examples: series   moose   deer

Possessive Nouns

Possession shows ownership. Here are the rules:

Add an apostrophe and an *s* to singular nouns.

Example: writer   writer's essay

With plural nouns ending is *s,* add an apostrophe after the *s.*

Example: writers   writers' essays

With plural nouns not ending in *s,* add an apostrophe and an *s.*

Example: children children's story book

Prepositions

Prepositions are words that link a noun or a pronoun to another word in the sentence. Prepositions are handy because they allow you to show how parts of a sentence are related to each other.

Here are some of the most common prepositions:

Common Prepositions

about	against	around	behind
between	despite	for	into
off	out	since	under
upon	above	along	as
below	beyond	down	from
like	on	outside	through
underneath	with	across	amid
at	beneath	but	during
in	near	onto	over
to	until	within	after
around	before	beside	by
except	inside	opposite	of
opposite	past	toward	up

A *prepositional phrase* is a preposition and its object.

Examples: on the wing   in the door

NOTE
Remember that possessive pronouns don't require an apostrophe. The possessive pronouns are *yours, hers, its, ours, theirs,* and *whose.*

Pronouns

Pronouns are words used in place of a noun or another pronoun. There are several different kinds of pronouns. The most common ones are *personal pronouns, possessive pronouns, interrogative pronouns,* and *indefinite pronouns.*

Personal pronouns point out a specific person, place, object, or thing:

	Singular	*Plural*
first person	I, me, mine, my	we, us, our, ours
second person	you, your, yours	you, your, yours
third person	he, him, his, she, her, hers, it	they, them, their, theirs, its

Possessive pronouns show ownership.

Examples: mine   yours   his   hers
            its   ours   theirs   whose

Interrogative pronouns begin a question.

Examples: who   what   which   whom   whose

Indefinite pronouns refer to people, places, objects, or things without pointing to a specific one.

Examples:	another	anybody	everyone	everything
	nobody	none	one	some

Pronoun Case

Pronouns often trouble us because they have different forms for different uses. *Case* is the form of a noun or pronoun that shows how it is used in a sentence. English has three cases: *nominative, objective,* and *possessive.* This means that the pronouns have one form as a subject, another as an object, and a third to show possession, as the following chart shows.

Pronoun Case

Nominative (as a subject)	Objective (as an object)	Possessive (to show ownership)
I	me	my, mine
you	you	you
he	him	his
she	her	hers
it	it	its
we	us	our, ours
they	them	their, theirs
who	whom	whose
whoever	whomever	whosoever

Here are some guidelines to make it easier for you to use pronouns with assurance.

Use the nominative case to show the subject of a verb.

Example: <u>We</u> took practice AP Language tests.

Use the objective case to show the noun or pronoun that receives the action.

Example: The book was helpful to <u>us</u>.

Use the possessive case to show ownership.

Example: The teacher gave us <u>her</u> advice about taking the AP Language test.

Punctuation

Punctuation is an important writing tool because it helps determine meaning. Each mark of punctuation provides important visual clues to readers, showing where sentences begin and end, telling readers where to pause, and so on. Here are the basic rules.

Apostrophes (') are used three ways:

To show possession (ownership)

Examples: Morrison's novel   Shaw's play   Charles' letter

To show contractions (where a letter or number has been omitted)

Examples: can't   won't   didn't

the '60s   the '90s

To show plural forms

Examples: three 8's or eight 3's   your n's look like h's

Brackets: Use [ ] to show words that interrupt a direct quotation.

Example: "Four score and seven years [87 years] ago, our fathers brought forth on this continent, a new nation, conceived in Liberty, and dedicated to the proposition that all men are created equal."

You probably won't be using brackets a lot, since it's not often that you'll have to interrupt a direct quotation to clarify it or add information.

Colons: Use a colon before a list. This is a colon :

Example: We proofread for the following issues: capitalization, punctuation, and spelling.

Commas: Use a comma after introductory words and expressions, to separate items in a series, to set off interrupting words and expressions, to separate parts of a compound sentence, and at the close of any letter.

Examples:

If you want to do well on the AP test, you must study hard.

You can study simulated test questions, write essays, and review novels.

This process, I know, will help you earn a high grade.

Dashes

Use a dash to show a sudden change of thought. A dash is a long hyphen, like this —

Example: Students can do very well on the AP Language and Composition test— if they prepare thoroughly.

Ellipses: Use these three spaced periods to show that something has been left out.

Example: (original quote) But in a larger sense, we cannot dedicate—we cannot consecrate—we cannot hallow—this ground.

(edited quote) But in a larger sense, we cannot dedicate. . . this ground.

Exclamation marks: Use an exclamation mark to show strong emotion.

Example: I can't believe I reviewed an entire novel last night!

Hyphen: Use a hyphen to show a word break at the end of a line, in some compound nouns, and in fractions and in compound numbers. A hyphen looks like this -

Example: mother-in-law   three-quarters   fifty-five

TIP
Can't tell if you're using too many commas? When in doubt, leave it out!

NOTE
Unless you're writing comic books, use only one exclamation mark at the end of a sentence.

Parentheses: Use parentheses to enclose additional information.

Example: Perhaps the best part about doing well on the AP test (despite the hard work) is the deep satisfaction it gives you to succeed at a difficult task.

Periods: Use a period after a complete sentence, most abbreviations, and initials.

Examples: Try to study for at least an hour a day.

I like to study before school or after 8:00 p.m.

Dr. Martin Luther King, Jr. was a superb writer.

Question Marks: Use a question mark after a question.

Example: Did you write that practice essay within 40 minutes?

Quotation Marks: Use quotation marks to set off a speaker's exact words.

Example: "This draft is astonishingly good," the teacher said.

The teacher said, "This draft is astonishingly good."

"This draft," the teacher said, "is astonishingly good."

Semicolons: Use a semicolon between main clauses when the conjunction (*and, but, for, or, yet*) has been left out and to separate items in a series when the items contain commas.

Examples: I study on my own, and I study in small groups.
                 I study on my own; I study in small groups.

Sentence Errors

A *sentence* is a group of words that expresses a complete thought. A sentence has two parts: a *subject* and a *predicate*. The subject includes the noun or pronoun that identifies the subject. The predicate contains the verb that describes what the subject is doing.

Example: Ernest Hemingway / wrote /   novels and short stories.
                subject   verb   predicate

Sentence Fragments and Run-Ons

Sentence *fragments* and *run-ons* are often used in dialogue to show everyday speech, but they are considered sentence errors when used in straight text.

A *sentence fragment* is a group of words that does not express a complete thought. It may also be missing a subject, verb, or both.

Example: Studied all night.   **I** studied all night.

A *run-on sentence* consists of two incorrectly joined sentences.

Example: My teacher advised us not to study all night we will not absorb much.

There are three ways to correct a run-on sentence:

1. Separate the run-on into two sentences:

Example: My teacher advised us not to study all night. We will not absorb much.

2. Add a conjunction. You might add a coordinating conjunction (*and, but, or, for, yet, so*):

Example: My teacher advised us not to study all night, for we will not absorb much.

You might add a subordinating conjunction:

Example: My teacher advised us not to study all night because we will not absorb much.

3. Add a semicolon.

Example: My teacher advised us not to study all night; we will not absorb much.

Select the repair method depending on your audience, purpose, and unique writing style.

Dangling Modifiers

A *dangling modifier* is a word or phrase that describes something that has been left out of the sentence. As a result, the sentence does not convey the correct meaning. It may also unintentionally cause humor. Correct a dangling modifier by adding a noun or pronoun to which the dangling modifier can be attached.

Example: *Dangling*: Coming up the stairs, the clock struck midnight.
    Correct: As he was coming up the stairs, the clock struck
    midnight.

Misplaced Modifiers

A *misplaced modifier* is a descriptive word or phrase that is placed too far away from the noun or the pronoun that it describes. As a result, the sentence is unclear. It may be confusing or unintentionally funny. To correct a misplaced modifier, move the modifier as close as possible to the word or phrase it is describing, as the following example shows:

Sam found a letter in the mailbox that didn't belong to her.

What the writer thinks this sentence says: Sam found a letter that didn't belong to her.

What this sentence really says: The mailbox doesn't belong to Sam.

Correction: Sam found a letter that doesn't belong to her in the mailbox.

Sentence Types

There are four types of sentences in English: *declarative, exclamatory, interrogative*, and *imperative*.

Declarative sentences state an idea. They end with a period.

Example: Good writers are made, not born.

Exclamatory sentences show strong emotions. They end with an exclamation mark.

Example: What a high score you will earn!

Interrogative sentences ask a question. They end with a question mark.

Example: When is the AP test given?

Imperative sentences give orders or directions. They end with a period or an exclamation mark.

Example :   Do Practice Test 3, please.

Sentence Variety

Unless you are writing certain kinds of dialogue, all your sentences should be grammatically correct. In addition, craft your sentences to express your ideas in the best possible way. Strive for rhythm, pattern, and variety as well. Here are some ideas to try:

Expand short sentences by adding detail.

Short: The plane took off.

Expanded: The plane took off, a shrieking golden ribbon in the morning sky.

Combine short sentences.

Short: O. Henry wrote a short story called "The Gift of the Magi." A husband sells his watch to buy his wife combs. They are for her beautiful hair.

Combined: In O. Henry's short story "The Gift of the Magi," a husband sells his watch to buy his wife combs for her beautiful hair.

Change sentence openings to create emphasis and rhythm.

Sentence: I unlocked the attic door with great difficulty.

Revised: With great difficulty, I unlocked the attic door.

Transitions

Transitions—words and expressions that signal connections among ideas—can help you achieve coherence in your writing. Each transition signals to the reader how one idea is connected to the next. You'll want to choose the transitions that link your ideas just the way you want. You can use the following chart to help you make your choices:

Transitions	Relationship
Addition	also, and, besides, too, in addition to, further
Contrast	but, nevertheless, yet, in contrast, however, still
Comparison	likewise, in comparison, similarly
Example	for example, for instance, thus, namely
Place	in the front, in the back, here, there, nearby
Result	therefore, consequently, as a result, thus, due to this, accordingly
Summary	as a result, in brief, in conclusion, hence, in short, finally
Time	next, then, finally, first, second, third, fourth, afterwards, before, during, soon, later, meanwhile, subsequently

Use transitions to show how ideas are linked.

Without transition: Frank completed his research. He started his outline.

With transition: *After* Frank completed his research, he started his outline.

Verbs

Verbs are words that name an action or describe a state of being. There are three types of verbs: *action verbs, linking verbs,* and *helping verbs.*

Action verbs tell what the subject does.

| Examples: | write | draft | revise | edit |

Linking verbs join the subject and the predicate and name and describe the subject.

| Examples: | appear | become | feel | turn | grow | look |
| | remain | seem | smell | sound | stay | taste |

Helping verbs are added to another verb to make the meaning clearer.

| Examples: | am | can | could | does |
| | had | might | will | would |

While all three types of verbs are necessary in writing, action verbs make your writing forceful, while linking verbs tend to make it wordy. As a result, you'll probably want to use action verbs whenever possible.

Verb Tense

Verbs can show time, called tense. Every verb has three parts:

Verb Part	Example
present tense	break
past tense	broke
past participle	broken

Some verbs are *regular.* This means they form the past tense by adding *-d* or *-ed* to the present form.

Other verbs are *irregular.* This means their form changes in the past tense. The following chart shows the most common irregular verbs.

Present Tense	Past Tense	Past Participle
arise	arose	arisen
bear	bore	born or borne
beat	beat	beaten
become	became	become
begin	began	begun
bend	bent	bent
bite	bit	bitten
blow	blew	blown
break	broke	broken

bring	brought	brought
burst	burst	burst
catch	caught	caught
choose	chose	chosen
come	came	come
creep	crept	crept
dig	dug	dug
dive	dived or dove	dived
do	did	done
draw	drew	drawn
drink	drank	drunk
drive	drove	driven
eat	ate	eaten
fall	fell	fallen
fight	fought	fought
fly	flew	flown
forget	forgot	forgotten
forgive	forgave	forgiven
freeze	froze	frozen
get	got	gotten or got
give	gave	given
go	went	gone
grow	grew	grown
hang	hung	hung
hang (execute)	hanged	hanged
hide	hid	hidden
hold	held	held
hurt	hurt	hurt
kneel	knelt	knelt
know	knew	known
lay	laid	laid
lead	led	led
lie (horizontal)	lay	lain
lie (falsehood)	lied	lied
lose	lost	lost
prove	proved	proved or proven
ride	rode	ridden
ring	rang	rung
rise	rose	risen
run	ran	run
say	said	said
see	saw	seen
shake	shook	shaken
show	showed	showed or shown
sing	sang	sung
speak	spoke	spoken
steal	stole	stolen
swim	swam	swum
take	took	taken

teach	taught	taught
throw	threw	thrown
wake	woke, waked	woken or waked
write	wrote	written

Verb Voice

In addition to showing time, most verbs also indicate whether the subject is performing an action or having an action performed on it. This is called verb *voice*. English has two verb voices: the *active voice* and the *passive voice*.

In the *active voice*, the subject performs the action.

Example: Angela took the practice AP Language exam.

In the *passive voice*, the action is performed upon the subject.

Example: The practice AP Language exam was taken by Angela.

The active voice is usually preferable to the passive because it is more vigorous and concise. For example, notice that there are six words in the second example but only four words in the first. Who needs that extra "was" or "by"? These words don't add anything to the meaning. Since they make the sentence wordy, they should be omitted.

Use the passive voice to avoid placing blame or when you don't know who performed the action.

Examples: A mistake was made.   A window was left open.

Tense

Avoid shifting tenses in the middle of a sentence or a paragraph.

Wrong: I *was walking* to class when a huge dog *jumps* up and *attacks* me.

Right: I *was walking* to class when a huge dog *jumped* up and *attacked* me.

Wordiness

Write simply and directly. Omit unnecessary details or ideas that you have already stated. Use a lot of important detail but no unnecessary words.

Omit unnecessary words.

Wordy: We watched the big, massive, black cloud rise up from the level prairie and cover over the sun.

Better: We watched the massive, black cloud rise from the prairie and cover the sun.

Rewrite sentences to eliminate unnecessary words.

Wordy: Sonnets, which are a beautiful poetic form, have fourteen lines and a set rhythm and rhyme.

Better: Sonnets are a beautiful poetic form with fourteen lines and a set rhythm and rhyme.

Study this chart:

Wordy	Concise	Wordy	Concise
honest truth	truth	revert back	revert
past history	history	partial stop	stop
foreign imports	imports	free gift	gift
true facts	facts	most unique	unique
proceed ahead	proceed	at this point in time	now
set a new record	set a record	at the present time	now
small in size	small	few in number	few
complete stop	stop	weather event	snow (rain, etc.)
due to the fact that	because	in order to	to

Sentence Structure

There are four basic types of sentences: *simple sentences, compound sentences, complex sentences,* and *compound-complex sentences.* Let's look at each type of sentence a little more closely to see how you can use them to create your own personal style.

Words Often Confused

Some pairs of words are mixed up with each other. Sometimes, it's because the words sound alike; other times, it's because they're spelled alike. The following words are often confused, misused, and abused.

Word	Definition	Example
accept	take	Accept my thanks.
except	leave out	Everyone except him.
affect	influence	This affects your grade.
effect	result	The effect of the law.
already	before	Elvis already left the room.
all ready	prepared	He was all ready to go.
all together	everyone at once	They yell all together.
altogether	completely	It was altogether wrong.
altar	table of worship	Put the candles on the altar.
alter	to change	Alter the skirt.
ascent	rising	The rocket's ascent took an hour.
assent	agreement	Nod to show assent.
bare	uncovered	The window was bare.
bear	animal	The bear growled.
	endure	Can you bear the noise?
brake	stop	Use the car's brake.
break	destroy	Don't break the dish!

capital	government seat	Visit the capital.
Capitol	where the U.S. legislature meets	Congress meets in the Capitol.
conscience	morally right	Listen to your conscience.
conscious	awake	She was conscious during surgery.
desert	leave behind	Desert a sinking ship.
	arid region	Camels travel in the desert.
dessert	sweet food	I love a rich dessert.
emigrate	leave a country	She emigrated from France.
immigrate	enter a country	To immigrate means to enter a new homeland.
lay	put down	present: The cat lies down.
		past: The cat lay down.
		future: The cat will lie down.
		perfect: The cat has lain down.
lie	be flat	present: Lay your cards down.
		past: He laid the cards down.
		future: He will lay his cards down.
		perfect: She has laid her cards down.
lead	writing material	That's a lead pencil.
led	conducted	We were led to safety.
learn	receive facts	You learn grammar.
teach	give facts	I teach grammar.
loose	not fastened	The clasp is loose.
lose	misplace	I might lose the necklace.
passed	went by	Voters passed the law.
past	gone by	They helped in the past.
principal	main	The principal road is Woodward Parkway.
	head of a school	Murray Cantor is the principal.
principle	rule	You know the principles of grammar.
rise	get up	The cost of living will rise.
raise	lift	Raise your arms.
respectfully	with respect	The audience clapped respectfully.
respectively	in the stated order	The red, blue, and green books belong to John, Billie, and Lee, respectively.
stationary	staying in place	The car was stationary.
stationery	writing paper	Hotels have nice stationery.
than	comparison	Kansas is bigger than Rhode Island.
then	at that time	The state was then very dry.
their	belonging to them	It is their book.
there	place	Put it there.

they're	they are	They're good friends.
weather	atmospheric conditions	The weather is rainy.
whether	if	Whether or not you agree.

NOTE

Remember that an *independent clause* is a complete sentence. A *dependent clause* is a sentence fragment, a sentence part.

NOTES

NOTES

NOTES

NOTES

NOTES

NOTES